THE CASE OF

ABRAHAM LINCOLN

THE CASE OF

ABRAHAM LINCOLN

A STORY OF ADULTERY, MURDER, AND THE MAKING OF A GREAT PRESIDENT

JULIE M. FENSTER

palgrave
macmillan

First published in 2007 by
PALGRAVE MACMILLAN™
175 Fifth Avenue, New York, N.Y. 10010 and
Houndmills, Basingstoke, Hampshire, England RG21 6XS.
Companies and representatives throughout the world.

PALGRAVE MACMILLAN is the global academic imprint of the Palgrave
Macmillan division of St. Martin's Press, LLC and of Palgrave Macmillan Ltd.
Macmillan® is a registered trademark in the United States, United Kingdom
and other countries. Palgrave is a registered trademark in the European Union
and other countries.

ISBN-13: 978–1–4039–7635–2
ISBN-10: 1–4039–7635–X

Library of Congress Cataloging-in-Publication Data

Fenster, J. M. (Julie M.)
   Case of Abraham Lincoln : a story of adultery, murder, and the making of a
great president / by Julie M. Fenster.
      p.   cm.
   Includes bibliographical references and index.
   ISBN 1–4039–7635-X (alk. paper)
   1. Lincoln, Abraham, 1809–1865—Career in law.   2. Trials (Murder)—
Illinois—Springfield.   3. Poisoning—Illinois—Springfield—History—19th
century.   4. Adultery—Illinois—Springfield—History—19th century.
5. Anderson, George, d. 1856—Death and burial.   6. Springfield (Ill.)—
Biography.   7. Presidents—United States—Biography.   I. Title.

E457.2.F46   2007
973.7092—dc22

                                                                    2007011364

A catalogue record of the book is available from the British Library.

Design by Letre Libre, Inc.

First edition: November, 2007

10 9 8 7 6 5 4 3 2 1

Printed in the United States of America.

To Ruth Fenster and Warren Fenster,
as ever

TABLE OF CONTENTS

Ten pages of photographs follow page 124.

ACKNOWLEDGMENTS

When I became interested in Abraham Lincoln's career as a lawyer about ten years ago, a person such as I, living far from Illinois, had very little access to original source material. In the year 2000, that changed with the release of *The Law Practice of Abraham Lincoln: Complete Documentary Edition.* A three-volume DVD set, it allowed anyone, anywhere to peruse the documents that describe Lincoln's legal work. This book owes a great deal to that supremely thorough effort to collect every document on every case on which Lincoln worked. The *Complete Documentary Edition* was edited by Martha L. Benner and Collum Davis; the assistant editors were Daniel W. Stowell, Susan Krause, John A. Lupton, Stacy Pratt McDermott, Christopher Schnell and Dennis E. Suttles.

The Lincoln Memorial University in Harrogate, Tennessee has a valuable archive especially rich in early publications on Lincoln. I am grateful to Dr. Charles M. Hubbard, a respected author and the director at that time, for his help and suggestions. LMU was the first research site that I visited for this book. It also has a handsome museum devoted to the Lincolns.

The Abraham Lincoln Presidential Library and Museum in Springfield, Illinois, encompasses the Illinois State Historical Society. It is a beautiful facility, and I am obliged to the ALPLM staff for assistance that benefited this book enormously. Glenna Schroeder-Lein and Jan Perone were very generous with their time in helping me. The very first item I re-

quested in the Manuscripts Department was the 1860 diary of one Philemon Stout, who was on the jury of the Anderson trial. To my surprise, I was
told that someone was already using it: the gentleman sitting across the
table from me. That is how I met Richard E. Hart, who immediately inquired in his enthusiastic way about my research. As a private research project, he has created an annotated directory of Springfield in the year
1860—not so far off from the year of my particular interest, 1856—and he
was kind enough to let me consult the portion of it relevant to this book.
Mr. Hart is currently the president of the Abraham Lincoln Association, a
venerable and yet vibrant organization located in Springfield.

The McLean County Historical Society's Stevenson-Ives Library in
Bloomington, Illinois, has a valuable collection, located in the old County
Courthouse. I am particularly grateful to Ardys Serpette for her patience in
finding many critical items for me. The Illinois Regional Archive Depository at the University of Illinois at Springfield found the probate records for
the George Anderson estate, along with many other items from the case. I
am also indebted to John Hoffmann of the Main Library at the University
of Illinois at Urbana-Champaign.

The Library of Congress was instrumental in the research. Two institutions near my home in Upstate New York have collections of Lincoln books
as fine as any outside of Springfield: Cornell University and the Buffalo &
Erie County Library. The Onondaga County Public Library Inter-Library
Loan Department was diligent, as usual, in bringing many dozens of micro-
filmed newspapers within my reach. I am also indebted to the State University of New York at Morrisville and Onondaga County Community
College.

My literary agent, Joelle Delbourgo, heard about my interest in Abraham Lincoln's life and career in Springfield, and believed even before I did
that it needed to open into a book. I am now in a position to be grateful for
her insistence. Alessandra Bastagli, senior editor at Palgrave Macmillan, has
given the project her fullest support since she first heard of it. She has been
encouraging at every turn. I also owe special thanks to Alan Bradshaw, pro-
duction director at Palgrave, who led the manuscript through the editing
process with uncommon care and insight.

My uncle and aunt, Howard and Lynn Berk, arranged my trip to the Lincoln Memorial University in Harrogate, Tennessee, a town all the more charming because it isn't near anything except chains of mountains and the Cumberland Gap. As far as I could see, there was no way to get there from Upstate New York, except in a canoe. But my aunt and uncle picked me up at the Atlanta airport and drove me, for which I will always be grateful. My uncle interrupted work on his latest novel to make the tour.

I owe Richard Harfmann more than can ever be repaid for his encouragement from the inception of this project. He went on innumerable research trips with me, chatting on the way about all the latest news (of 1856) and seeing nothing of the local sights except the stacks at the libraries.

Douglas Brinkley has been a friend for many years, a born teacher and historian who has become a leader in the field. I was very fortunate that he took an interest in this book from the start.

My father was supportive in every way, from learning to use the photocopy machine at the Buffalo & Erie County Library to giving me dispensation to miss his birthday, in favor of working on the book. Thank you to him, to Paul, and always Neddy.

Wisconsin

Lake Michigan

Galena ○
JO DAVIESS

Iowa

OGLE
○ Oregon

○ Dixon
LEE

Chicago ○

COOK

Princeton ○

○ Ottawa

Indiana

KANKAKEE

WOODFORD
○ Metamora
Peoria ○
○ Eureka
○ Pekin
TAZEWELL

McLEAN

○ Bloomington

VERMILION

Mississippi River

Lincoln ○
DeWITT
○ Clinton
LOGAN

Urbana ○

Danville ○

MACON

CHAMPAIGN

Quincy ○

MORGAN
Springfield ●
○ Decatur
SANGAMON

EDGAR
Paris
○

Jacksonville ○

COLES
○ Grand View
Charleston ○

MACOUPIN

Shelbyville ○

Jerseyville ○

FAYETTE
○ Vandalia

Alton ○

LAWRENCE

St. Louis ○

Missouri

ST. CLAIR
○ Belleville

ILLINOIS
showing sites
of importance to
Lincoln in 1856

Kentucky

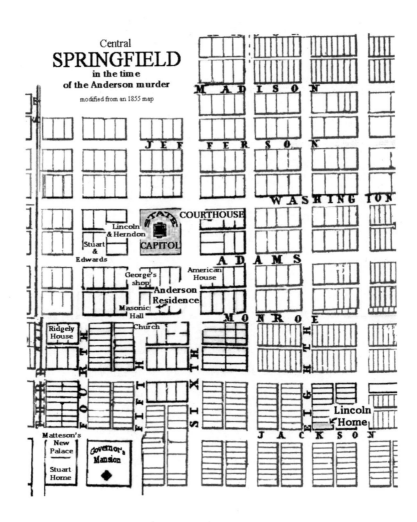

Central
SPRINGFIELD
in the time
of the Anderson murder

modified from an 1855 map

M A D I S O N

J E F F E R S O N

W A S H I N G T O N

COURTHOUSE

Lincoln & Herndon

Stuart & Edwards

STATE CAPITOL

George's shop

American House

A D A M S

Anderson Residence

Masonic Hall

M O N R O E

Church

Ridgely House

F O U R T H

F I F T H

S I X T H

S E V E N T H

Lincoln Home

E I G H T H

J A C K S O N

Matteson's New Palace

Governor's Mansion

Stuart Home

LINCOLN IN HIS ELEMENT

BY DR. DOUGLAS BRINKLEY

E ven as President Abraham Lincoln's two inaugural addresses and the Gettysburg Address live on in history for their literary eloquence, the Emancipation Proclamation (issued January 1, 1863) gets short shrift. Terse, unemotional, and carefully worded, the Proclamation was tactically written with the U.S. Supreme Court in mind. Always a constitutionalist, Lincoln knew that to truly abolish slavery he would have to argue his case in a court of law. To liberate African Americans he needed the skill of a circuit lawyer, not the impassioned zeal of William Lloyd Garrison. Recognizing that only judicial logic would free the slaves, Karl Marx, reporting for a European newspaper, saluted Lincoln, writing that the "most formidable decrees which he hurls at the enemy and which will never lose their historic significance, resemble—as the author intends them to—ordinary summons, sent by one lawyer to another."

Marx was on to something. For, more than any other U.S. president, Lincoln was a master lawyer. According to the Lincoln Legal Papers, which historian Julie Fenster consulted in writing this rich narrative, from 1836 (bar admittance) to 1861 (presidential inauguration) Lincoln was involved in over 5,100 cases. That is a truly staggering number. Most were in Sangamon County, but he also "rode the circuit" around Central Illinois, trading his legal services as wares. A specialist in debt-related law, Lincoln was also involved in nearly thirty murder cases. More than just a seasoned lawyer, he was a hardened one. Gawky and full of moral rectitude, he was to become one of the premier lawyers in Illinois. His *aw-shucks*, homespun advocacy grew into the stuff of legend. While it's true that Lincoln's most steadfast client was the Illinois Central Railroad, Lincoln, a first-rate lawyer for hire also worked on over sixty cases *against* the booming railroad industry.

Lincolnania is a cottage industry, yet just when it seems that we've learned as much about our prairie leader as is historically possible, this book is chock-full of new insights on his pre-presidential years. Based on first-hand anecdotes (most of them unpublished before this), it tells the story of Lincoln's life as a middle-class professional man. Fenster's portrait doesn't at all resemble Henry Fonda in the 1939 movie, *Young Mr. Lincoln*, or Carl Sandburg's honest rail-splitting hayseed of poetic lore. There is no overt romanticism in these pages. Following Lincoln's legal and political career in chronological fashion, she brings to light important new legal cases previously unknown to 1850s history. Fenster shines a clear light on the all-too-human legal draftsman nicknamed Honest Abe. With battered old stovepipe hat in hand, his ambition knew no bounds.

Like Doris Kearns Goodwin in *Team of Rivals*, Fenster deftly profiles a group of Lincoln's steadfast peers. While Goodwin focused on Lincoln's national adversaries, however, Fenster showcases law partners, circuit riders, and courtroom duelers like William Herndon, Usher Linder, John Stuart, and John Palmer. Her groundbreaking treatment of the Anderson Murder Case—in which Lincoln cohorts with the dregs of society—rescues from oblivion a truly important flashpoint in our sixteenth president's march to greatness.

Fenster's longtime interest in Lincoln's legal career has now grown into a seminal study of Abraham Lincoln. Fenster insists that it's crucial we understand Lincoln the lawyer, if we're to honor Lincoln the president whole-heartedly. In this, her eighth book, she delivers the goods.

Douglas Brinkley
New Orleans
March 15, 2007

CHAPTER 1

MARCH, 1856

LIKE A CATHEDRAL

Dr. George Angell grew up in Providence, Rhode Island, and returned there to settle into a predictably comfortable life after graduating from Harvard Medical School in 1847. Six years later, in 1853, it occurred to him that his life was perhaps a little too predictable.

"About this time, many favorable reports were coming from the western country," he wrote, "and being seized with the land fever, I determined to go west and buy some land."[1] No sooner did word spread that he was in the market, than a man named Remington K. Webster showed up at his door in Providence, offering a farm for sale in Logan County, in the heart of Illinois. Angell took note.

Central Illinois, a generation removed from its frontier days, was in the grip of a new kind of momentum, propelled by improvements in agriculture and enticed by the progress of the railroad. In the short time since Dr. Angell started his career, land prices in Springfield had more than doubled.[2] Returns such as that looked slick in Providence, where money invested in a typical bond took almost twenty years to double. Even beyond the rates and the numbers, though, Angell wanted to move out west someday.

Webster fully understood Dr. Angell's fascination with the West. He had likewise grown up in New England, a place that tied ambition to patience. In some hearts, however, the two traits resided as natural enemies. Illinois in the 1850s offered a more buoyant scenario. Its population was burgeoning with the usual migrants, of course, people bereft of prospects back home, but it also drew another sort: the well-educated and well-heeled, assured of success anywhere they chose to live. The difference was that in Illinois, they didn't have to wait their turn.

In 1848, Remington Webster had purchased three tracts in Logan County, Illinois,[3] and as it turned out, he could hardly have chosen a better section. His land was close to the proposed route of Illinois' first north-south railroad. For years, the line had been delayed in a frustration of rumors and false starts. Webster bided his time. Then, in 1853, with the railroad not only under construction but nearing completion, he was ready to cash in. Moreover, he had a plan by which to improve on his windfall.

Webster was going to sell land he didn't own anymore. Someone else, a man named Gill, held an order of execution against the farm, the residue of a legal skirmish over an unpaid debt amounting to about one-sixth the value of the land. Within a few months, the deed would automatically transfer to Gill. So it was that in June 1853, Webster was rushing Dr. Angell out to Illinois from the east to see the land, sign the papers, and make payment.

Farmers in the older states devoted season after season, a whole life through, to making their fields more level and fertile, and less rocky. In central Illinois, the land beckoned as though the hard work had already been done. Webster's farm was uniformly flat and fertile. That was the geography of the place, all the way to the horizon. "Surpassingly beautiful," said a former settler, recalling his first sight of the Illinois prairie, "Covered with luxuriant grass, interspersed with flowers of every hue, which gracefully bent with every passing breeze."[4]

As the two New Englanders stood on the prairie, looking over the acreage for sale, Dr. Angell had only one complaint: there wasn't enough of it. He had more money and he wanted more land. With a customer in that frame of mind, Webster just so happened to have another tract, and he offered it up at just $2.25 per acre—quite a bargain. Webster didn't own that tract, either, but at least he was on good terms with the man who did.

While Dr. Angell was scurrying around Logan County, marveling at the sheer infinity of the sky, and signing checks, he unexpectedly heard "that Webster's reputation was not of the best."[5] Soon afterward, he learned that that assessment was, if anything, generous. A search of the county's court records revealed the looming specter of the execution order. Angell was aghast at the situation, but nonetheless he sprang all over it. For a medical man, he not only understood real estate law but something about combat. First, he paid off the old debt and obtained the execution order from Gill. While that wouldn't likewise convey the deed, it did mean that Gill, unwittingly cast as the tip of Webster's whip in the swindle, was effectively removed from the scenario. Then, before Angell left to return to his practice in Providence, he faced off with Webster. Producing a fresh agreement he said that he would let the matter drop without pressing charges if Webster signed it. The agreement stipulated that Dr. Angell didn't have to make further payment on the land until Webster provided a document proving his outright ownership. As Dr. Angell knew full well by that point, Webster didn't have any such document, nor could he get it without obtaining the execution order, which was in Angell's possession. Regardless, the agreement was signed. "Webster was now at my mercy,"[6] Angell concluded with a sinister air. If and when the doctor was ready to make payment on the land, the sale would be completed.

In March of 1856, Dr. Angell was ready. He returned to Logan County exquisitely prepared for his final triumph over R. K. Webster. On his arrival, though, he learned that his plans would have to change somewhat. Webster was in the process of suing him.

Webster's contention was that all previous agreements were void, since his wife, a co-owner of the farm, hadn't signed them.

"I was advised," Angell recalled, "to go to Springfield and consult Abraham Lincoln about the matter."[7] He may well have wondered why he couldn't hire a local attorney. In truth, several lawyers operated offices in Logan County, but they had yet to match the reputation of anyone from

Springfield, one of the three cities in the state that veritably collected great lawyers. The other two were Chicago and Bloomington. Springfield was the state capital and Chicago had grown into the biggest city in the region. Bloomington's legal strength was more of an anomaly, but in all three places, good lawyers apparently brought out the best in one other, raising expectations as they stirred competition. While some of Illinois' other cities had their stars, the serious work and the big cases typically found their way to the attorneys from the three towns that hit the hardest, when it came to legal matters.

Dr. Angell, as intent on victory as anyone who is being sued by their swindler, was on the next morning's train to Springfield. A little less than three hours later, he arrived, stepping down off a car at the Chicago, Alton, and St. Louis Railroad station, which consisted of a small warehouse and a place where the train could stop on the north side of town.

The whole city of Springfield, population 7,250,[8] was only about fifteen blocks-square. From the station to Lincoln's office downtown was a distance of five blocks. It was a short walk, but probably an arduous one—in Springfield at the time, the only thing more stubborn than the mud was the city government's reluctance to spend money on sidewalks. Because Angell's path took him along several commercial blocks, he could depend in some measure on the plank-walks provided by building owners. That left him with only one problem: crossing the streets. When he made his way across the intersection of Jefferson and Fifth, he had to plan a route around a sink-hole big enough to have become a pond and old enough to have wildlife.[9] It was the same all over the state; Chicago, already fond of superlatives, was said to have the streets with the deepest, stickiest mud of them all.

As Dr. Angell looked up and down the cross-streets of Madison, Jefferson, and Washington (with more presidents—Adams and Monroe—just beyond his route), he could see that most of Springfield was no more crowded than a village. Even near the center of the city, wide lawns surrounded most of the homes and empty lots aired out the rest. Before long, though, Angell would not be looking around, but up, as every visitor did when the State House came into view. The home of all Illinois' state gov-

ernment, the State House was very much the center of the city of Springfield, presiding from its own spacious square. The first part to come into view
from a distance was the wooden dome, painted white and jutting up more
than a hundred feet. Roundly colonial in style, it was anything but a harbin-
ger of the building itself. Instead, it was a contrast to the main building, presiding so sternly in its Greek Revival style and buff-colored sandstone.

By the time Angell had a full look at the State House, he was in downtown Springfield, where rows of three- and even four-story buildings cra-
dled the square. Directly across from where he stood was the County
Courthouse, tall and thin in whitish brick. A veritable second home for
Springfield's lawyers, it was as loyal to Greek architecture with its Doric
columns and classic pediment as the State House before it.

Lincoln's office was on the opposite side of the square from the County
Courthouse, on the second floor of a red brick building at 103 South Fifth
Street.[10] Dr. Angell was probably muddy by the time he reached the build-
ing, but it didn't matter much. Most business offices then, especially in the
West, were little more than workrooms. Law offices tended to be even more
rustic than others.

Dr. Angell disappeared into the building on the square and started up
the stairs. The office that Lincoln shared with his partner, William Herndon, was at the back of the building. Spartan by any standards, it was decorated mostly by unfiled papers and abandoned books. The office consisted
of just one room dominated by two long tables arranged in a "T" and covered by the coarse green felt known as baize. The comforts consisted of a
wood-burning stove and a spittoon; pictures of George Washington and
Andrew Jackson hung on the walls.[11] Aside from some chairs and a bench,
there were exactly two other pieces of furniture. The first was a bookcase
and the second, a secretary. It was a modest secretary, at that, just an upright
desk with pigeon-holes overlooking a writing surface.

Throughout the month of March, 1856, Lincoln was to be in court,
either Federal or County, nearly every day. Although he handled dozens
of matters during that span, most were dispatched rather quickly with in-
dividual filings or motions. Only eight went to trial, each typically lasting
less than a half-day.

Lincoln was devoting a lot of time in March to questions of land use—ones on a grander scale than Angell's 380-acre squabble. He had been hired to compose two opinions on real estate law. Running to about a half-dozen handwritten pages each, they were on the subject of pre-emption, the right of settlers to claim ownership of lands ultimately sold by the government to, for example, a railroad. One was written for a lawyer representing such settlers in Beloit, Wisconsin; the other for the Illinois Central Railroad, Lincoln & Herndon's steadiest client.[12]

Researching precedents on which to rest such opinions was not Lincoln's favorite aspect of the law. The year before, however, in a moment of self-doubt during a case in conjunction with a team of nationally known attorneys, he'd resolved to concentrate on his practice, "to study law,"[13] as he bluntly expressed it, more deeply than had been his habit. His objective was to keep from slipping in the profession as its standards rose. In that vein, he made a thorough survey for both of the opinions he wrote, delving into copies of *Land Laws, Land Opinions* or snatches copied from the U.S. statute books at the State Capitol library.

"I immediately went to his office and found him in," Angell recalled of his meeting with Lincoln,

> He was seated with his arms resting on a table and his long legs crossed. He was so different from any person I had ever seen that for a moment I was dazed. The man looked like a cathedral.
>
> I stated my business, and feeling in my vest pocket, produced a ten dollar gold piece which I offered him as a retainer's fee. He was silent for a moment, and then said as he pushed my money toward me, "I'm sorry, I'm sorry, but that fellow [Webster] was here not half an hour ago and I took five dollars of his money. But I'll tell you what to do; you go see John T. Stewart [sic], he's a better lawyer than I am anyway."[14]

Angell had lost the first round to Webster, and by a factor of only a half-hour. Within a few minutes of leaving Lincoln, though, he was at the office of Stuart & Edwards, around the corner, and just off the square. Both John Stuart and his younger partner, Benjamin S. Edwards, were socialites around Springfield. They were also both related to Lincoln's wife, Mary: Stuart as a cousin and Edwards as an in-law. That made them relatives of Lincoln's, as well, but the referral wasn't based on nepotism. For one thing, socialites who were related to Mary Lincoln were a remarkably common item in Springfield.

Anyway, Lincoln was not alone in his appraisal of John Stuart's ability. Usher Linder, a fellow lawyer from eastern Illinois, said of Stuart, "He had the reputation of being the ablest and most efficient lawyer in the State, especially in trespass and slander cases."[15] Stuart, a college-educated lawyer from Kentucky, had been Lincoln's mentor and his first partner, nineteen years before. They dissolved the firm without rancor after four years; apparently because Stuart didn't believe in splitting fees equally and Lincoln couldn't live on his percentage.

Both Stuart and Lincoln had long been interested in politics, standing as candidates for various offices, though with no particular success on either side. Stuart had, however, accumulated a fortune, mostly through land investments. His house faced the governor's residence in Springfield and was next-door to the most stupendous residential construction project south of Chicago: the showplace mansion of the outgoing governor, Joel Matteson, who was planning to remain in the capital city after his term ended at the end of the year. Even half-finished, Matteson's house was impressive, with a four-story tower and a gaggle of outbuildings. Stuart lived in his own substantial house with his wife, Mary, and five of their six children; their oldest daughter, Betty, was away at boarding school.

"When I first saw him," said Linder of John Stuart, "which was in 1837, I thought him the handsomest man in Illinois. He had the mildest and most amiable expression of countenance I nearly ever saw. He is eminently cheerful, social and good-humored, and a man would be a fiend to pick a quarrel with him."[16]

Stuart's amiability was sincere, but it was also a factor in his professional technique. Colleagues couldn't say what, if anything, was at work behind his playful nature. The same might be said for Lincoln, his former protégé, except that he was a much more moody man. Stuart was all smoothed out, and in a legal case he investigated his adversary's position meticulously without ever seeming to do anything of the kind. As a fellow lawyer, Joseph Gillespie, said, "He keeps his own batteries* masked, while those of the opposite side are closely scrutinized."[17]

Less fastidiously, other lawyers nicknamed him "Jerry Sly."[18] In March 1856, Stuart was not investigating people, though, but pipes. He was on a special committee studying the feasibility of a water system for the city based on artesian wells.[19] It was one of his frequent forays into civic issues—of the type that held no interest for Lincoln. The committee report was due on March 14, and so Stuart's desk was more likely piled with water-table charts and treatises on hydraulic engineering than with law books when Dr. Angell arrived.

Dr. Angell explained his case for the second time that morning and Stuart agreed to represent him. Then they sat talking. The conversation eventually turned to Lincoln, the only other person in Springfield that Angell knew.

"I have never seen Mr. Lincoln before, but he appears to me to be a remarkable man," Angell said, according to his account of the meeting.

"He is," Stuart agreed.

"Has he any political ambitions?" Dr. Angell asked.

Stuart replied in a stage whisper. His big eyes glistened. "I think," he said, "he has."[20]

---

* cannons

CHAPTER 2

APRIL

AT THE ANVIL

On the night of March 19, a Wednesday, the four children in the Anderson family heard the sound of men outside: talking, sometimes shouting, their boots shuffling against the street. Dozens and then hundreds of men were walking by the front windows of the Anderson house on Monroe Street, making their way in the dimming twilight to a meeting at the Springfield Masonic Hall next door. George Anderson, who owned the house with his wife, Jane, knew about the gathering: his brother William was one of the organizers.[1] But the people in the houses hadn't been expecting such a big crowd or so much noise, not on a Wednesday night.

Anyone could have been frightened by the strangers so suddenly outside the windows, anyone who didn't already know that the men had business in the neighborhood. Anderson knew. He was still uneasy as darkness fell on Wednesday night—even if it was, as he'd told his children, just a meeting at the Masonic Hall.

On Monroe Street between 5th and 6th streets, it was practically always the Masonic Hall. It was the main source of news and incident in the neighborhood. Otherwise, the block was so quiet it could have been a still-life. On the far corner was the Third Presbyterian Church, with the Andersons' place and a couple of other houses in between. The Methodist Church was across the street, built without a steeple, and shaped like a bank vault. It was next to the block's finest residence, the home of a man who described his occupation only as "gentleman." On the block, he was known as a land speculator.

Springfield wasn't as yet well-defined in its neighborhoods. Monroe, within a block or two of Fifth Street, boasted more than its share of ostentatious homes, and in the very midst of them was a sprawling blacksmith shop, strewn with carriages and parts. Another smithy, Talbott and Anderson, co-owned by George Anderson, was located around the corner on Fifth, just past the Masonic Hall. Anderson could go to work every day just by walking through his backyard and then turning into the service alley that ran behind the houses. As a Free Mason,[2] he could also attend meetings of the fraternal order at the Hall every month, without much exertion.

Anderson fit well into Springfield: he was prosperous in his business, and yet no one noticed him much beyond that, in either a laudatory or a derogatory way. He could have been the city's median citizen, its everyman. Or just another emigrant from the east, hoping the boom wasn't over yet. Raised on a farm in New Jersey, Anderson went west in the early 1840s and settled in Springfield, as did two of his brothers. He was a well-trained blacksmith and was welcomed from the start in the growing city. For a few years, he worked for an older smith named R. F. Coflin, and over that same span he married and started a family. Eventually, Anderson came to the conclusion that working for Coflin's blacksmith shop was not the way to grow rich. Coincidentally enough, Coflin came to the same conclusion. With a bad case of gold fever, he dropped everything to go to California with the Forty-niners.

Anderson was no doubt tempted to go to California, too, but he had to stay home for the sake of his family. Taking over Coflin's smithy, he wrote out an ad for the newspaper, to announce his proprietorship. "Farmers and others may depend on having their work done promptly," Anderson promised. No mere shoer of horses, he was an all-around metalworker, listing his lines of work as reinforcing wagons with iron, making plows and other implements, and even repairing pumps.[3]

All the while, Anderson longed for a partnership, regarding it as a shortcut to a bigger shop. In no time, however, he learned that it is far easier to form a partnership than to survive one. As the 1840s turned into the 1850s, he was learning the same lesson about once a year, making and breaking partnerships with the passing seasons. In 1851, he finally had a better start and the opportunity to join forces with someone he already knew.

After two years in California, Mr. Coflin, Anderson's old boss, drifted back to Springfield and placed a jovial announcement in the paper: "R. F. Coflin, having returned from the Gold Diggings, has concluded to try his old trade, and 'dig gold' by hammering at the anvil, and for that purpose he and George Anderson have entered into partnership."[4] The pair were not only old comrades, they were among the city's best-known blacksmiths. And that gave Anderson the chance to learn two more lessons.

Friendship didn't matter and neither did fame. When Anderson and Coflin dissolved the business less than a year later, an announcement in the paper plaintively requested all those still owing money to the firm to leave the funds at a local store—Wright & Brown crockery—"as we must have money to pay our debts."[5]

Late in 1852, Anderson made one final try at a partnership, signing with a reliable blacksmith named William Talbott. Anderson had been right to keep taking chances; their partnership was so productive that they soon moved into the two-story shop on Fifth Street near Monroe. They employed a platoon of employees to keep the work moving along, and Anderson was able to provide his family with a larger house—the one on Monroe—with a neat front lawn behind a decorative iron fence. In the spring of 1856, he and Talbott took yet another step forward. Realizing that they had already outgrown the shop on Fifth Street, they made plans to move into even bigger quarters. The business was humming along just the way Anderson had always hoped, but it wasn't enough. His neighbors, all the while, were accumulating fortunes.

When people in New Orleans had money to invest, they participated in ship cargoes. In New York City, they took shares in railroads, but in

Springfield, extra cash went into land speculation. Residents of Central Illinois were consumed by the dream of acreage. Whether or not they did anything about it, they knew good land was out there, surrounding the city like a different kind of gold. Over the years, Anderson purchased a few tracts in the countryside, and several lots in town, one of which he co-owned with Talbott.

At thirty-six, George Anderson lived quietly, looking to the Masons for most of his friendships. He had come a long way, and he was edging toward the comfortable end of the middle class, with hired help for the house, tuition for the children's school, and new clothes for his wife whenever she had the whim. That's what Anderson wanted. More work and more money, and then he went home through the alley to the big backyard and the house with the iron fence in front. Unlike others, who gave in to drinking or gambling, George Anderson just liked to go home and rest. In March of 1856, it wasn't working out that way, though.

Three young men boarded with the Anderson family: two apprentices, and George's nephew, Theodore. The Andersons were not unusual in having paying guests. In Springfield, homeowners were expected to make room for relatives from back east, acquaintances from the country, and anyone else looking for a start in the growing city. The newcomers were predominantly young men, with money for room and board, but not much else. The Andersons managed to find places for all ten of the people under their roof, putting the children in one bedroom, along with the hired girl, and turning the dining room into a kind of men's dormitory—when family meals weren't being served there. In the latter part of March, however, George decided that one of the boarders was going to have to move.

The two apprentices were all right, they knew their place. The problems were with Theodore, who had arrived from New Jersey in November. At twenty-three, he wasn't doing anything about getting a steady job. He was a mason by trade; Springfield would have offered plenty of work, if he had been interested. In fact, Theodore wasn't interested in anything at all, except hanging around the house with his aunt and with the children, when the three older ones weren't at school.

George Anderson was in the position, yet again, of having to go to someone and have it out, to bust it up and clear the way. The amount of turmoil he faced must have surprised him. He lived along a little path from the backdoor to the shop and back, yet it was a challenge to defend even that small strand of an empire. Altogether, the house no longer felt comfortable, inside or out. Anderson was convinced that a man was casing the property, lurking in the yard, waiting for his chance to—Anderson wasn't sure what. And he wasn't glad to see anyone on his block at night, least of all hundreds of strangers in their boisterous mood, streaming toward the Masonic Hall on Wednesday the 19th.

The two hundred men on their way into the Hall were the stuff of the People's Mass Meeting. William Anderson almost certainly convinced his brother right next door to join them.

With voters smoldering over two national issues in 1856—the extension of slavery and the suppression of Catholicism—the political parties were in flux. During the month of March, however, residents of Springfield were more captivated, or at least more amused, by the search for municipal candidates. Because people were alienated from one another the instant that party affiliations were discussed, though, a group of Springfield citizens decided to bypass the parties altogether and nominate a slate of candidates by acclamation. That was the purpose of the People's Mass Meeting.

The favorite for treasurer was Presco Wright, the receiver for George Anderson's broken partnerships.[6] He had broken up his own partnership, Wright & Brown, the previous week. The crockery was gone and so was Mr. Brown. John Cook, a lawyer who was already mayor, was nominated for a second term. One of Anderson's fellow blacksmiths snatched a nomination for alderman.

Once the roster of candidates was complete, the meeting broke up and the men started for home, each one of them having "become a worker for the city's good," as the chairman had put it.[7] With that, they lit their lanterns and disappeared into Monroe Street, east or west.

After George Anderson returned home, he took off his clothes and climbed into bed. The room he shared with his wife was on the first floor, in the back corner of the house. For weeks, he hadn't been sleeping very well. If Wednesday night was like every other one, he didn't shut his eyes, even after he snuffed out the candle by the bed. Long after the meeting broke up and the voices disappeared from the street, Anderson would be lying awake in the dark, listening.

Within two days, the People's Ticket was tottering. Presco Wright wrote a letter to the Springfield *Register*, arrogantly denying that he would ever, under any circumstances, deign to run for office in Springfield. Another man was selected and publicized, though in the enthusiasm to forget the Presco Wright affair, no one asked him if he wanted to run. He didn't. He said so in his own subsequent letter to the newspaper. The problems mounted: Mayor Cook, who had always been an upstanding citizen, was publicly accused of stealing $47 from the Odd Fellows annual festival.[8] He responded in the manner of a guilty schoolboy, explaining, when pressed, that he didn't exactly steal it.

William Herndon, of the Lincoln & Herndon law firm, remained aloof from such dust-ups. He regarded himself as a humanitarian far above the level of local issues, of artesian wells, and Odd Fellows. "A man," he wrote the day before the Mass Meeting, "who, in this crisis and in this age, has no opinion on slavery is a miserable thing." He pondered that for a while and then continued, "He who dares not express that opinion respectfully is not an uncommon one." It was a vague reference, but Herndon was frustrated that more people, such as his law partner, for example, were not entirely open with their anti-slavery convictions.

Abraham Lincoln had begun to express his views two years before, most notably in a speech delivered at Peoria and later published in its entirety in the Springfield *State Journal*. More recently, though, he'd been laying low. That was something Herndon would never do. With frequent letters to the editor and an active speaking schedule, Herndon had become Springfield's leading abolitionist: he believed in an immediate and outright end of slavery. His position was only a little surprising, because his younger brother, Elliott, also a lawyer, was staunchly in favor of maintaining the status quo: letting the South keep its slavery and letting most of the West choose, state by state, whether to allow it or not.

William, 38, and Elliott, 36, had spent most of their lives in Springfield, where their father owned a tavern and enough other enterprises to give them a comfortable start. William took after his father, a tall man, energetic and emotional in temperament.[9] A trifle spoiled, the two brothers had come into adulthood as something like Springfield's first modern citizens: not pioneers humbled by the difficulty of life, but headstrong, enticed by their own potential.

The two Herndon brothers stood on opposing lines in the debate over slavery. In between them were other opinions, vehemently held, that would grant the existence of slavery in some places, not others, or under certain circumstances, duly described. The most contentious issue was the extension of the slavery question by the 1854 Kansas-Nebraska Law, championed by Senator Stephen Douglas of Illinois. Douglas' law replaced the Missouri Compromise, which was discussed at least as often and as passionately in the mid-1850s as when it was first passed in 1820. The Missouri Compromise constituted a trade-off. Anti-slavery forces allowed Missouri to come into the Union as a slave state, so long as pro-slavery forces accepted that Maine would come in as a free state, and that Western states lying north of 36 deg. 30 min. (a continuation of Missouri's southern border) were to be free when they came into the Union.

For thirty-four years, the Compromise remained in effect, and was regarded by many Americans the same way the Dutch regarded a dyke. As long as it stood, the country was safe. Then in 1854, when pro-slavery forces in Congress blocked attempts to organize and open new lands in the West so long as they were under the provisions of the Missouri Compromise, the Kansas-Nebraska Law replaced the Compromise. It gave those same prospective states, north of 36 deg. 30 min., the right to decide for themselves whether to allow slavery or not. The law infuriated those who were against slavery, not to mention those who just didn't like getting clipped in a trade. That disgruntled faction labelled itself "Anti-Nebraska."

Early in 1856, the crisis over slavery was a national obsession, yet the argument was ill-defined—except in the Herndon family, of course. And a powerful third party was pulling the swirl even further askew. The Know Nothing movement had started in the early 1840s as a secret society. The name derived from the members' habit of replying to prying questions by repeating the same refrain: "I know nothing." In 1854, the furtive Know

Nothings had made a strong political debut, placing nine governors and forty-three Congressmen in office.[10] They intended to exert even more influence in 1856. (Officially, they were by then called the American Party, but that title was rarely used.) The overriding concern of the Know Nothings was with blocking Catholic immigration into the United States. Yet they weren't racists. It was perfectly common, especially in the northeast, to favor freedom for slaves, and deportment for Catholics.[11] Never were the labels, "liberal" and "conservative" so meaningless as in the presidential election year of 1856.

Party designations were fairly meaningless, too. The Democratic Party was looming large, but most Democrats qualified their affiliation with a prefix—a Douglas Democrat, a Slave Democrat, an Anti-Nebraska Democrat, a Free Soil Democrat, and so forth—all of which indicated that the behemoth was on the verge of shattering. The opposition was in far worse shape. People who called themselves Whigs likewise gave themselves prefixes (many of the same ones used by the Democrats), despite the fact that their party had disappeared under them, like a waterlogged barge. Abraham Lincoln described himself as an "Old Line Whig," which was a benign way of clinging to the old wreckage without offending too many of the other prefixes.

Early in 1856, however, Lincoln had begun to sense that a major shift was imminent. He knew that a strong party would arise to face the Democrats, but he didn't believe that it would be the Know Nothings. In February, Lincoln had a preview of one effort to bracket a new political party around the confusion left by the shifting—and disappearing—affiliations. On Washington's Birthday, he was invited to a meeting of newspaper editors in Decatur, about 35 miles east of Springfield, an easy hour's trip on the Great Western Railroad line. The purpose of the meeting was to organize Anti-Nebraska political forces in Illinois, without rgard for previous party affiliations. In other words, the meeting was intended to encompass all those people incensed at the idea that slavery was even a possibility in the West.[12] Around the country, others were giving in to the same inclination toward *fusion*, in the expression of the day, pulling disparate elements into an opposition party. The Illinois editors were among the earliest to act formally. Though Lincoln was not an editor, he had al-ways maintained friendly relations with journalists, and he received a spe-cial invitation to the Decatur meeting from George T. Brown, a good friend and the proprietor of the *Courier* in Alton, near the southwest cor-ner of Illinois.

The poor *Courier* was a money-losing proposition, but it couldn't die. The little paper was too important as a symbol of the passions at work all around it. Because Illinois was a microcosm of the United States on the issue of slavery (the northern part was against it, and the southern part was for it, with the middle part blurry), George Brown may as well have run an anti-slavery newspaper in the heart of Alabama as in Southern Illinois. Alton was a special case, though. The city had its own abolitionist roots that made the *Courier* more of a declaration than a business. One night nineteen years before, in 1837, an armed crowd had set out to destroy the printing press of an earlier abolition newspaper in Alton. The mob was doubly dan-gerous: unleashed by the moral climate, and unrestrained by the deputies in town. The editor of the newspaper, Elijah Lovejoy, tried to protect the printing press, courageously, and stupidly. When he was spotted in the open, more than one person in the crowd opened fire. He was hit with five bullets, and died on the spot. That was part of the reason Brown brought out the *Courier*, whether Alton would read it or not.

No picture or physical description of George Brown, a bachelor, is known to exist today, but in early 1856, he actually gave an endorsement to a grooming product. It was something called Professor Wood's Hair Restora-tive. Perhaps he had to do it, in order to sell an ad to Professor Wood. How-ever, in black and white, the angry rabble-rouser announced "that a few applications of it made him look so young and handsome that he felt like getting married."[13] He would, apparently, do anything for the *Courier*.

After receiving Brown's invitation to join the editors at their Conven-tion, Abraham Lincoln refused to accept—or to decline. The most he said, in a conversation about a week in advance, was that he thought he would "try and have some business in Decatur at the time of the Convention."[14] He ultimately made good on that promise and showed up, but he entered into the effort to organize a new party trepidaciously. Lincoln gave the editors suggestions on the platform of the proposed party, and was later described as "a very genial and capable advisor."[15] He also accepted the invitation to speak at the concluding banquet. At that, the Springfield *Register* chided that when it came to giving a speech, Lincoln was "ready at the tap of the fusion drum, on all occasions." Yet Lincoln was careful to keep his distance from the nascent party, declining any official role in the organization. Instead, he stood aside as the attendees appointed William Herndon to their central steering committee. Lincoln was apprehensive about aligning with factions that he regarded as unelectable, most notably those spearheaded by outright abolitionists. Likewise, he was considered by the abolitionists to be too conservative in his own anti-slavery position. In all things and at all moments, they wanted action.

William Herndon was among them. He immediately wrote a letter for publication in the Springfield *State Journal* proclaiming his role on the central committee of the editors' Anti-Nebraska party. In his righteous way, he reflected, "The appointment is deemed by me the highest honor of my life."[16] He went on in two full columns to explain why. Herndon often sent letters-to-the-editor to the *Journal.* So it was that in March of 1856, everyone who read the paper knew what Herndon was thinking, feeling, predicting, and demanding, but no one, anywhere, was sure where Lincoln was headed politically.

Aside from John Stuart, not many people were convinced that Abraham Lincoln still did have political ambitions. Not many people cared. "No one here during Lincoln's active life as lawyer and politician looked on him as likely to have a greater, grander, and more glorious place in the history of his country than any one of a half dozen others then living here," commented a lawyer from Bloomington, Peter Whitmer.[17] In early 1856, Lincoln was inclined to the same opinion. He even professed himself a failure in terms of his earlier ambition to hold office in Washington. "None of us thought much about him one way or another," said John M. Palmer, a lawyer who was active in politics, "I regarded Lincoln as a good lawyer and a fair sort of speaker."[18]

Lincoln had delivered effective addresses, but then, everyone in his circle could say the same. In the manner of actors in a producer's ante room,

Stuart, Palmer, Edwards, Herndon, and at least twenty other figures in Illinois politics in 1856 could, if they wanted, pass around tattered clippings referring to their own triumphs in front of an audience.

Illinois may have been young, but it had no shortage of sophisticated politicians, anxious to go to Washington in one capacity or another. The competition within the state helped to propel those who did break through, preparing them for anything the national stage might demand. Nonetheless, with the terrific concentration of talent, it was a daunting time to pretend to political ambition in Illinois. Lincoln was certainly part of the upper echelon in the state's political circles, but while some were noticeably moving ahead, it wasn't clear where he was.

The favorite of the state's Anti-Nebraskans in early 1856 was William Bissell, a former Democrat. A wellspring of excitement arose at the mere mention of his name, especially in relation to a run for the governorship. Bissell was, by all accounts, the man to watch in Illinois politics.

A country boy raised in unpretentious circumstances in upstate New York, Bissell possessed natural elegance and "great force of argument," in the words of a neighbor in Illinois.[19] He had been to Yale and earned a medical degree in Philadelphia, before moving to Illinois to start a practice. He was only there a short time before he realized that nearly all of the influence in the state belonged to the lawyers. He thereupon became a lawyer— and then, at the start of the Mexican War, a soldier. With the troops voting for their officers, Bissell was unanimously chosen to lead the regiment, and was, withal, a hero in battle. Elected to Congress upon his return, the dashing doctor-lawyer-colonel-Congressman took a stand against the extension of slavery into the territories, and entered into vitriolic arguments on the subject with Jefferson Davis of Alabama. When Davis threw down the challenge of a duel, Bissell accepted in a flash. As it happened, the duel was canceled before any shots were fired, and in Illinois they never failed to point out that it was Davis' side that canceled it.

Abraham Lincoln was one of those promoting Bissell's candidacy for the governorship. Lincoln was one of the smarter political strategists in Illinois. He was also one of the better lawyers and more popular speakers in the central part of the state, but none of that anointed him for anything, except more of the same. Had he been struck by lightning that winter, no one would have lamented the political career that might have been. At times, he was resigned to believe it himself: at the age of forty-seven, the career that might have been was the one he had. He was a busy lawyer.

And yet "Jerry Sly" John Stuart thought something was still there, churning in Lincoln, or trying to.

As March came to a close, it was still possible that Lincoln would decide that 1856 was his year to make a move politically. Of course, he'd decided that same thing in other years, without materially changing his prospects. Eighteen-fifty-six was different, though. It held out more potential than any previous year in his career. That didn't make it a safe or pleasant time for a politician. With people dodging treacheries that had been planted long before, most pointedly in relation to slavery, the world all around Lincoln was in motion. The unsettled year before him demanded taking sides—and in all things, not just politics. Although Lincoln was innately a man of accord, he was going to have to respond. He would have to take sides. The matters of a nation would depend on it. So would those of a single family in Springfield.

CHAPTER 3

THE BEGINNING OF MAY

STRANGER IN THE YARD

As of the end of March 1856, Dr. George Angell had yet to return to Rhode Island. He was still in Logan County, impatiently waiting for the Circuit Court to arrive. Because Angell had never stopped yearning for the prairie's embrace—and the ruination of Remington K. Webster—he'd been biding his time in Illinois since the beginning of the month, looking forward to his day in court.

The case of Angell's disputed land purchase fell within the jurisdiction of the nomadic Eighth Circuit Court, which covered eight counties in Central Illinois. Its first stop was Springfield's Sangamon County Courthouse. When it adjourned there on Saturday, March 29, the presiding judge, David Davis, and the lawyers who traveled the circuit with him prepared to push north to Logan County.

That was the circuit: after hearing cases in Logan County, the judge would move on to Bloomington in McLean County, then Metamora in Woodford County, Pekin in Tazewell and so on, over the course of two months. Abraham Lincoln's routine was to travel with the judge, committing himself to practically every single day of the traveling court throughout its spring and fall terms. Saturday the 29th was probably the last day he spent at his house, knowing that he would be away for the better part of eight weeks.

Lincoln's home, seven blocks from the office, was a sturdy one-and-a-half story clapboard house, painted brown and lined with rose bushes in the front. The plants may even have been showing signs of green, encouraged by mild weather during the week. Normally, the property was very neatly kept, inside and out, but when Lincoln went home from court on Saturday, his house was on its way to becoming something of a wreck.

The Lincolns had decided to expand their house, after living in it for twelve years. The second floor was the problem. In its original configuration, it consisted of two bedrooms, with a pitched ceiling so low at the sides that even Robert, twelve, was in danger of hitting his head.[1] Willie, six, and Tad, three, were probably safe. The ground floor of the house had a kitchen and dining room toward the rear, a family room, and a more formal front parlor. It also had a back parlor that was being used as a bedroom.[2] That made for three bedrooms, which simply wasn't enough. In addition to the five Lincolns, the house had to accommodate at least one maid. And, whenever Lincoln was away, he paid a neighbor boy to sleep at the house, since Mrs. Lincoln was uncomfortable when her husband wasn't home.

H. M. Powel, a next-door neighbor in his early teens, had been hired by Lincoln for night-duty at the house several years before. "Mrs. Lincoln was very nervous and consequently easily scared," he recalled, "I remember one night some miscreant came and made a hideous noise against the weather-boarding of the house and Mrs. Lincoln promptly fainted. As soon as the two servant girls and I could restore her to consciousness, I went out to see if any one was there. Of course he was out of sight. As soon as we were all in bed again, the noise was repeated and again Mrs. Lincoln fainted."[3] Powel was authorized by another neighbor, a deputy, to borrow a shotgun, stand guard, and shoot anyone who came near the house. The rest of the night, however, was quiet.

With no simple way to call for help, people were isolated, even in city homes. Some thrived on it, finding peace in the solitude. Some hated it, and stayed in boarding houses long after they could afford homes of their own.

For the wives of traveling men, such as the Circuit-Court lawyers, the strain was wearing. Mary Stuart and Hellen Edwards both suffered from nervous problems, as did Mary Lincoln.

Isolation told on men, as well as women, of course. George Anderson had had a scare at the end of March, when someone told him that a man had been seen lurking around the house at night. Anderson had harbored his own suspicions along those lines, but with the new corroboration, he was sure. The person who reported the trespasser was nineteen-year-old John Morgan, one of the apprentices living in the house. He had heard Anderson talk about his fear of a stranger on the property and said later that he was only trying to warn him. Morgan told Anderson the man was wearing a dark cloak and standing on the side of the house. Anderson decided to take action and he knew just what to do. He had a friend in the Masons who owned guns and would be willing to loan out an Allen pistol for as long as it was needed.

A few days later, on Saturday the 29th, Anderson finally took his nephew Theodore aside. He told him that he could no longer stay at the house; he'd have to find another place to go. By way of explanation, George told other people that Mrs. Anderson had complained that she couldn't continue to keep house for the extra man. It was too much work. Theodore didn't contradict that story.

In fact, Theodore didn't appear to take offense. He packed his trunk and left, as he had been told. George hadn't said anything to incite Theodore. He wanted him out of the house and once that was done on Saturday, he was satisfied that things would go back to normal.

The construction at the Lincolns' house may or may not have begun as of Saturday; the precise date was not recorded. The house was almost certainly in upheaval that day, though, as the interior was prepared for the work. The firm of Hannon & Ragsdale, architects and builders,[4] had been engaged to undertake the expansion, at a cost of $1,300. No builders in Springfield had a better reputation. Their other projects at the time included $7,000 worth of improvements to the Governor's Residence. They were also building a few standard houses at $900 each, along with Matteson's mansion, at fully one hundred times that much.

In the remodeling that was about to begin, the Lincolns would gain three bedrooms and a storeroom upstairs by raising the second story to full height, while expanding it over the one-story wing at the rear. The work would double the family's sleeping space, and free up the back parlor downstairs for entertaining. But it was a major undertaking, at least for the Lincolns.

Once the work began and tarpaulins were all that separated the second floor from the sky, the family would have to camp out on the first floor. Abraham Lincoln was not known to care about his personal comfort, but as the schedule worked out, he wouldn't be troubled by the remodeling. He apparently left town late Sunday or early Monday morning. After that, he was to be gone for a long time, and before he came home again, the job would be finished.

When dark came on, Mrs. Lincoln had a neighbor boy sleeping in the house to make her feel safer. Over on Monroe, George Anderson had a loaded pistol by the bed, and even then, he kept listening to the dark.

On Monday afternoon, March 31, the Circuit Court convened in Lincoln, Logan County. The town of Lincoln had been named three years before for none other than Abraham Lincoln. He wasn't famous then, but he was present at just the right time. The town was founded by a trio of land dealers who knew the same thing that everyone did in the early 1850s: the new railroad planned as an axis for the state couldn't do much for local prosperity unless the trains passed through one of Logan County's towns. The announced route, however, missed them all by miles. The three land dealers soon remedied that, selecting an empty field alongside the tracks as a likely site for a city, and then hiring Abraham Lincoln to draw up the legal papers and some of the municipal plans.

Because the new place couldn't possibly be named after one of the partners (that is to say, just one of them), they sent the honor across the table to their lawyer. Lincoln was apparently delighted, as anyone would be, and he participated in the ground-breaking ceremonies in 1853. The following year, the three founders built a fashionable hotel, the Lincoln House and, more cunningly, a Courthouse. With that, they handily arranged to have the county seat moved to the town of Lincoln. The spring term in 1856 represented the first time that the Eighth Circuit Court convened there. As one of seventeen such Circuit Courts in the state, the Eighth applied the law in just about all matters above the level of municipal citations and short of Federal statute. Because the Court heard cases in every type of criminal law, as well as financial, family, property, and liability law, the attorneys on hand had to be as versatile as the caseload was varied.

Dr. Angell, pacing around the lobby at the Lincoln House or busily rocking on the front porch there, was fortunate that he had only had to wait three or four weeks for the circuit to land in Logan County. The court toured through its eight counties only twice a year, in spring and fall. If his problems had occurred a little later in the spring, he would have had no choice but to wait six months for the court to swing through again. Many people found themselves in just that predicament; people who were in far worse trouble than he.

The Court that traveled to each of the counties actually consisted of just one person: the judge. As many as a dozen lawyers swept along in his wake, though, and for a very simple reason. The work was where the judge was. During the first few days of court, clients in need of counsel drifted around the courthouse, searching for someone to hire. And looking remarkably like trout in a barrel to the attorneys on the circuit. Lawyers consulted with prospective clients in the privacy of a park bench or the shade of an old tree. Those taking a case might then have less than a day to prepare before it went to trial.

Though the process might seem hectic and perhaps slapdash by later standards, the Circuit created a dynamism that soon separated out fumblers, leaving only the deft, quick, or confident. Lincoln happened to be all three, and was in demand, with his fair share of new clients whenever he arrived at a courthouse. He was in his element, but the days of the Circuit Court, as he knew them, could not last. He saw that as clearly as anyone. In the 1850s, Illinois' circuits were shrinking, almost by the year. With the population increasing, judges were added, schedules extended, and travels reduced. As a style of legal proceeding, and as a way of life, the very spirited first era of Illinois' circuits was drawing to a close.

In 1855, Abraham Lincoln compared the prevailing style of the circuit to that of Eastern trial work, where lawyers employed a more modern approach: "They study on a single case perhaps for months, as we never do," he reflected, "We are apt to catch up the thing as it goes before a jury and trust to the inspiration of the moment."[5]

Lincoln wasn't beyond admitting to a little nervousness about the more bookish kind of lawyers. "They have got as far as Ohio now," he said, "They will soon be in Illinois."[6] For the time being, however, the circuit life was well-tailored to Lincoln, a man who needed the stimulation of fresh sights, unreported news, and lively gatherings, just as much as he needed solitude and time to think.

For the duration of the Logan County spring term, Abraham Lincoln and John Stuart both stayed at the Lincoln House hotel, more specifically in what was known as the "Lawyers Room." It was practically a dormitory, with a fireplace and four beds, but while the Circuit Court was in session, the room was filled with more lawyers than beds. "Some of us thin fellows doubled up," recalled Lawrence Weldon.[7] Judge Davis was the only one accorded his own bed, not out of respect, but because he was so round he didn't leave room for anyone else. Lincoln was willing to double-up, as Weldon had put it, especially if it reduced his expenses. He was well-used to sharing a bed on the road, as were all of the lawyers on the circuit.

The practicality of the arrangement, however, didn't foster any informality as far as Lincoln was concerned, and neither did his affability and his self-deprecating humor. For all of his humility, he was careful to maintain his dignity. Wherever he was, including the Lawyers Room, he was addressed as "Mr. Lincoln" by those who knew him. Only his very closest friends, Stuart and Davis among them, took so much of a liberty as to call him "Lincoln."[8] People who didn't know him at all tagged him with a nickname, which wasn't unusual in the case of a longtime politician; around Springfield, he was "Old Uncle Abe."

Back in Springfield, the city elections were held on Tuesday, April 1. The big news there was that someone had finally agreed to run for treasurer. (And he won.) John Cook, however, lost his race for mayor, either due to the scandal surrounding the $47 picnic money or because, as one of his supporters pointed out, the number of votes cast in the election was greater than the total number of adults who lived in the city. Lincoln, Stuart, and the other Springfield lawyers on the circuit missed the holiday atmosphere of Election Day. But then, they also avoided the recriminations and lawsuits that followed in the days afterward.

"Father is away and we are very quiet and lonely here," Mrs. Mary Stuart wrote to her daughter from Springfield two days after Election Day, on Thursday, April 3. "I know so little that is going on I can hardly make out incident enough to fill a short letter," she continued, "It is quite bright and pleasant today." The fair weather precipitated the one bit of incident that Mrs. Stuart could report: "Mr. Lincoln has commenced raising his back building two stories higher," she wrote, "I think they will have room enough before they are done, particularly as Mary seldom ever uses what she has."[9] She was referring to the fact that the Lincolns didn't host many parties, compared to other couples in their circle. In the Lincolns' defense, the inclination to entertain might have been tempered by the bedroom separating the two public rooms in the house. A wall had been constructed to block it from the front parlor, but even so, the configuration was awkward. In fact, the men from Hannon & Ragsdale were under orders to rip out the wall, and so the old reluctance may have been coming to an end, even as Mrs. Stuart was trying to fill up the page.

In Lincoln, as the spring term drew on there, Lawrence Weldon woke up one morning in the Lawyers Room in the hotel, and noticed that Abraham Lincoln's place in bed was already empty. "Up early and dressed," Weldon recalled, "he sat before the big, old-fashioned fireplace."[10] Lincoln pensively began to recite his favorite poem, "Oh, Why Should the Spirit of Mortal be Proud?" He had woken up in one of the troubled, sad spells to which he was subject. The other lawyers stopped what they were doing in getting ready for the day and listened.[11] Praising the poem and his recitation, they even tried to help Lincoln think who the author might have been.*

---

* Weldon later learned that the poem was attributed to the Scottish poet, William Knox (1789–1825).

On Friday afternoon, Lincoln met with Remington Webster. The Circuit Court was scheduled to hear the case of *Webster v. Angell* the next day. After the meeting with Webster, Lincoln probably had dinner at the hotel with Judge Davis and some of the other lawyers; robust meals every evening were a regular feature of the Eighth Circuit. Davis enjoyed Lincoln's stories and his conversation so much that his presence at the table was even regarded as something of a command performance.

"I was sitting on the verandah of the old Lincoln House the evening before the case was to be called," Dr. Angell later recounted, "when Lincoln came out and drew up a chair beside me."[12] Although Lincoln was representing Webster, the plaintiff, he was curious about the visitor from Rhode Island. Dr. Angell recalled the conversation, as Lincoln struck it up:

> "Angell, our case comes up tomorrow," he began.
> "I know it," I replied, "and I'm very glad of it."
> "I had a talk with my client this afternoon and from his account I couldn't see that you wanted anything of him but about what was right, do you?" continued Lincoln.
> "Mr. Lincoln," I replied, "I never had a lawsuit in my life. I don't want anything but my rights and I don't expect to get it."
> With that I handed him the written agreement between Webster and myself together with several of Webster's letters to me.
> "You look those papers over tonight," I said, "and tell me tomorrow what to do and I'll agree to do it."
> "No, no," replied Lincoln, "that wouldn't be right for I'm Webster's attorney; but I'll tell you how we can fix it. You find Stewart [sic] and I'll find Davis and Webster and we'll see if we can't come to an understanding tonight."[13]

Angell found John Stuart, his attorney, and they made their way to the Lawyers Room, along with Lincoln, who had Remington Webster in tow. Lincoln was an arbitrator at heart, and liked nothing better than to bring parties together to try for a little common sense. He probably didn't consider himself a profound peacemaker in such efforts. He just preferred the simple path in everything he did, so long as there was nothing to be lost by it. On that basis, the hotel room boded better than the courtroom, though the hour was getting late.

Davis suggested that each of the clients have a say first. "Before beginning my story," Angell said, "I requested that if I should say anything to which Webster did not agree, he should have the privilege of asking me any questions, and then I asked that I have the same privilege when he was telling his story. When I made this request I was looking straight at Lincoln. At the beginning his countenance was perfectly impassive and placid. When, however, I asked the privilege of questioning Webster, he stretched his legs out to their full length, leaned back in his chair and laughed loud and long."[14]

After Angell and Webster spoke, Judge Davis told them to leave the room momentarily. It was nearly midnight when they were called back. Davis then announced that he had decided in favor of Angell, who would have the farm free and clear for a sum that was actually less than he had offered Webster sometime earlier, in the long history of their disagreement. "Webster sulkily remarked that I had offered him $200 more than the decision gave him," Angell recalled. Lincoln heard that and lost his patience.

"You old fool," he shouted at Webster, his own client, "you'll keep on until you won't get a cent."[15]

Judge Davis then asked Angell if he were satisfied with the out-of-court settlement. Apparently, the doctor could be sulky, too. He replied that he had agreed to be satisfied, and so he was satisfied. With that, he took out his wallet and started to pay Webster the $125 cash down-payment ordered by the judge, while Lincoln wrote out the details of the agreement.[16] Angell soon realized, however, that he only had $109 in cash. Lincoln offered to loan him the balance, sixteen dollars, and Angell gave him an I.O.U. for that amount.

"What did you mean, Angell," Judge Davis inquired, "when you said you agreed to be satisfied and you were satisfied?"

"Just what I said," Angell answered.

"But I judged by that remark that you were hardly satisfied with the decision," said Davis.

Dr. Angell turned to Lincoln. "Mr. Lincoln," he said, "do you think it was just right that nothing was said in the decision about that quarter section which Webster agreed to sell me for $2.25 per acre?"[17]

By then it was past midnight. "This deponent sayeth not," Lincoln replied in what Angell described as a grave tone. Lincoln hadn't made anyone happy. He had sought a graceful way to forego the unlikely chance of a victory in favor of acceptable justice, but in the end, his client, the plaintiff Webster, felt that he hadn't fought hard enough for him.

Lincoln must have gone to bed that night thinking that he was the only lawyer in the world who could end up having the defendant likewise grousing that he hadn't fought hard enough for *him*.

CHAPTER 4

EARLY MAY

SOMETHING ABOUT STRYCHNINE

John Stuart was undoubtedly happy to have the negotiations in *Webster v. Angell* settled on Friday night. He wanted to go home.

On Saturday morning, Stuart checked out of the Lawyers Room and left for Springfield. Though he returned home as often as possible, his absence on the circuit was hard on his wife. "He will be at home on Saturday, but will leave again on Monday," Mrs. Stuart explained in a letter to her daughter that week, "He will be about [away] most of the time for several weeks. Cousin Liz said she was going to stay with me most of the time during Father's absence, but she has been here but little as yet."

The absences were even harder on Mary Lincoln. Lincoln didn't go home on weekends. From the city of Lincoln, he took the train and went directly to Bloomington for the start of McLean County Court on Monday.

Bloomington was something of a favorite with Lincoln, as it was a cauldron of strong personalities and fast-moving politics. And both were rising to new intensity even as his train pulled into the station over the weekend. Word was spreading throughout the state that Bloomington would be the site of the Illinois Anti-Nebraska Convention scheduled for the end of May.[1] Of course, Lincoln knew about the Convention in advance of the general announcement, but his fascination lay in seeing the unfolding effect on others, through conversations with everyone from fellow lawyers to hotel porters, and his habitual perusal of every newspaper that came his way. If anyone turned the tables and asked him about the Bloomington Convention, though, he would have had to admit that he didn't have any plans to attend.

On Monday, John Stuart arrived in Bloomington and rejoined the court. The same day, he and Lincoln were suddenly swept up in a case that was roiling the city's medical community. The previous October, a livery stable in Bloomington had caught on fire; so many thousands of people had flocked to watch that the firemen couldn't get through to put it out. The blaze then spread to other buildings, one of which had collapsed on a carpenter, breaking both of his thighs. A few weeks later, the same doctors who had set the fractures found that one of the legs wasn't healing straight. They prepared to reset it, but the carpenter had refused further treatment. The doctors begged him to change his mind, predicting that otherwise he would be left with a crooked leg and a pronounced limp. "Leave it alone," he insisted.[2]

Five months later, the carpenter filed a malpractice lawsuit against the doctors for leaving him with a crooked leg and a pronounced limp. The two doctors scrambled to hire a defense team, but the six toughest lawyers in Bloomington were unavailable—they had already been hired by the carpenter. The doctors resorted to Springfield lawyers, hiring John Stuart and Abraham Lincoln. The two were formidable when they were on the same side. Nonetheless, they weren't ready to face the big guns of Bloomington in such an unusual case. Lincoln, for his part, had never argued a malpractice suit before, though he had been faced with practically every other type of legal circumstance, outside of maritime law. He and Stuart had to think quickly, not about how to win the case, but how to delay it. Fortunately—that is to say, conveniently—one of the defendants was ill. Not only that, he was in Cincinnati. Lincoln wrote a legal declaration, detailing the facts of the case, and contending that the defendant, whose testimony was crucial, couldn't attend court.[3] Judge Davis granted a continuance, postponing the trial until the fall term. (The case, which was actually heard a whole year later, became known as the "Chicken Bone Case," in reference to the props used by Lincoln at the trial; it ended in a hung jury and was eventually dismissed.[4])

By April 22, the Eighth Circuit Court had moved on to the town of Metamora, well north of Springfield. Lincoln was there all week, and almost certainly aware of a flurry of editorials from as far away as Chicago, discussing a new name for the governorship, a name "which bears with it a prestige of greater force; a true, firm and abiding statesman; one in whom the highest trust might be committed without fear of principles being sacrificed, or interest peddled off—a man that spurns to lick the hands of the political tricksters for the emoluments of office, but who would if selected as a candidate of the free party endeavor by the pure advocacy of lofty measures, to gain a seat in the gubernatorial chair." The suspense finally ended in the last line, "It is Wm. H. Herndon, Esq. of Springfield."[5]

As to Lincoln, he still wanted Colonel Bissell to run for governor. Bissell had been at home all spring in the town of Belleville, in the southwestern part of the state. As he learned through letters of the growing hope in the state that he would stand as a candidate for governor, he remained aloof. The invincible hero, at forty-five, was still recovering from the effects of a paralytic stroke suffered two years before. He couldn't walk very easily, if at all. But that fact didn't deter his supporters, including Lincoln. They were sure that Bissell was still the same old warrior and, more to the point, that he was still the people's favorite, the man who had never lost an election, not even in the army.

Bissell was not as optimistic. That spring, he wrote a letter to Senator Trumbull, a fellow resident of Belleville, then serving in Washington; both were vocally Anti-Nebraskan and nominally members of the Democratic Party. And both were aware that a person could no longer be, in good conscience, an Anti-Nebraskan Democrat. Nonetheless, the way forward was by no means clear. Colonel Bissell insisted in the letter that he wasn't interested in being a candidate for governor. He certainly didn't want to run with the newly coalescing Anti-Nebraska party, not if it was nothing more than a scheme of the radicals, by which he meant abolitionists, to overwhelm the moderates, by which he meant former Democrats—and he was convinced that the new party was exactly that.[6] On the same premise, he didn't approve of the upcoming Bloomington Convention, saying it would only succeed in "killing off the nominees."[7] He wasn't worried about their lives, but their prospects for a political future. Most of the state's experienced Anti-Nebraska politicians had the same foreboding, but Bissell was uncharacteristically sour and abrupt in voicing his intention not to run. Trumbull apparently didn't act on the letter in any way; he let others continue to promote Bissell's candidacy.

It was understandable for a man who was largely confined to bed to decline an arduous campaign, as well as for that same man to decide against entering the tumult of politics in the 1856 season. It was perfectly understandable. But not if that man was William Bissell: intrepid, fearless, and as committed as anyone to reversing the Kansas-Nebraska Act.

During the week of April 22, Dr. Rufus Lord was summoned to an emergency at the Anderson house in Springfield. George Anderson was ill.[8] And that was a rarity. The doctor was used to visiting Monroe Street to see the children or even Mrs. Anderson, but for the first time, George was sick, complaining of cramps in his abdomen and a high fever. Because both symptoms came and went through the day, Dr. Lord didn't think it was anything serious. George didn't go to work, though, which may have been a sign that it was very serious indeed.

Outside George's window, Monroe Street was coming alive in the warm spring air. His own four children, ranging from George Junior, three, to Mary, thirteen, were playing in the backyard, and he could hear their voices. Normally, they would be out and about, going for walks with their mother, and following her on errands, but she was busy taking care of their father. Theodore was around, too. After he left the household, at George's insistence, he'd been away for the first two weeks of April, visiting the town of Jerseyville, southwest of Springfield. He said he had been looking for work there, but apparently didn't find anything. As soon as he returned, he found his way back to the Andersons', where he passed some of his time talking to the children in the backyard.

Up the street from the Andersons, Robert Lincoln spent free time on Monroe Street, too, often visiting the Conkling's boy, Clinton, who lived on Monroe at Fourth. They both attended parties at the home of the Ridgley family just across the street. Nicholas Ridgley, a banker and the owner of the new gasworks, had reigned as Springfield's richest resident until Governor Matteson decided to move in permanently. The Ridgley teens and their friends referred to Nicholas as the "Emperor," because as near as they could tell, he had the same bearing as his namesake, the Russian czar. The czar may not have been as austere. Nicholas was vastly outnumbered, however, by the thirteen Ridgley children, so there was usually something going on with them and the young people who were invited to come to their house.

Not every kid in town, of course, was invited to the Ridgley house. Clinton Conkling was part of the in-crowd by virtue of his mother having been a socialite in Washington, and his father being a Princeton man, as well as a respected lawyer in town. Robert Lincoln's pedigree gave him the same entree. In his own neighborhood on Jackson Street, the children called him "Cross-eyed Bob" (because of his roving right eye), and so perhaps it is understandable that he seemed anxious to slide into more polite circumstances. On his own, he was a somewhat awkward boy.[9]

All of the Lincoln boys were notoriously undisciplined. They weren't wild or bullying, but more like untrained puppies, following their own whims, come what may. The Lincolns wanted them to be that way: free, with a happy outlook. "We never controlled him much," Lincoln wrote later of Robert.[10] He could have been speaking of any of the boys. "A more devoted father I have never known," said one of the Lincoln family's physicians, speaking of Lincoln, "His sympathy was almost motherly, and his patience with the children, whether sick or well, opened my eyes."[11]

J. P. Kent lived on the same block as the Lincolns. In fact, he was one of the youngsters who stayed with the family when Lincoln was away. "I recall that Bob, the elder, and Tad, the younger, were *Mamma* boys," he wrote, "They neither one had the slightest personal appearance or deliberate easy manner of Mr. Lincoln. They both resembled their mother in looks and action."[12]

As the eldest, Robert seemed to crave more self-control, but he didn't know how to adopt it as a young teen. The previous winter, when Matteson had thrown a fancy ball at the governor's mansion for the socialites of Springfield, the Lincolns attended—Abraham Lincoln temporarily overlooking his antipathy for Governor Matteson. The next night, the young people from the same families were invited for their own soiree. John Stuart described it in a letter to his daughter Betty, noting the mansion's new gaslight lamps. "The house was full of boys and girls," he wrote, "The gas was in full operation—the band was in attendance—all the rooms were thrown open, and all the children danced or at least hopped around. John [Stuart Jr.] danced all evening *in his way*. Next day he and Bob Lincoln were hunting up the dancing master."[13]

Even at thirteen, Robert knew what he needed. He sought out the company of his upper-class friends, and was welcomed in their homes because of his father's reputation and his mother's connections. It was the kind of entree that George Anderson's children couldn't even buy. For a small town and a young one, Springfield was settled, if not ossified, in terms of its social strata. Education and gentility counted for even more than money; a degree from one of the good eastern colleges was the best passport of all. George Anderson had nothing to offer in those respects. He had no education to speak of. And his wife, Jane, was illiterate. At thirty-one, she was presentable, she was no hillbilly, but she had never learned to read. Whenever she was required to sign a deed or another legal document, someone who could read had to explain it to her first. Only then would she take the pen into her fingers. She wasn't used to holding such a thing, though, and so her mark, her "X," was tentative and shaky. Someone else would then sign next to it to affirm that the mark represented Jane True Anderson.

Born in Kentucky, Jane True had originally moved to Springfield with one of her sisters. They were very poor, and Jane had to find work to support herself. Another of the True sisters had moved to New York City and became rich, through marriage or some enterprise of her own. Jane, for her part, married Anderson in 1843, and a little more than a dozen years later, she was starting to enjoy her status as a lady of leisure, with a maid of her own to do the work.

Although George Anderson was dabbling in real estate, he was only a small player. As with most of the other propositions in Central Illinois, the business of land speculation was especially congenial for the attorneys; of the sixteen expansions of the city of Springfield in the 1850s, more than a quarter involved tracts owned by practicing lawyers.[14] Benjamin Edwards, John Stuart's partner, for example, made some excellent deals, buying acreage on the outskirts of town, waiting for the city to engulf it, and then selling it, lot by lot.

Politics in the region was even more elitist than the social and business worlds. Leadership of the parties was assumed by professional men and prosperous farmers. Of the eleven appointees for the Central Committee of the Anti-Nebraska Party—the selection of which William Herndon was so proud—seven were lawyers, two were gentleman-farmers, one was a portrait painter, and one a land agent. That was a typical picture of party leadership in Illinois. And the other parties were similar in composition—except for the portrait painter, of course. Clerks, workmen, small-business owners, and craftsmen were nowhere to be seen in the decision-making process. Neither were farmers with average or small holdings, despite the fact that farm families made up eighty percent of the population of most Illinois counties, including Springfield's Sangamon County. With larger businesses and institutions not yet developed, Central Illinois was still a lawyer-led society, making it hard to tell who was in the profession for its own rewards, and who was just on the way through, awaiting a different field of opportunity.

After William Herndon saw his name mentioned for governor in the newspapers, he hastened to protest that he didn't want "to be a candidate for anything." Still, he couldn't resist clipping out the articles. He sent one set of them to a friend, the famous abolitionist Theodore Parker in Boston, emphasizing that he had no intention of running and wasn't sure he could be elected, anyway.[15] He was right. William Herndon might have made a viable candidate in Boston, but in Springfield, he was far too well-known as an abolitionist.

"I knew Bill Herndon well," recalled a Springfield resident, "He was of a nervous temperament, quick-spoken and impulsive." He also noted that "Herndon's clothes were of the latest fashion, rich and snappy."[16] Herndon loved to clip the newspapers, and he dutifully kept a scrapbook of articles and editorials related to the slavery issue. He often pressed it on his senior partner, hoping it would exert some influence, but he should have known better. The formula for changing Lincoln's mind was never that simple.

Lincoln resisted inflammatory editorials of the very type that Herndon took so seriously, but then, he wasn't known to seek out opinions or advice on any topic. He thought out questions, large and small, in the isolation of his mind. And when he needed someone to follow, he looked to leaders long dead.

For four years, the Anderson family had been treated by Dr. Rufus Lord, a graduate of the medical school at New York University. At the age of thirty-four, he was the senior partner in a busy office complete with a lab. Doctors provided their own medicines in the mid-nineteenth century, and Lord employed a dispensary clerk to fill his prescriptions. Lord shared the office with Dr. Edward Fowler, a twenty-six year-old physician from Pennsylvania.[17] On May 1, when George Anderson was in the midst of another attack, his wife sent the apprentice, John Morgan, for Dr. Lord. The doctor had been called to the house every day but one since his first visit on April 22. Whether Morgan found Lord in the office or at his home nearby, the two of them immediately made their way to Monroe Street.

Dr. Lord found Anderson vomiting and "sick at his stomach." A fever had been surging and receding all day, with the result that he was exhausted, wet and groaning. The cramps he felt at the onset of the condition had become full-fledged spasms, contorting his body beyond his control. Whenever the spasms came on, the groans turned to shrieks of pain.

The doctor couldn't detect any obvious cause for the malaise. He assured Anderson that the whole thing was probably going to be quite temporary. On the basis that it wasn't a serious illness, but a case of some sort of grippe, Dr. Lord gave Anderson pills to quiet his stomach and then he left the house. There wasn't much choice. Only big cities had hospitals then. Springfield, for its part, was struggling just to construct sidewalks. The seriously ill and wounded had to stay at home, although in dire cases, such as Anderson's, visiting nurses were hired to provide care around the clock. Meanwhile, the doctor typically came by every couple of days.

Dr. Lord returned to examine Anderson two days later, but he didn't notice any particular change. Jane Anderson was in the bedroom almost all the time, taking care of her husband, with the help of a nurse. Back at the office, Lord discussed Anderson's case with Dr. Fowler, but both were baffled. Anderson was only thirty-six, a man with an otherwise strong constitution. Yet, he seemed to have no digestive tract left.

Another two days later, on May 5, Dr. Fowler was stunned by the latest turn in the case. He met George Anderson on the street. Anderson didn't look entirely well, but he was walking under his own power. The fevers were gone and he said he was feeling better. Dr. Lord stopped by the Anderson house later that day to see for himself. Anderson, he reported, "told me that he was doing well, and believed he would take no more pills."[18] The visiting nurse didn't come back, and the next day the household began to return to normal.

During the first week of May, Abraham Lincoln was in Pekin, the seat of Tazewell County. On May 6, he was having a fairly usual day—very usual, inasmuch as he was filing papers in *Opdycke v Opdycke and Opdycke*, a case that had been dragging on for five years. Every spring and most autumns, Lincoln filed a decree ordering the guardian Opdycke to sell land belonging to the minor Opdyckes. On May 6, a Tuesday, he wrote another. He also lost a case on appeal, in a farm-labor dispute over nine dollars' worth of harvesting, stacking, and masonry.

Not many of the regular Circuit lawyers had made it to Pekin. Judge Davis was there, of course, but John Stuart had gone home for good during April. Local lawyers provided the opposing counsel in both of Lincoln's cases on May 6. One of Lincoln's friends was in Pekin, though. And if Lincoln needed cheering, it was the right one. Amzi McWilliams, at 32, had recently moved to Springfield from Bloomington in search of a new start.

He was good in his profession—"very talented," said a colleague[19]—but an aggressive new generation of lawyers was crowding in. Among them was, for example, his next-door neighbor, John Scott, who was already a favorite with Judge Davis.

Davis couldn't abide Amzi McWilliams, who possessed two things that clean-cut John Scott did not: a temper and a sense of humor, both of them irrepressible. "A low vulgar man," Davis said of McWilliams, while admitting with a kind of disdain that the man was witty. Lincoln, he said "attached himself to this poor unfortunate Creature" and others like him for the sake of the wit and the jokes. "Lincoln used these men," Davis said, "merely to whistle off sadness—gloom & unhappiness. He loved their intellects, minds and felt sorry for their failings—and sympathized with them."[20] Lincoln, who was well used to being called upon for a funny story whenever someone else needed a laugh, was probably glad to have Amzi around on Wednesday after the dull defeat of Tuesday's day in court.

Late on Wednesday, John Morgan was on Monroe Street in Springfield, running at top speed to fetch Dr. Lord. George Anderson was back in bed, in far worse shape than ever. He had the intermittent fever, along with nausea, just as before, but everything was more painful, even the fever. Anderson's stomach hurt more than it ever had in his life. Also, he was having spasms, moments when the illness overwhelmed him, and made him curl up in an almost paralytic state. Dr. Lord prescribed morphine in powder form to release Anderson's racked system.

Back at the office, Lord talked over the case with Fowler. He carefully suggested that he couldn't help suspecting that Anderson was being poisoned. Dr. Fowler had already come to the same conclusion. He thought it was significant that Anderson had rebounded the day before, and had been out on the street, feeling fine. Then, another twenty-four hours later, he was worse than ever. Fowler's theory was that if the spasms had been caused by a disease, or some condition that originated within the body, they would remain for days at a stretch. They wouldn't stop abruptly. Then start suddenly again.

The next morning, the bell at Fowler's home started ringing at 6 A.M. Anderson was in terrible trouble, the spasms were nearly killing him. Fowler rushed to the house and found Jane Anderson trying to alleviate her husband's agony. Elbowing the night nurse aside, she tried to help the doctor, anticipating his actions, and imploring him to tell her how to help. Fowler took stock of the situation as he worked; he "gave him purgative medicine to open his bowels," he recorded. He also took note that the cycle of the illness seemed to begin in the late afternoon, with numbness in Anderson's fingers and toes. At about six, the fever started to take hold: a higher temperature, weakness, delirium, profuse sweating. After about four hours, at ten o'clock or so, the spasms began and Anderson's body, already racked, was unable to fight them off. He was helpless. It was as though he were under attack from two different directions: his digestion and then the muscular contractions. Fowler gave George Anderson a morphine pill to alleviate the spasms. Before he left, he gave a bottle of the pills to Jane Anderson.

Dr. Fowler returned to his office convinced of one thing: Mrs. Anderson couldn't be poisoning her husband. She was obviously in her own agony seeing her husband lying there, pleading to someone, anyone for help. However, the doctor made a mental note to check his own medicine supply. The subject of strychnine was on his mind.

William Herndon had been scurrying around town all week, gathering names for a notice he intended to place in the newspaper. It was an announcement related to the Anti-Nebraska Convention in Bloomington on May 29, and in his peculiar style, it was more thunderous than clarion. It said something about the undersigned being against the repeal of the Missouri Compromise, and against President Franklin Pierce, but in favor "of restoring the administration of the General Government to the Policy of Washington and Jefferson." To that end, they planned to assemble on May 24 to choose delegates for the state Convention.

Herndon collected over 120 names, from John Armstrong, a carpenter, to Job Fletcher Jr., a longtime Whig who had been a State Senator many decades before. The list included some august and very current personalities, such as James Conkling. Stephen T. Logan, a rather eccentric man who had a towering reputation as a lawyer, was also included—Lincoln had once been his junior partner. Lincoln's family doctor, and brother-in-law, Dr. William Wallace, was listed, too. All three of those impressive personages were buried in the middle of Herndon's list. The one name that wasn't anywhere to be seen was that of Abraham Lincoln. He was as disturbed over the extension of slavery as anyone on the list, but he was holding back, not ready yet to endorse the nascent Anti-Nebraska party. He knew it was to be a fusion party, but he didn't yet know whose version of "the Policy of Washington and Jefferson" would hold sway over it. As ever, he was wary of being connected to the more vehement "radical abolitionists."

At the end of the week, on Friday, May 9, Lincoln was still in Pekin, arguing cases that seemed to be headed nowhere. One pertained to John T. Scates' cattle, which had apparently committed a little vandalism "breaking into" Philip Davin's enclosure, according to the ensuing lawsuit.[21] A justice of the peace had ruled in favor of Davin the previous September, awarding him $25 in damages.[22] John Scates thought the judgment outrageous and decided to fight it. And he felt confident of victory, too, either because his cattle were patently harmless or because his older brother, Walter, was chief justice of the Illinois Supreme Court. Walter Scates was also a warm friend of Abraham Lincoln, who took on the appeal, in conjunction with a local lawyer. After the testimony of twelve witnesses[23] and arguments on each side, the jury failed to reach a verdict. Another trial was scheduled for the fall term.

In Springfield, Herndon was excited about unveiling his plan for the pre-Convention meeting. He was ready to submit his notice to the Springfield *State Journal*, but it needed one more name, that of Lincoln, the most respected Anti-Nebraskan in town. What is more, Herndon was convinced that Lincoln needed the notice. He considered that his senior partner was adrift. "Mere hatred of slavery and opposition to the injustice of the Kansas-Nebraska legislation were not all that were required of him," Herndon wrote many years later, "He must be a Democrat, Know Nothing, Abolitionist, or Republican, or forever float about in the great political sea without compass, rudder or sail."[24] To that end, Herndon filled in "A. Lincoln" at the very top of the long column of supporters for the new party, and then submitted the petition to the paper. It appeared on May 10.

When John Stuart picked up his copy of the Springfield *State Journal* that Saturday and turned to page two, he could hardly believe what he saw. At one time, he and Lincoln had been quite similar in their politics. While Stuart was aware that Lincoln had moved to the side of anti-expansion while he was leaning in the other direction, toward his roots in the slave state of Kentucky, he was aghast to see his old Whig comrade associating with an untried and potentially damaging new party.

Herndon was sitting in his office when John Stuart burst in, his big eyes wide with excitement. He asked if "Lincoln had signed the Abolition call in the *Journal*." Herndon explained that he had himself signed Lincoln's name. "Did Lincoln authorize you to sign it?" Stuart pressed. With that, Herndon had to say no, but he was quick to protect his dignity by being emphatic about it. Stuart was taken aback. "Then you have ruined him," he said in an accusatory tone, tinged with finality.[25]

Stuart wasn't the only one in Springfield to think that Lincoln had been ill-used. Through it all, Herndon was unremorseful. "I was by no means alarmed at what others deemed inconsiderate and hasty action," he wrote, "I thought I understood Lincoln thoroughly, but in order to vindicate myself if assailed I immediately sat down, after Stuart had rushed out of the office, and wrote Lincoln, who was then in Tazewell County attending court, a brief account of what I had done and how much stir it was creating in the ranks of his conservative friends. If he approved or disapproved my course I asked him to write or telegraph me at once."[26] Herndon then left Springfield, taking the train to Decatur, where he was scheduled to deliver a speech in the Anti-Nebraska cause.

Lincoln was in Pekin on Saturday when he received Herndon's message. He was having a remarkable day: a case was actually coming to a close. That was unusual enough, with the Circuit Court's capacity for continuances, demurrers, changes of venue, appeals, and motions of all kinds. But the case in question, *Roberts v. Harkness*, had been on the docket every term for three years. Edson Harkness had owed money to the Roberts family since 1837: nineteen years later, after five trials and one motion for a new trial, the case was finally settled on May 10.[27]

That night, Herndon was announced as the speaker at the Anti-Nebraska meeting in Decatur. He probably had yet to hear from Lincoln and, as he took the stage, he must have been wondering whether, perhaps, he had indeed ruined him. His speech went well, later receiving outsized praise in the local paper, but then, most political speeches in 1856 received rave reviews in those newspapers that supported the same position on the slavery question.

Lincoln eventually sent a response to Herndon's blunt question. Herndon opened it and found to his relief that it was entirely friendly.

Lincoln was being generous with his partner. He could have yanked back his own right of self-determination by sending a letter of repudiation to the Springfield *State Journal*. That's what almost all of the candidates for city treasurer had done, under similar circumstances. Lincoln was normally too kind-hearted to do anything so rash, but to assume that he was just being polite by going along with Herndon's stunt is to give the junior partner too much credit for goading Lincoln out of his inertia. Lincoln did have the characteristic trait of shrugging off setbacks. John Stuart was right, though, in thinking that when it came to affiliation with a post-Whig political party, the stakes were high for Lincoln. For that reason, Lincoln's reluctance to hurt Herndon's feelings wouldn't have kept him from writing a letter to the editor.

Out on the Circuit, traveling from Logan County to McLean to Woodford and then Tazewell counties, Lincoln was alive to the news. Whenever a political leader around the state announced plans to go to the Bloomington Convention, he heard about it. By early May, he knew that Rev. Owen Lovejoy of Princeton, Illinois, was going to attend. Lovejoy, whose brother had been assassinated by the pro-slavery mob in Alton nineteen years before, was a militant abolitionist. His name alone was enough to energize slavery sympathizers of all stripes: they despised him. A lot of moderates did, too, fearing that he would, if he could, tear the country apart and make it a wreckage, all for the sake of his single-minded cause.

Lincoln abhorred slavery, but he was not an abolitionist, believing it to be a politically futile position. In the effort to harness Anti-Nebraska sentiments in Illinois, Lovejoy loomed as a rival. "On the slavery question," wrote Isaac N. Arnold of Lovejoy, "as a stump speaker, it would be difficult to name his superior."[28] Many people praised Lovejoy's ability to rouse the emotions of a crowd, yet if the likes of Lovejoy were to dominate the new party, Lincoln would want no part in it.

In early May, though, other political players were making known their intention to join the new party. Displaced Whigs such as Orville Browning, a widely respected lawyer from Quincy, and Stephen T. Logan, Lincoln's former law partner from Springfield, were committing support for the fledgling effort. That was important to Lincoln. He was himself a Whig, after all, and he knew that the new party wouldn't get anywhere if it couldn't pull in the Anti-Nebraska wing of the disintegrated party. Even more important to him, though, were the Democrats who were being displaced. If the new party could attract the Anti-Nebraskans from the Democratic Party, as well as the Whig, it would have a kind of integrity that would attract other factions as well.

Before the start of May, Gustave Koerner, the Democratic lieutenant governor of Illinois, had been as cagey as Lincoln about affiliating with the new party. Koerner was unique among Illinois politicians, being, for one thing, the most educated of them. He had earned a doctorate at the University of Heidelberg, in his native Germany. Not long afterward, he was forced to flee Germany; an uprising of militarists and reactionaries had reversed the democratic Revolution of 1848 and persecuted those, such as he, who insisted on clinging to its ideals. Koerner moved to the United States, learned English, and gained admission to the Illinois Bar, earning the respect of both the American-born electorate and the influential German-speaking one. Elected lieutenant governor in 1852, he was a Democrat, but he had always been against slavery and in the aftermath of the repeal of the Missouri Compromise, was openly against its expansion. John M. Palmer, an influential lawyer who was also known as a conservative Democrat, felt similarly betrayed by his party's—and Senator Douglas'—championing of the Kansas-Nebraska Law.

Abraham Lincoln was well aware that the Illinois State Democratic Convention at the beginning of the month had been devoted to the cult worship of Stephen Douglas, dismaying many party members, including John Palmer, Chicago's Norman Judd, and Lieutenant Governor Koerner. By mid-May, he knew with certainty the extent of the alienation. All of them had broken ranks with the Democrats and were making plans to go to Bloomington. They represented a critically important block: old-school Democrats, ready to start over in the Anti-Nebraska cause.

The commitment of Koerner, Palmer, Browning, Logan, and a growing list of other conservative and moderate figures convinced Lincoln that Bloomington would be the right place to look for the soul of what was to be the Republican Party, and at the same time, to find a home for himself in politics. With all that he knew as May unfolded, Lincoln sent his reply to Herndon, and he could even afford to be jovial about his greatest fear: "All right," he wrote, "Go ahead. Will meet you—radicals and all."[29]

George Anderson had a good night on Saturday. Dr. Lord came to see him and found that he was "in a comfortable condition, the skin was in good order, and the pulse good, but had a slight burning in the stomach, like heart-burn."[30] Anderson may have been feeling better, but Dr. Lord wasn't. The manner in which the symptoms came and went kept bringing the thought of poison to mind, one in particular: strychnine.

Strychnine had come into vogue during the previous decade, gaining what one report of the day called "so worldwide a celebrity."[31] In the form of clear crystals, it was derived from the berries of a tree that grew naturally in India. In the Far East, people actually managed to become addicted to strychnine for its stimulant qualities, learning to take it before or after food to control the negative effects, while finding satisfaction in its power to sharpen the senses. Introduced into Western medicine, strychnine was adopted in tiny doses as a laxative, with other uses later added to the pharmacology. It was, however, also well-known to be a deadly poison in even slightly larger amounts, bringing on agonizing convulsions by which the muscles, no longer controlled by the brain, twist the body into distorted positions, arching the back almost to the point of breaking and then overpowering the internal organs. Eventually, victims suffocated.

Dr. Lord was reluctant to confront Jane Anderson with his suspicions, but he was curious enough about strychnine poisoning to do a ghastly thing. Finding a dog, he poisoned it in his backyard with strychnine to see what would happen. The dog died in five minutes, after suffering the same type of spasms that were besetting Anderson. On Sunday night, Lord was called again to Monroe Street. Anderson was in the throes of a particularly violent spasm, his body contorted with a drastic arch in his back. It was painful even to look at him. Lord had had no success with the purgatives; he resorted to a bulb syringe to open Anderson's bowels. At the same time, because he was convinced that the convulsions were caused by poison, even though he didn't know the source, he administered camphor as an antidote. Anderson was already taking morphine.

The next day, Lord was called again, and when he arrived at the house, he found Anderson in the midst of another violent spasm. By that point, Lord was certain that Anderson was somehow ingesting strychnine. There could be no other explanation. But the doctor kept quiet. He wanted to rule out the possibility that his own dispensary clerk, back at the office, had put the wrong pills into the morphine bottle. Privately, he examined the pills in the morphine bottle, and they seemed to be correct. He gave Anderson one and the spasm was reduced.

Looking around the house, Dr. Lord considered the possible means of delivering the poison. The household included Mrs. Anderson and the four children. The oldest was a girl, Mary, thirteen. Then there were two more girls and the boy, three. Aside from the family, two apprentices, John Morgan and Cyrus Youst, lived in the house. There was also a maid, Rebecca Law, a twenty-four year-old farm girl from a village near Springfield. And there were nurses who were on duty night and day, since Anderson was so acutely ill. However, the only person who gave Anderson his meals, his drinks, or his pills was Mrs. Anderson. As his wife, she insisted upon that.

Dr. Lord waited out a driving rainstorm at the house, and when it weakened to a drizzle, he left for home.[32] Later in the day, Lord and Fowler went together to call on Anderson. They found him weak, but fairly comfortable under the circumstances. Later, the two doctors discussed the case. They both thought it very likely that George Anderson was being poisoned with strychnine, but they decided not to take any action. When asked later why they didn't, Dr. Fowler could only repeat what he'd heard his partner say many times, that Mrs. Anderson was the most devoted of wives, constantly anxious for her husband's recovery.

CHAPTER 5

MAY 15

THE OLD MAN WENT OUT

The day was the finest of the year, May 15, and it was spring in every dimension. "Although we have had many beautiful days this spring, yet the present one surpasses all others," wrote a resident of Springfield, "the sun shines bright and warm, the grass and vegetables are growing luxuriantly and we are not exaggerating very much when we say that we can *almost* see them grow . . . the blue sky is without a speck. The flowers have already begun to bloom."[1] May 15 was the finest day of the year and it was to be George Anderson's last.

To everyone in the household, Anderson seemed to be over his sickness. One day earlier, on Wednesday, he'd gotten dressed and walked over to the blacksmith shop, spending some of the afternoon looking over the work that the men had done during his illness. On Thursday, he was there almost all day—but first, he had an errand. He stopped to see the clothier on the same block, and bought a pair of black pants and a shirt.[2] He'd lost so much weight, his own clothes were loose. He also picked out socks and underwear, and splurged on a new satin stock (the flowing style of tie worn at the time). After changing, Anderson went to his shop and did a little work. A few people came in to see him. The atmosphere was quiet.

Jane Anderson was even more anxious than George to get out of the house on Thursday. She was bursting with things to do and the inclination just to be out and away. Everyone around town had the same idea on that sunny spring day, making the streets more crowded than usual, but no one else had been through what Mrs. Anderson had. She wasn't just out of the house, she was out of the role of nurse. She was out of the smell of the sickroom. She had dresses to make, patterns to buy, and shops to visit downtown. Theodore went along, too, since he had the time. Altogether, he had been in Illinois for about four months, and he was still living off the savings he'd brought from New Jersey. A tall, lean young fellow,[3] he was entirely unlike his uncle; he was in no hurry.

In the bright sun, scurrying around on one errand or another, Mrs. Anderson looked carefree, whether because she was out of the sickroom or out with her young nephew. Whatever the reason, she seemed to throw her old habits aside. Normally, she took at least one of the children with her when she went out, but on Thursday, she left them at home in the care of the maid.

On the other side of Springfield, Hannon & Ragsdale were finally finished with the construction on the Lincoln house. The Lincolns had a roof over their heads. Over the weekend, Mrs. Lincoln had purchased wallpaper at John Williams and Co.,[4] a department store. The decorating was apparently set to begin. In overseeing the construction, Mary Lincoln had received help and advice from a neighbor named James Gourley, a shoemaker by trade.[5] Between the two of them, they probably noticed that neither Hannon nor Ragsdale were on hand for the project, leaving the whole job to assistants.[6] And indeed, the work was far from expert. Almost a hundred years later, when the Lincoln homestead was undergoing a general restoration, Richard Hagen, a trained building-archeologist, inspected the workmanship of the 1856 addition. "The methods used in joining the 1856 work to the 1839 structure would dismay a good carpenter," he wrote, "For example, odd pieces of wood were indiscriminately nailed together for studding, showing the carpenter to have felt that work which would be covered with lath and plaster could be done in any fashion."[7] However uneven the under-

lying quality, Mary and the boys could go upstairs and walk through a warren of new rooms without bumping their heads on the ceiling. What is
more, Abraham Lincoln, at 6'3", would be able to do the same.

Lincoln was in the town of Clinton, about forty miles northeast of
Springfield, still on "the tramp around the circuit," in John Stuart's phrase.[8]
On Thursday, May 15, he was trying to wrap up a divorce suit. It was a ser-
pentine case, twisted by misunderstandings purposefully set, like traps. The
year before, Lincoln, working for the husband, had almost become part of
the squabble when the wife claimed that the only reason she hadn't com-
plied with court schedules was that she had been waiting to hire Lincoln
herself.[9] By the time the case returned to the docket in May, 1856, she had
her own counsel in the form of John Stuart, along with two well-known
lawyers from Bloomington, Leonard Swett and John Wickhizer, but the
case was only postponed again.

Jane Anderson came home on that afternoon, May 15—without
Theodore—and had tea in the front parlor. On most days, she did a share of
the work around the household, but she had her luxuries, too: fine clothes,
for one thing, and someone to bring tea on a tray in the afternoon. As in
most households, dinner was served at noon and supper at eight or nine,
with tea in late afternoon as a bridge between the two. On that day, Mrs.
Anderson had been invited to the home of her husband's nephew, Charles
Anderson, for high tea. Charles and his wife, Mary, wanted to celebrate
George's return to good health. Mrs. Anderson, though, didn't attend. She
had been out all afternoon with Theodore, and she decided to stay in and
have tea alone. Just before supper, George arrived home. As soon as he came
in, he told Jane something she already knew: she hadn't been to tea at
Charles' house.

"No," she confirmed, she hadn't.

"If you're above going out with me," he said, "you can go back where
you've been and stay there."

"I will," she said.

"You can go now," George said.

"Well," Jane said, "I didn't hear you say anything about being able to
take care of the children."[10] Their voices carried notes of both stridency and

humor; even those who were in the room were too bewildered to say whether they were fighting or flirting.

Later, the Andersons had supper, and everyone in the household went to bed early. John Morgan had been living in the house for two years, without having his own room. His place in the house was a cot pushed against one wall in the dining room. Cyrus Youst, the other apprentice, was staying somewhere else in town, as he usually did; when he slept at the Anderson house he had a cot in the dining room, too. The children and the hired girl slept in another room, adjoining the dining room on the north side of the house. The bedroom that George and Jane shared was on the south side.

In the evening, George started to feel ill again. He hadn't bothered to put on a nightshirt. He had just taken off his new shirt and pants and lain down. At about nine o'clock, with the fever starting higher, he woke up. He sat up and then climbed out of bed. He wanted to go to the bathroom, which took the form of an outhouse, or privy, in the backyard. Anderson didn't bother to get dressed; he was hot anyway. He climbed out of bed without waking his wife, pulled on his coat and made sure he had his Allen pistol. Then he went outside. The air was cool and clear, and it was fresh, compared to that in the bedroom.

At about ten o'clock, John Morgan was sound asleep on his cot in the dining room when he heard something and slowly woke up. Mrs. Anderson was calling him. "The old man went out while I was asleep," she said, "Go see where he is." Morgan stood up and then went out the back door. He made his way down the steps and across the yard toward the privy. It was a moonlit night, but anyway he wouldn't have needed a lantern to get to the little shack. He knew the way perfectly well. Morgan figured he'd need both hands to help Anderson back to bed. Before he reached the privy, he found Anderson lying on the ground. Even in the dim light, he knew in an instant. Anderson wasn't moving. He was dead. Something told Morgan not to touch him. He called out his name, just to be sure. Nothing moved.

Morgan rushed back into the house to tell Mrs. Anderson. He told her that he thought Anderson was dead. "Go out and bring him in," she said. He wouldn't. He told her to go out and see for herself, but she wouldn't do that. She was frightened; the death was out there in the dark. She refused to go outside, but finally she went to a window in the back of the house and peered out until she saw the blur of George's body lying crooked in the yard. Then, as Morgan told it, she "commenced crying and taking on dreadful."

The simplest of facts had come through the back door: George Anderson was dead. But it may as well have been that the winds of a hurricane found their way inside the house. Ranting and roaming, Jane Anderson couldn't go outside to see what had happened and John Morgan insisted that he couldn't either. "Go wake up the hired girl," Jane implored. Morgan started for the other side of the house and she followed him to the room used by Rebecca Law. Apparently, the children remained asleep. Mrs. Anderson and Morgan squeezed in to the bedside. Rebecca was from a farm, where people learned about death firsthand in their daily chores, killing animals with their own hands. She was unfazed. "If you think he's dead," she told Mrs. Anderson, "you better not go near him, because the law won't allow anybody to touch him." Mrs. Anderson accepted that advice with a degree of relief. She told John Morgan to fetch the doctor. Morgan decided to go to see Dr. Fowler, rather than Lord. Fowler lived closer.

While Mrs. Anderson was waiting in a frantic state at the house, word began to circulate that her husband was dead. Morgan must have told people he met on the street, because the first person to show up at the house was Thomas Connor, a forty-six year-old Irishman[11] who lived seven blocks away. Connor worked as a chairmaker in a shop near the house, and knew the Andersons slightly.[12] He wasn't like Mrs. Anderson and John Morgan, not at all. He wanted to look. In a rush, like the crowd who went to see the livery stable burn down in Bloomington, Connor scurried down the side of the house and into the backyard.

Dr. Fowler was the next to arrive, and he carried out a preliminary examination of the body. No sooner had he touched Anderson's head than he realized that Anderson hadn't been alone when he died. He later said that he "found him lying in the back yard near the privy, with his head towards the house. His head had a severe wound on the back part, a large fracture, sufficient to have produced immediate death . . . as though it was made by a blow from some blunt heavy club or other article. The wound was a rough, ugly one, near four inches from the ear."[13]

F. Irwin Dean and Benjamin Watson were the next ones to make their way into the yard. Theodore Anderson showed up not long afterward. Dean, twenty-three,[14] worked as a clerk at Whitmer's department store in Springfield.[15] He noted that Anderson "had on nothing but his coat, drawers and socks." Dean didn't wait for the law, but took it upon himself to search the body, finding as he later said, "an Allen's revolver in the coat pocket." Connor saw him take it out.[16] Dean put the gun in his own pocket for safekeeping. Seeing the wound, and hearing Dr. Fowler assert that it was undoubtedly the result of an attack, he looked around the yard. "There was no stick or cane laying close to the body of the deceased," he said, adding that he "found a pine stick about five or six feet long and $1^{1}/_{2}$ by $3^{1}/_{2}$ inches, within about twenty feet of the body."[17]

At midnight, the deputy sheriff, John T. Jones, arrived on the scene. He made note of the position of the body. The head was away from the privy, as though Anderson had just come out of the little shack when he was hit. Anderson's remains were then carried into the house, which was becoming crowded with people: onlookers and neighbors. Of those later interviewed as having been there, a large number admitted that they didn't know the Andersons, had no medical or police connection, and had nothing to contribute. They were just there in the middle of the night, in somebody else's house, in the aftermath of somebody else's murder. The new mayor, John W. Priest, was in the throng. In the midst of the confusion, Dean put the pistol he'd found into a drawer in the house. Anderson's body was on the sofa in the sitting room, with sheets underneath it and pillows holding up the head, as though to make it comfortable.

Two more doctors arrived. One was Rufus Lord. The other was Sanford Bell, his former mentor who was, at forty-seven,[18] an elder in the profession in Springfield. They hovered over the body, the sheets and pillows underneath it stained with blood. Dr. Bell recalled of Anderson's remains that he "saw the wound on his head; it was sufficient to have caused instant death."[19] Fowler and Lord agreed, yet they insisted that there was more to it. Anderson had shown signs of strychnine poisoning over the previous two or three weeks; he may have been murdered twice over. They decided to perform an autopsy on the spot.

Jane Anderson was in her bedroom, crying. When she heard that the doctors were about to conduct an autopsy, her sorrow turned to anger and she screamed that "the physicians were cutting up her husband to gratify themselves." She swore vengeance on them. Mayor Priest went into the bedroom and tried to take her in hand. He gave her his assurance that, "they were only examining the wound in the head. She then became a little quiet, and said she wished they would all leave the house."[20]

The doctors weren't "only examining the wound in the head." They were cutting out the stomach and a piece of the small intestines. In the Anderson's sitting room, they removed the organs, and those who wanted to watch did so. The doctors then performed preliminary tests. Dr. Bell said that he "assisted in the examination of the stomach; and was of the opinion that it contained poison of some kind."

Dr. Fowler reached the same conclusion, but was more specific. He said of the stomach that, "so far as the tests made upon it, it was evident that some poisonous substance had been introduced into it, and from all indications, it appeared to be strychnine."[21]

Deputy Sheriff Jones heard other things, lots of other things, in the snatches of conversation that were wafting through the rooms of the Anderson house. The place was overheated with stories about the Andersons. When Jones heard the opinions of the doctors regarding the poison, he searched the house. Then he took heed of another theory, another rumor. Disregarding the hour, and appointing Benjamin Watson, a candy-maker, to accompany him, he went to the home of Charles Anderson, where Theodore boarded. He demanded to be shown to Theodore's room. It was mostly bare, but they found a trunk with the name "Theodore Anderson" painted on one end. They broke it open.

Inside, the deputy found a picture of Jane Anderson. He started to pick it up, and noticed a vial right next to it. He handed the picture to Watson. As he picked up the vial, he could see that it was half-filled with a clear, crystalline substance. They assumed it was strychnine. Jones handed the bottle to Watson. As he continued to search through the trunk, he found a bundle of letters, addressed to Theodore but unsigned. They took them away, too.

By the time Jones and Watson returned to the Anderson's house, Amzi McWilliams was there in his official capacity as State's Attorney in Sangamon County. Watson handed him the vial and the picture. The doctors had already left, taking the body to Dr. Fowler's office.

By lantern light in the Andersons' backyard, someone found a hammer in the grass. It was the sort of tool that could have been used in the blacksmith shop or around the house. The hammer head corresponded exactly in size to the wound that killed Anderson. It was taken to the sheriff's office.

As dawn approached, the Andersons' house emptied out. Theodore was among those few who stayed. With the morning, news of the murder spread throughout the city. The fact that a "well known and respected citizen"[22] had been struck down was a frightening development in a city that had gone years without a single murder. That it happened in the victim's own backyard was chilling; he may as well have been killed inside the house. Everyone in town, after all, made the same trip outside to their own privies, day and night. If people weren't safe in the backyard, they weren't safe anywhere. And if a killer was loose, then the whole city was under siege.

The coroner convened an inquest during the morning. With testimony from the doctors and other witnesses, the basic details were collected. Anderson had gone out of the house between nine and ten o'clock at night, and was killed by a blow to the head. With that, the verdict was "death by the hands of some person or persons unknown."[23]

A second wave of reports circulated through the city. Except for the verdict of murder, though, everything that people heard was unconfirmed. "Touching the ground of suspicion, there are numberless reports which do not agree with one another," reported the Springfield *Register*.[24] People picked through all of the allegations and observations, to find an explanation that made them feel better about the murder and the safety of their own houses. The most comforting of them denied that there was a killer on the loose. That theme was summed up by the statement in the *Register*.

"Delicate domestic affairs," explained the paper, "are mingled with this lamentable tragedy."[25]

"There are a thousand rumors in circulation," acknowledged the Springfield *State Journal*.[26] At least one was proved true later that morning, when the sheriff set out to locate Theodore Anderson, on orders from Amzi McWilliams. He found Theodore at the scene of the murder with Jane Anderson and the children. The sheriff bluntly told Theodore that he was under arrest for the murder of his uncle. Theodore balked, denying that he'd had anything to do with the crime, but the sheriff ignored all of the talk and took him away to jail.[27] Theodore was formally charged with the murder.

That night, Lord and Fowler met at their office to conduct a full autopsy. In all, five physicians were present. Among them was William Wallace, Lincoln's brother-in-law and close friend. In addition to performing the post-mortem on the body, McWilliams had asked the medical team to positively identify the substance in the vial. That was easy. After a test, they confirmed that it was unquestionably strychnine. Then they turned to the post-mortem and further analysis of the contents of the victim's stomach.

Theodore spent Friday night in jail, awaiting an arraignment hearing before a police magistrate. Springfield's magistrate was Turner King, forty-three, a sand dealer and landowner who often performed civic jobs on the side.[28] With King scheduled to hear facts in the case on Monday, Theodore was to be confined to the jail all weekend. He was sitting in his cell on Saturday morning when his uncle was buried.

The funeral was carried out with Masonic rites, a well-attended and impressive ceremony that began with four huge carriages leading a procession through the city. Jane Anderson was in one of the carriages, surrounded by her children. Her sister and George Anderson's relatives were also part of the procession and stood by her at the funeral. They were either in shock or they couldn't bring themselves to believe the stories they were hearing about her. Rebecca Law, the Andersons' hired girl, didn't lose her cool, though, nor did she go to the funeral. On that Saturday, she went to a wedding in a nearby village. Word came back to Springfield that Rebecca was telling people that Mrs. Anderson had killed her husband with a shovel to the back of the head.

McWilliams, the marshal, and the deputy continued their investigations. They weren't just looking into the murder, but into the relationship of Jane Anderson and Theodore. On Saturday afternoon, they made a tremendous find: bloody sheets and pillow cases stashed in an extra outhouse on the property—and a wide plank covered with blood on one end that was found in an adjoining lot. The new evidence suggested that Anderson had actually been killed in his bed, and then moved outside.[29]

On Saturday afternoon, the sheriff took new action and went looking for Jane Anderson. She was arrested, just as Theodore had been. A female prisoner was unusual enough in Springfield, but a female murder suspect was entirely new. Mrs. Anderson was taken from her house, led into a carriage, and put in jail. Her sister took charge of the children. The house was left empty. McWilliams, sorting through the facts, which were few, and the lurid rumors, which were swarming, had come to the conclusion that if Theodore Anderson was guilty, so was Jane Anderson. With her arrest, the murder was reported in newspapers from Missouri to Wisconsin. As to Springfield, there was no other topic discussed on the streets.

Benjamin Edwards, Stuart's law partner, heard all of the details, even though he spent most of the weekend at his estate on the northern edge of Springfield. That Saturday, he was out-of-sorts, trying to be glad for his wife and two younger children, who'd left on a vacation to Niagara Falls the day before. His wife hadn't been feeling well and the trip was supposed to help steady her nerves. Knocking around in his huge house on Saturday, Edwards wrote to his oldest daughter, Helen, who was away at school. "I felt very lonesome last night," he said, "and do not doubt but I shall feel more so, until I am compelled by the business of the office and in court to devote my whole attention thereto." He sounded like a lawyer, even in addressing his fifteen-year-old daughter, but she was probably used to it. "There is nothing new here," he added toward the end of his letter, "except that George Anderson, the blacksmith, was murdered night before last. He was found in his yard, but the suspicion now is that he was murdered in his bed, and carried into the yard."[30]

At thirty-eight, Edwards was a haughty man, who had a way of making sure no one forgot that he was the son of a former governor. A graduate of

Yale and the law school connected with it, he was meticulous in his profession. "He is a very fine lawyer," the attorney Usher Linder allowed, "liberally educated, but I may say without giving any offense to him, that he is one of the vainest men I ever knew."[31] Unfortunately, Linder didn't reveal how one might make such a remark without giving offence. But there is other evidence that Edwards must have been a difficult man. Among other things, the amiable Abraham Lincoln couldn't stand him.

Lincoln and Edwards were related by marriage, and saw each other often at social gatherings, in addition to working in the same profession in the same small city. Edwards had taken Lincoln's place as Stuart's partner, and while Stuart had denied Lincoln a fifty-fifty split, he had accepted Edwards as a full partner. Judge Davis once said that Lincoln "despised" Benjamin Edwards.[32] The two certainly had disparate backgrounds, a fact that Edwards refused to forget.

When Mrs. Anderson's sister in New York heard about the murder of George Anderson, she headed for Springfield. The family intended that Jane have the best defense team that money could buy, and apparently, the sister from New York could buy the best. Springfield, of course, counted its attorneys by the dozen. There were young pups like John Rosette, with his matinee-idol looks. There were local legends like Stephen Logan, with his long hair and fanciful clothes. Then there were the plainer non-conformists, like Abraham Lincoln. There were workmanlike lawyers like James Matheny, and those like Thomas Lewis, who were more interested, it seemed, in anything but the law. They all circled around each other, filling the newspapers with their opinions and their exploits, filling the city with their aspirations. Mrs. Anderson's relatives wanted the most aggressive attorneys in Springfield. Abraham Lincoln, out tramping the circuit, couldn't even be considered.

Stuart & Edwards were hired over the weekend. On Monday, William Campbell and Thomas Lewis were also engaged for the defense team on behalf of Jane Anderson. The court scheduled her hearing first, before Theodore's, in consideration of her imprisonment and the hardship it presented to her children. Theodore's examination would come later. In the meantime, they would each stay in prison at least until their respective arraignment hearings. Illinois had no provision for bail in cases of murder or manslaughter.

Turner King, the police magistrate, was scheduled to preside. Because the Anderson murder was such a troubling case, though, a magistrate with more solid legal knowledge was added. The second justice was Lucien B. Adams, a lawyer who officiated at municipal court hearings.

Jane Anderson's case was to be heard on Monday. That gave Edwards, Stuart, Lewis, and Campbell just one day, Sunday, to prepare. Amzi McWilliams had been working on the case since Friday. He was planning to have the indictments in place within a week or ten days, so that when the Circuit Court arrived in Springfield for Sangamon County's term in early June, Judge Davis could hear the case. Just that quickly, he could have it concluded.

CHAPTER 6

MID-MAY

EXCITEMENT IN THE CITY

O n Sunday, John Stuart wrote to his teen-aged daughter, Betty, who was away at school:

My dear Betty

Another week has passed and you are that much nearer the time when you come home to remain when the Schoolday times are over and when you will begin in earnest the business of your life—we are all looking anxiously to the time when you will return and we will have a young lady at home . . .

There was a murder committed in town on Thursday which has been the cause of great excitement in the City. Mr. Anderson living between Masonic Hall and 3d church and a member of the firm of Talbott and Anderson black Smiths was found about eleven o'clock at night dead in his own yard with a fractured skull evidently caused by a blow with a heavy club. A cousin [sic] of Anderson's has been taken up and is in jail charged with the crime and only yesterday the wife of Anderson was arrested and put in jail charged with being an accomplice. Tomorrow Mrs. Anderson is to be examined before the magistrates and I hope will be proven innocent of the charge. Mr. Edwards, myself defend her.[1]

Normally, an arraignment hearing might be expected to take an hour or two. Jane Anderson's took three days, starting on Monday. Moreover, each session lasted twelve hours or more, from mid-morning until late at night. The prosecution was organizing its argument as the hearing went along. So, of course, were Stuart and Edwards, Campbell and Lewis. Sometimes, a witness would be called and questioned carefully, only to reveal that he or she didn't know any of the Andersons and had no information whatsoever about the murder. Then there would be a delay while another witness was selected, located somewhere in the building or elsewhere within the city, and then sworn in. When the time came for the defense attorneys to present their side, they had no real evidence of their own. They could do little more than recall prosecution witnesses and probe for new shafts in the dim light cast by previous testimony.

As meandering as the hearing was at times, it faced a vexing challenge: convincing people to stand by the rumors they'd been spreading all week. McWilliams first called the two doctors, Lord and Fowler, who went over the details of the separate attacks on Anderson: the poisoning and the blow to the head. They both described their treatment of Anderson's illness as starting on May 1, which was odd, considering that their own account book showed that they had been treating him almost daily since April 22.[2] If nothing else, the doctors helped to clear up the mystery surrounding the bloodied sheets and pillowcases found stashed away in the Andersons' backyard. They were apparently the cloths on which the body lay after the murder and during the initial autopsy at the house. That quashed the speculation that Anderson had actually been killed in his bed and then moved to the backyard. One mystery was solved. But then there was the relationship between Jane Anderson and Theodore Anderson.

None of the witnesses could explain why George Anderson had told Theodore to find another place to board, though the time of his departure was universally placed in late March. Mr. Smithers, the owner of a local daguerrean room—portrait studio—was called to testify about the daguerreo-type picture of Mrs. Anderson that had been found in Theodore's trunk. A daguerreotype represented a substantial expense, unlike snapshots in a later age. Smithers looked at Theodore's picture of Jane and confirmed that he had taken it. He then testified that in February the couple had come into his da-guerrean room, located on the square near the Courthouse. They'd returned not long afterward for another picture of Mrs. Anderson, in a different dress.[3]

The court next learned that John Morgan, the apprentice, had made re-markably few observations about the Andersons during his two years in their household. Taciturn by nature, he seemed particularly aloof on the stand. He did say, as reported in the transcript of the hearing, that "Mrs. Anderson told him that he must be careful how he talked about the murder around town."[4] In his sullen testimony, he reported that during all the time that Theodore had lived at the house, he'd seen him walking with Mrs. An-derson just once, and her in-law, Mrs. Charles Anderson, was with them, he added quickly. Pressed by McWilliams, Morgan said that the two of them did frequently walk down to the front gate and back.

John Armstrong provided much more titillating testimony than that. Armstrong, who owned a carpentry shop next door to Anderson & Talbott, was fairly well-known in town. In fact, he was among those who signed William Herndon's May 10 call for the Anti-Nebraska meeting in Spring-field. Armstrong came to the stand right after Rebecca Law, the Andersons' maid, had confirmed that on the day of the murder, Mrs. Anderson left the house by herself at about quarter to three, not returning until five-thirty. Next, Armstrong testified that he had seen both Theodore and Jane on that afternoon, and they were together. He said that he first saw them in the northern part of the city. Asked where they were going, he said that they ap-peared to be going out of town. Under questioning, he explained that at about four o'clock "they went into a lot belonging to Dr. Jayne, adjoining to B. S. Edwards' residence; they went into the bushes and set down; remained there a short time, and then came out and went in the direction of the lane west of B. S. Edwards."[5] Armstrong said that he couldn't see them the entire time they were sitting on the grass in the bushes, but at one point, he did notice them talking together. Just as the image that Armstrong provided was settling in—a rather vain woman sneaking off with her husband's nephew while the husband was at work, getting over the effects of poison—he suddenly backed off, adding that, "he saw nothing of any familiarity between them."[6]

Armstrong wasn't through, though. Later in the day, he was recalled. Under questioning by Amzi McWilliams, he said that he "had noticed something in the conduct of the young man that appeared strange." Theodore, he said, was at George Anderson's shop more often in the wet weather than dry. When it rained, the young man would stand just inside the shop door for an hour at a time, behind a board that hid him from people passing on the street. From that vantage point, he could peer diagonally across the backyards and see part of the Andersons' house. Sometimes, he went upstairs for a different view. Armstrong could easily explain why Theodore only used the hiding place in the rain. In clear weather, according to the testimony, Theodore walked up and down the alley leading from the shop to the backyard of the house. "He acted very strange," Armstrong said, "so much as to elicit remarks from the workmen in the shop; [he] appeared to be watching some one in the house."

Other witnesses testified to seeing Mrs. Anderson and Theodore walking around the north side of town together on the previous Thursday or on other occasions. One identified them as a couple he'd seen going into an empty house on the next block three times during the month of February. Another confidently recalled that he'd seen them in a daguerrean room— not Smithers' room, but another one—for a long period of time "sitting on the lounge, conversing and laughing."[7] A neighbor named Northerner picked up the story of their actions on the Thursday George Anderson was killed. That would have been just after they returned from the fields near Benjamin Edwards' house. Northerner passed the Anderson house on Monroe Street at six-thirty in the evening and saw Jane and Theodore at the fence. They separated when he approached. "She afterward called him back," Northerner said, "he then went back."[8]

Mr. Smithers was recalled to the witness stand to clarify something regarding the daguerreotype. He said that Theodore and Jane had visited the studio together for the second picture, and that at that time, the first one was returned to Smithers. He was thereby able to confirm that the picture found in Theodore's trunk was no cast-off, no extra copy; it was the picture Mrs. Anderson had approved and accepted.

Somewhere amid the innuendo, a motive was trying to arise. McWilliams was presenting the crime as one of two murders and one victim. The testimony of the prosecution witnesses implied that Jane Anderson had tried unsuccessfully to poison her husband throughout the three-week period ending May 15. Oblivious to the fact that the doctors suspected strychnine poisoning all along, she was, McWilliams alleged, trying to give George Anderson just enough poison to kill him, but not enough to betray the true cause of death. With Lord and Fowler watching all the time, so the prosecutor supposed, she was too tentative. She was afraid to raise the dosage. His conclusion was that when Jane's efforts didn't progress, Theodore used the hammer in the dark.

The story that had gone around town all week was at last out in the open in the courtroom. It was a good story, but it didn't arrange itself quite as neatly in court as it had on the street. Even the prosecution witnesses, particularly the doctors, painted Jane Anderson as a woman above reproach during the long illness of her husband. Fowler and Lord were at pains to praise her attentiveness and compassion, but then, they were on trial, too, in a sense. They had been treating the victim for weeks, and had privately identified the cause of his malady as poison. More, they had speculated that the specific poison was probably strychnine, had proved the seriousness of their suspicions by killing a dog in the name of educating themselves—and then had refrained from telling Anderson himself, confronting those around him, or notifying the sheriff. They each went to extremes on the witness stand to explain their failure to act.

Dr. Fowler told the court that in nursing George Anderson during late April and the first half of May, "Mrs. Anderson appeared very devoted, attentive and anxious for his recovery." In case that sounded as though it were only an outsider's opinion of the woman, he added that, "Mr. Anderson appeared to place a great deal of reliance and confidence in his wife, so much that I took particular notice of it; her attention was very marked and affectionate."[9]

Fowler's partner corroborated. "She willingly did all, and more than I advised her to do," Dr. Lord told the court, "Mr. Anderson's confidence in her was so great that he could not bear the idea of not having her wait upon him; [I] had perfect confidence in the nursing." Then he said that he would have "tested for poison had anyone else been nursing." It was a strange medical investigation, though, that was built upon an intended conclusion (Mrs. Anderson's innocence), rather than the evidence.

Overall, the testimony did suggest a motive: that Jane Anderson and Theodore Anderson were committing adultery, and tried to kill George Anderson, first by one method, and then by another. All of the facts fit that scenario, even Jane Anderson's overtly careful nursing, which could be painted as diversionary.

Just when Justices Adams and King were well-acquainted with that theory, another witness took the stand: Mary Anderson, the thirteen-year-old daughter of George and Jane Anderson. She swore an oath to tell the truth, with her hand on the Bible, and then, in answer to McWilliams' first question, acknowledged that she knew what an oath was. First, she was asked if she knew Theodore Anderson. She said she did, that he had boarded at their house.

"He was a lover of mine," Mary blurted out. McWilliams asked her if she was "in much trouble about his situation."[10] She said that she wasn't. When he tried to ascertain if she had written the love letters found in his trunk, Jane Anderson's defense attorneys objected vociferously, on the basis that the letters would have to be brought in as evidence before the prosecution could try to prove anything regarding them. The justices sustained the objection. With that, Mary Anderson was dismissed.

Mary Anderson presented a complication. If her story was accepted, it would offer a different motive for the crime. In the nineteenth century, the word *lover* didn't necessarily indicate a physical relationship, as it would today, nor did it rule one out. Using the word was akin to calling someone a boyfriend today, with its wide range of implications. Mary's use of the word introduced the possibility that she and Theodore might have been the ones having an illicit affair. At the time, no one took Mary's story seriously, but it muddled the prosecution's case.

The defense concentrated instead on a mysterious man seen lurking around the Anderson's house: a tall, thin man dressed in black with a hat.

John Morgan said that he had seen a man of that description in early April, a few weeks after Theodore Anderson stopped boarding at the house. Asked if it could have been Theodore, Morgan said that the figure he'd seen had been wearing a black hat; Theodore had a reddish one. It was soon after Morgan made that sighting that George Anderson borrowed a pistol.

William Planck, a candymaker, was asked if he'd seen Theodore Anderson on the night of the murder. He said he couldn't swear to it positively. For a moment, it seemed as though he were just another stray, resting his feet in the witness box. Under further questioning, however, he did say that on Thursday night, he'd seen a man dressed in black standing around in the lot at the back of Owen's Drugstore. The store was on the south side of State House Square. That is, in the four-sided city block where the murder took place, Owen's Drugstore faced north into the square, and the Anderson House faced south, onto Monroe. Their backyards adjoined the same alley, which cut through the middle of the block.

Planck said that he saw the man stir from Owen's backyard and walk into the alley toward the Anderson's yard. "He corresponded in size with Theodore Anderson," Planck said, "but was dressed different from what he was in the fore part of the evening."[11]

In no particular order, a long parade of neighbors testified at Jane Anderson's hearing. Sometimes the prosecution witnesses made the defense's case, and sometimes the defense witnesses underscored Jane Anderson's potential as a murderess. Inasmuch as the attorneys on both sides exerted so little control over the testimony—barely knowing themselves what anyone had to say—the hearing was at least an open airing of information from the witnesses. On Wednesday, court was still in session, to the fascination of all those following the case in Springfield—and Illinois' other cities. In a report of the trial on Thursday, the *Illinois Chronicle* in Decatur was one day behind, but otherwise well-informed: "The examination," noted the paper, "which was still in progress up to yesterday, had failed to elicit evidence sufficient to convict the parties, though we learn that the citizens of that city have no doubts as to their guilt."[12]

While Springfield was looking forward to each new tidbit that emerged from the Anderson hearing, the cities of Urbana and Kankakee, in the eastern part of the state, were distracted by a different kind of *cause célèbre.*

A feisty priest named Father Charles Chiniquy had built up a vibrant parish in Kankakee since arriving there in 1851. With his strong personality, he was beloved by his parishioners. Yet, a little storm of controversy followed his dealings with almost everyone else. Father Chiniquy didn't get along with the bishop in Chicago, and he proved too strong-willed for a few of the local Kankakeeans, too, especially when he used his pulpit to tell shocking stories about individuals in the community. Some of the accusations were perfectly true, but it was nonetheless unfair, since the victims were mostly private citizens who had no means of rebuttal or defense.

A businessman named Peter Spink got off easy, compared to some of Father Chiniquy's other targets, but he still didn't like the idea of people being told in a sermon that he was a perjurer. In 1855, Spink filed a $10,000 slander suit. As the case made its way to trial in Kankakee, he filed a petition for a change of venue, "on account of the prejudice of the judge of said court against him."[13] The case was duly moved to Champaign County Circuit Court in Urbana, a stop on Judge Davis' Eighth Circuit Court. For most of those involved in the case, the move was an inconvenience. For Father Chiniquy, it was a personal cataclysm that brought him to the very brink of doom. But then, to him, everything was. Fortunately, he was a man who savored nothing so much as evidence of his own martyrdom.

According to Father Chiniquy's account, he almost fainted when he heard the news that he would have to go to Urbana for his trial. A friend mopped his forehead, while a stranger made a suggestion. "Though your lawyers are expert men, you will want something better at Urbana. Try to secure the services of Abraham Lincoln, of Springfield." His lawyers concurred, as Father Chiniquy described it:

> "If you can secure the services of Abraham Lincoln, by all means do it. We know him well; he is one of the best lawyers, and one of the most honest men we have in our state."

Without losing a minute, I went to the telegraph office with that stranger and telegraphed to Abraham Lincoln to ask him if he would defend my honour and my life (though I was a stranger to him) at the next May term of the court at Urbana.

About twenty minutes later I received the answer:

"Yes, I will defend your honour and your life at the next May term at Urbana. Abraham Lincoln."[14]

Although that response sounds cheeky, as though to chide the self-righteous Father Chiniquy, it was the priest's version of the story, and probably his version of what was in the telegram, as well. In any case, Lincoln came to Urbana prepared to defend the priest. The trial largely coincided with the Anderson hearing in Springfield, taking up the Circuit Court docket on Tuesday afternoon and all of Wednesday, May 20 and 21. The streets of Urbana were crowded with witnesses and partisans in the confrontation between Spink and Father Chiniquy. Half of Kankakee seemed to have descended on the town, with empty lots transformed into campsites for the visitors, their pets, and their musical instruments.

Many of the witnesses from Father Chiniquy's church spoke only French. Though an interpreter was providing translations,[15] the trial presented challenges for Lincoln, whose strength was his facility with the English language. Anyway, *Spink v. Chiniquy* was the sort of case that Lincoln regretted. He had handled such cases consistently throughout his career: disagreements that exploded far beyond their negligible effect on "the honour and the life" of either party. He performed his duties in Urbana for Father Chiniquy, but his usual method would have been to look for a better way out of the tussle rather than to thread it through the rules of court—and take up so much of the court's time, to boot. With the lawyers from Kankakee, Lincoln conducted the defense at the trial all day Wednesday. He and the others wended their way through a long list of witnesses, doggedly trying to sort out the feuding, bickering, and griping, most of it in French, from the facts, which had to be presented to the court in English.

"When the tedious trial was nearly through," recalled Henry Whitney, "a juryman was detected crying: the court noticed it, and said promptly

'What is that juror crying about?' 'My child is dying,' sobbed he." In the midst of the crowded courtroom, someone had sidled up to the jury box and passed a message to that effect to the juror. Judge Davis looked into the matter himself, found that the story was true and had no choice but to dismiss the stricken man. Since no provision had been made for an alternate, he then asked the attorneys for each side if they would proceed with eleven jurors. Lincoln said, "We will." Then it was the turn of Spink's attorney. "We decline" he said.

The trial started over.[16]

Back in Springfield on Wednesday night, the final arguments in the Anderson hearing were being heard. Amzi McWilliams insisted that Jane Anderson shared "a criminal intimacy" with her nephew, Theodore. It was proved, he said, that they had been seen together in unexplainable situations, that a bottle of strychnine had been found in Theodore's possession, and that George Anderson had suffered from poisoning, most likely with strychnine, before his death. McWilliams' summation tried to show that, according to a report of the trial, "the poison was administered by the wife for the purpose of getting rid of her husband, but that not taking effect soon enough, the nephew did the deed in a more summary manner."[17] That was the prosecution's version of life on Monroe Street.

Benjamin Edwards, in his final speech, dwelt on the fact that Jane Anderson had "hitherto borne a good character."[18] That was the defense's version.

The following day, the verdict was in. John Stuart could hardly wait to tell Betty about it, and dashed off a letter to her as soon as he could:

My dear Betty,
    I received your letter of yesterday which has given me a great deal of pleasure—I write this in the office immediately after its receipt and with a good many talking around me. There is nothing new in the City. We have great excitement with the case of Mrs.

Anderson which I mentioned to you in my last. We commenced the investigation of her case Monday morning and only closed it last night at 10 o'clock when she was acquited and discharged . . . [19]

Justices King and Adams had not found enough evidence to hold Jane Anderson on the murder charge.[20] Nothing indicated that she had been the one who attacked George Anderson in the backyard, and that was the charge at hand. While the justices noted that strychnine had been found in Anderson's stomach, they could not consider it as a cause of death. Late Wednesday night, she went home once more to her children.

Theodore Anderson was next. His hearing was scheduled for May 28, meaning that he faced another five days in jail, but with the news of the first verdict, his cell took on an atmosphere of relief, compared to that in the first wretched week. In view of the conclusion in his aunt's case, in which the assault and not the poisoning was at issue, most people in Springfield predicted that he would be exonerated as a matter of course.[21] None of the testimony positively connected Theodore with the bashing, anymore than it did Mrs. Anderson.

Lincoln was still in Urbana on Thursday, awaiting the verdict in the retrial of *Spink v. Chiniquy*. Not many people were happy when it came in. The verdict was that there was no verdict, the jury was hung. Father Chiniquy chalked it up to the fact that his two local lawyers had allowed an Irish Catholic to sit on the jury, a sheep according to Chiniquy, taking orders from the man whom Chiniquy regarded as an unsleeping enemy: the bishop. However it was that the jury came to its indecision, Judge Davis continued the case until the fall term in October. Father Chiniquy no doubt felt faint all over again. For Lincoln, though, delay was an integral part of the Circuit Court. He moved on to Danville on Friday; the term there began on the next day, Saturday.

William Herndon was on a more exciting errand, as one of the two key speakers at an Anti-Nebraska rally in Menard County. The other was Richard Yates, a leader in the Illinois' Anti-Nebraska movement along with William Bissell and Senator Trumbull. Yates had been elected to Congress in 1850 when he was only thirty-two. At the time, he was the youngest man to serve at the Capitol. He completed two terms, and retained the aura of a rising star in Illinois politics. In the popular estimation, he was the most eloquent Anti-Nebraska orator in the state.[22] Yates, who lived in Morgan County, adjoining Sangamon to the west, was a handsome fellow with a ruddy complexion, high forehead, and curly red-brown hair. The chance to share a stage with Yates was an opportunity Herndon would not have missed, though it did mean shirking a crucial appointment in Springfield.

While Lincoln and Herndon were each away on Saturday, the 24th of May, the Sangamon County Anti-Nebraska contingent met at the Courthouse in Springfield. It was the gathering to which Lincoln had attached his name—to the great consternation of John Stuart. In fact, Lincoln's other former law partner, Stephen Logan, helped to run the meeting. Two hundred people were in attendance, a good number for a fledgling party. Nothing came easily that night, though, perhaps because no two people had the same idea as to why they were there, or what the new party was supposed to represent.

Job Fletcher, Jr., the elderly Whig politician, stood up near the beginning of the night and asked just that question: what was the object of the meeting? After a long pause, someone at the front of the room blurted out that the idea was to fuse with anybody in order to beat the Democrats. That was enough for some people, but it didn't bode well for the longtime success of the party. "Why fuse in Sangamon?" countered Fletcher, referring to the county in which Springfield is located, "Have we whigs not 600 majority? Why fuse at all?"[23]

A reporter wrote that Fletcher "insisted, then, that the whole affair looked too woolly for him." *Woolly* was a euphemism at the time, denoting sympathy toward African Americans and toward slaves. But then Fletcher didn't need euphemisms; as the report continued, he stated quite clearly that he had "no taste for fusion with abolitionists, know-nothings, and renegade democrats. He was a Whig and nothing else. He had signed the call, but he had no leaning to niggerism."[24]

Although the leaders of the Sangamon County Convention would never use the word "niggerism"—common as it was in pro-slavery and Democratic parlance—many of them had no more sympathy for the slaves than did Fletcher. They were, as the word from the front of the room had said it, against the Democrats, which translated in Illinois into a vehement sentiment against Stephen Douglas. In fact, a very successful, if limited, political party could have been formed in Illinois (and elsewhere) on nothing more than the Anti–Stephen Douglas platform. "How does that poor fallen wretch Stephen A. Douglas look and act?" wrote a constituent to Senator Trumbull in Washington in 1856, "Pity he will not do his country some service now by committing suicide."[25]

"You may think I hate the man," Herndon wrote to a friend about Senator Douglas, "I can say I do not; yet I do loathe him."[26] At least he cleared that up.

Still, the fusion had to be more than hating (or even loathing) Douglas. It also had to go beyond the passions behind "Anti-Nebraska." Something more inspiring had to pull the party together. For the moment, though, in local meetings all over the state, the only issue that brought people together at all was the one that dominated the Springfield meeting: "we regard the repeal of the Missouri Compromise as a wanton reopening of the slavery agitation."[27] That included a good slap at Senator Douglas, since it was his Kansas-Nebraska Act that had displaced the Missouri Compromise. With that, the nascent party was clinging to its issue, too timid to look any further past it or around it.

As part of the business of the meeting, Lincoln was duly appointed as a delegate to the State Convention, which was to be held the following Wednesday, May 29, in Bloomington. So were Herndon and Logan (and another man who declined the appointment the same day). The Democratic *Register* called the meeting "a flash in the pan, a fizzle,"[28] and while it would have taken a dim view of the proceedings no matter what had happened, there was indeed something missing from the party—a name, if nothing else. Someone had suggested "Republican" a few weeks before. It was already attached to similar political activity in other states.

As a name, "Republican" had been kicking around American politics for decades, used by one ill-starred party or another. When Senator Douglas heard that it was being resurrected yet again in early 1856, he labeled the new uprising against him and his party "Black Republicans." The epithet stuck, and made the whole issue of the name of the party uncomfortable.

That was the trouble with the new party: one way and another, it was all a reflection in the eye of Stephen Douglas. If the Bloomington Convention couldn't be powered from within, by its own ideas, then it really would be a flash in the pan or, at least, a fusion easily disintegrated with the help of Senator Douglas and his well-placed barbs.

The appointment as a delegate didn't come as a surprise to Abraham Lincoln. He planned to wrap up his work with the Circuit Court in Danville on Monday, and then travel by train to Decatur on Tuesday, on the way to Bloomington. As he prepared to leave, the big news in the newspapers around the country was the violent attack in the U.S. Senate on Senator Charles Sumner of Massachusetts. A telegraphed account published throughout the West reported that on the previous Thursday:

> Preston S. Brooks, of South Carolina, a member of the lower house, entered the senate chamber and approached the seat of Mr. Sumner, and struck him a powerful blow with a cane, at the same time accusing him of libeling South Carolina and his gray-headed relative, Senator Butler. Mr. Sumner fell from the effects of the blow. Mr. Brooks continued beating him.[29]

Sumner was seriously injured. In fact, he wouldn't be well enough to return to the Capitol for three years. Whether the beating really reflected the tension between the regions, or just the violent temper of Brooks, the response galvanized those in the North who were tired of the Southern will in all of its forms. Anger over the Sumner attack swept delegates toward Bloomington on Monday and Tuesday. So did news of a similar sort, which received much less publicity.

Paul Selby, the young journalist from Morgan County who had organized February's Anti-Nebraska meeting in Decatur, was also the driving force behind the Bloomington Convention. During the preceeding week, he was still in his quiet town of Jacksonville, preparing for his trip, looking forward to the things that could come of it and the role he was set to play. Over the weekend, a man named Phil Warren and two of his relatives found Selby on a street, and clubbed him with their walking sticks, in retribution for his Anti-Nebraska writings, so they said as they beat him. The attackers couldn't have been inspired by the Sumner attack—word of it had yet to reach Illinois on the weekend. But they were acting in the same spirit. Selby survived, but he couldn't travel. He lay in bed, recovering, as the other delegates made their way to Bloomington.

Political violence might have been sporadic, but what raised it into a phenomenon, an attitude known as the "Bludgeon Democracy," was the cheering that followed. Satisfaction in the attacks came from otherwise respectable sources, indicating that the slavery crisis had already started a kind of war, a dehumanizing of the enemy. "We understand from the public prints that Mr. Paul Selby, the abolition editor at the Morgan Journal got himself most *delightfully* caned a few days since," wrote a fellow editor in nearby Vandalia, Illinois, "You served him right, Phil, in all things save one. You didn't give him enough."[30]

The days leading up to the Bloomington Convention were crisscrossed with disturbing trends, all growing stronger. The town of Lawrence, Kansas, founded two years before by abolitionists from New England, had been attacked and partially destroyed by a pro-slavery mob on Wednesday, May 21. Details of the attack trickled into Illinois communities the following week. It was a peculiar time: at the clap of fear, each person in Illinois seemed to be reacting to something else, and running in a different direction.

Joseph Gillespie, a well-tempered Whig politician who had worked his way up from a job in the lead mines at Galena to a thriving law practice, arrived in Bloomington for the Convention, and immediately reported to Senator Trumbull, by means of a letter. "There is great excitement here in regard to the attack made upon Senator Sumner and the proceedings in Kansas," he wrote, "The general opinion here is that the Union is in great Danger and that some decisive steps must be taken by the people to arrest this downward tendency of things." He went on talking soberly of legislators needing to carry pistols and Bowie knives.[31]

Gillespie was present of his own free will at the Anti-Nebraska Convention, but he had been associated earlier in the year with the Know Nothing political party in Illinois. The Know Nothings were of immediate concern to Abraham Lincoln. They had established themselves quickly through the 1855 elections and, in spring of 1856, they were positioning themselves with some success as the most viable anti-Democratic party. They were founded on anti-Catholicism, but knew that they had to address the slavery question in the upcoming presidential election. That represented a sticky problem.

Know Nothings were anti-slavery, but in their own obtuse way, as outlined in a resolution passed at one of their conventions: "Roman Catholicism and slavery being alike founded and supported on the basis of ignorance and tyranny; and being, therefore, natural allies in every warfare against liberty and enlightenment . . . there can exist no real hostility to Roman Catholicism which does not [include] slavery."[32] Put more succinctly by of one the organizers, the plan for 1856 was to "take care of the Dutch and Irish after the nigger question is settled."[33]

Tepidly opposed to the expansion of slavery, virulently against immigrants, and offering a dependable alternative to the Democrats, the Know Nothings appealed to a surprisingly diverse body of supporters. It was itself a remarkable kind of fusion, in view of the fact that many of those who came out strongest for the party wouldn't have been allowed to set foot in a Know Nothing meeting. Established Louisiana Catholics tried to join the Know Nothing Party, because they didn't like recent Catholic immigrants. Their applications for membership were rejected.[34] The Know Nothings were gathering pockets of support all through the country in early 1856, though their strongholds were the cities of the north.

Abraham Lincoln predicted that the Know Nothing party would collapse,[35] but it was still thriving in May, with plans for a national convention in June. Lincoln eyed the support that was going to the Know Nothings, and wanted it very badly for the new party. He couldn't, however, see any way to accommodate them in a direct way. The previous year, in a letter to Joshua Speed of Kentucky, one of his oldest and best friends, he'd elucidated his feelings with the clarity that was his:

I am not a Know Nothing. That is certain. How could I be? How can anyone who abhors the oppression of negroes, be in favor of degrading classes of white people? Our progress in degeneracy appears to me to be pretty rapid. As a nation, we began by declaring that "all men are created equal." We now practically read it "all men are created equal, *except negroes.*" When the Know-Nothings get control, it will read "all men are created equal, except negroes, *and foreigners, and catholics.*" When it comes to this I should prefer emigrating to some country where they make no pretense of loving liberty—to Russia, for instance, where despotism can be taken pure, and without the base alloy of hypocracy [sic].[36]

If Abraham Lincoln was an idealist, it was only because he insisted on bringing the Declaration of Independence into more modern times. His confidence in the strength of that document made him manifestly confident in his positions on the slavery crisis. At unsettled junctures, such as May of 1856, other people spoke at length about the documents that founded the nation, without connecting the issues of the different eras with anything more conclusive than their own opinions. Whatever Lincoln's political inclinations were, he habitually tested them and himself against the possibility of betraying the intent of the Founding Fathers. He was more loyal to the Founding Fathers, in actuality, than to any particular party, than even to his own opinions. None of Lincoln's philosophy would matter, though, if he didn't have the political ingenuity to induce people to be as loyal to that intent as he was himself. That was the potential of the new party.

Lincoln didn't have the luxury of leaving the Know Nothings out of his calculations for the new party. Whether he wanted to or not, he had to consider ways to appeal to the rabid ones—those who wanted to "take care of the Dutch and Irish"—but he was even more concerned about those many well-meaning people who supposed that the Know Nothings offered a moderate alternative to the Democrats—people who were, like Joseph Gillespie, decidedly un-radical old Whigs.

In Springfield on Tuesday morning, Theodore Anderson was taken out of prison and transported to the Courthouse for his hearing before Justices Adams and King. Around town, onlookers were saying that he was going to have the same hearing, and the same outcome that Mrs. Anderson had the week before. Influential people in Springfield didn't like the way things were going, though. The hearing had been loose and ill-planned on both sides, but especially on the prosecution's part. No one was putting any pressure on the sheriff to find the tall man in the black hat seen near the house. But then, as far as most people in Springfield were concerned, he was already in custody: Theodore Anderson. The pressure was on Amzi McWilliams to prove it.

As Theodore entered the courtroom, he was no longer feeling quite as confident, having just heard the latest news in the case. Jane Anderson had been arrested again.

CHAPTER 7

LATE MAY

AN OLD BATTERED
STOVEPIPE HAT

Sometime in 1856, Abraham Lincoln wrote a paragraph of unusual introspection. Several people said that they had heard it used in one of Lincoln's speeches during the campaign season that year. Though the argument is ultimately rhetorical, proving a political point about Senator Stephen Douglas, the supposition is borne of plain, if cruel, self-assessment:

Twenty-two years ago Judge Douglas and I first became acquainted. We were both young then; he a trifle younger than I. Even then, we were both ambitious; I, perhaps, quite as much so as he. With *me,* the race of ambition has been a failure—a flat failure; with *him* it has been one of splendid success. His name fills the nation; and is not unknown, even, in foreign lands. I affect no contempt for the high eminence he has reached. So reached, that the oppressed of my species, might have shared with me in the elevation, I would rather stand on that eminence, than wear the richest crown that ever pressed a monarch's brow.[1]

In fact, Lincoln couldn't be generous about the misuse he felt Douglas made of his position. The last line makes the point that he did indeed have a great deal of contempt for Douglas' enviable success, built as it was on complicity with those who promoted the extension of slavery and oppression. Still, Douglas' success was to be envied: he was a leader with more of a following than the president. Regarded as the finest speaker in the nation, he was actually idolized across a wide swath of the country, attracting a crowd whenever he went out in public. "He walked the streets in all the pride of his manly beauty and the full consciousness of his power," said a fellow resident of Chicago, who noted that Lincoln could walk down the street without being noticed at all, despite his height.[2] Millions of people looked to Douglas as the nation's savior, intrepidly working to hold the Union together. As of late May, he was driving fast toward the Democratic nomination for the presidency, and in any case, he moved with the weight of the Democratic Party behind him.

Abraham Lincoln had no party behind him, as he sat in the town of Danville for Vermilion County Circuit Court on Monday, watching a verdict in a debt-collection case go against his client, to the extent of $35 in damages.[3] Even if Lincoln didn't envy Stephen Douglas, the thought at least occurred to him that he ought to. Lincoln was forty-seven, a helpless age, really. He was old enough to see people his own age who had attained his dream and were living it. And old enough, moreover, to be aware of the new people on the rise, people younger than he who were either ahead of him in the "race of ambition," or crowding fast with the momentum so attractive in youth. Lincoln, too young to be an elder statesman, was perched on a plateau.

Of course, there were avenues for just such people: excuses for falling short that eventually become a more comfortable way of life. And Lincoln took one, for a while, throwing himself into his office work with renewed application, if not quite zeal. It apparently didn't make him feel any different, though; it was in the midst of his focus on legal work that he described himself as a flat failure.

Many of Lincoln's friends later pointed to the passage of the 1854 Kansas-Nebraska Law as the re-awakening of his interest in politics. The following year, he ran for the U.S. Senate, an office that was decided, in those days, by a vote in the State Legislature. Lincoln lobbied hard to secure the necessary votes, but fell short. One of those who turned away at a crucial moment was John M. Palmer, Lincoln's erstwhile friend from Morgan County. When it became clear that he could not win as an Old-Line but anti-Slavery Whig, he ceded his support to Lyman Trumbull, who came to the election from the more popular, even fashionable, vantage of an Anti-Nebraska Democrat. Lincoln and Trumbull espoused just about the same positions, but a liberal from the (conservative) Democratic ranks was considered more trustworthy than a self-described conservative from the (utterly rudderless) Whig ranks. Lincoln was embittered by the loss, quashing as it did whatever political dream had been reawakened the year before. Friends who applauded his selfless surrender in the 1855 election assured him that he would *undoubtedly* be the nominee next time around, in 1858. It was faint consolation. In the first place, that prospect would have him pitted him against the apparently unbeatable Stephen Douglas. In the second place, nothing was undoubted in politics, especially not in 1856, with the Whigs dissolved, the new party in a state of flux, the Know Nothings grasping at whatever was left, and the whole country just about out of patience and wanting to club the opposition in the head—a fantasy which Representative Brooks had indulged on the floor of the Senate.

In so unhappy a season in American politics, the one-day Convention in Bloomington had the potential to be a debacle, a blazing public display of animosity rather than unity. Just as disastrous for Lincoln, the delegates might unify behind a faction that either he could not support or one that he calculated could not prevail. He wasn't the only one aware of the risk of even attending. Senator Trumbull, still nominally a Democrat, and as ambitious as any politician in the state, decided at the last moment to keep his distance. Judge Davis opted to remain on the bench in Danville, where the Eighth Circuit Court was meeting all week. Under other circumstances, he would have been perfectly capable of taking time off, but the Convention represented uncharted territory, and it was not in his character to undertake any sort of risk.

In some places, there was lingering doubt as to whether Lincoln, the most guarded of players, would show up, but in actuality, he was fully prepared to enter the fray. That race that he worried about, the one of ambition, wasn't over. Something still forced him to believe that he was more than just a good lawyer tramping the circuit. The week before the Convention, Herndon had noted the change in Lincoln. He wrote to Senator Trumbull, "I have never seen him so sanguine of success, *he is warm*."[4]

While Lincoln was in Danville, he used his spare time to encourage others to attend the Convention, as well, whether as delegates or observers, and about a half-dozen men responded. They were all together at the station to catch the train to Decatur on Tuesday. "Our company with him as the leader, was the result of his effort," recalled J. O. Cunningham, an editor from Urbana, "He seemed happy at the result and, as we were all known to him as young attorneys and editors of his faith, politically, spoke in his most familiar manner to all, calling each by his familiar name, and indulged in stories and reminiscences with the greatest abandon and freedom from conventionalism."[5]

Although the Bloomington Convention was only to last one day, it represented a five-day commitment for a great many of the participants, including Lincoln, who needed the better part of two days just to get there. The city of Bloomington is northwest of Danville, but none of Illinois' trains ran on the diagonal then. The easiest way to make the trip was by rail: west to Decatur and then, a day later, north to Bloomington. Orville Browning, the influential lawyer from Quincy, faced an even longer trip. In order to go to Bloomington, which was due east of Quincy, he traveled due south, boarding a Mississippi steamboat on Monday evening and making his way down river. Arriving in St. Louis at dawn, he had to take a ferry across the Mississippi and then a train to Springfield. He would stay overnight there, at the American House, the best hotel in town, before catching another train to Bloomington.[6]

Born the year after Lincoln, Orville Browning was forty-six, an attorney who had made a large fortune in Quincy. He and Lincoln were sincere friends, yet in many ways, they were perfect opposites, Browning being strict with himself and others, and quick to pass moral judgment.[7] He was prominent in his church, and his daily life was structured by its teachings. Lincoln's religious feelings were so private that no one could even be certain that he had any. The list of differences went on. Gustave Koerner wrote of Browning:

> He was of an imposing stature, a really handsome man, with speaking darkish eyes, and in dress a most exquisite dandy. He always wore a dress-coat of peculiar cut—Prince Albert fashion—with an outside pocket, from which the ends of a white or light yellow pocket handkerchief dangled out. What made him particularly conspicuous was his ruffled shirt and large cuffs, then hardly ever seen . . . I came into very pleasant relations with him, but I should have liked him better if he had been a little less conscious of his own superiority.[8]

Sartorially, Abraham Lincoln never had a good day in his life (or a ruffled shirt, for that matter). And he could match his friend Browning's outward hauteur only with his own trademark humility. Which of the two men was, in truth, the more self-assured was less apparent.

Browning, a former Whig loyalist, was closely aligned with Lincoln politically. Both were against the extension of slavery, yet regarded themselves as conservatives. Browning had a grudging admiration for Lincoln's intellect but didn't take him seriously as a potential candidate. In fact, Browning nurtured his own unrestrained ambitions, being the sort of man who would like to be president—if he could be appointed. He had, as he wrote to Trumbull just before the Convention, "uncontrollable repugnancies to political life and political contests."[9] Lincoln had felt the same way the year before, after his defeat for the Senate. But then, everyone laboring their way to Bloomington felt some stirrings of new hope. Browning wasn't immune. "I am teazed to the point of desperation to take the field," he wrote.[10]

On Tuesday, the day before the Convention, Lincoln also had a lot on his mind: strategies and contingencies in pursuit of the political game so soon afoot. He eased his thoughts in typical fashion, by finding good company. And talking. If he harbored any indulgence at times of pressure, it was just that: lively conversation. Otherwise, Lincoln lived without vices on the road, as at home.

"He never drinks intoxicating liquors of any sort, not even a glass of wine," said an associate of Lincoln, "He is not addicted to tobacco in any of its shapes. He never was accused of a licentious act in all his life. He never uses profane language."[11]

In terms of profane language—that is, an expression that insults religious sensibilities—Lincoln might let loose with a common exclamation of the day, "by Jing,"[12] which was regarded in some circles as a substitute for "by God." That would be a particularly emphatic moment. A single instance of his saying "damn" was noted, and only because it was so extraordinary. There were those among his fellow lawyers, of course, who could have merited similar documentation of any sentence in which they didn't say "damn," or worse.

Words regarded as profane were more plentiful and more offensive in the nineteenth century than today. Lincoln generally steered clear of them all. His language wasn't entirely sanitized, however. In the realm of storytelling, he delighted in coarse words and impolite imagery. A relative by marriage remembered being in a store and seeing a gaggle of lawyers around the stove, taking a break during a recess from court. He noticed Lincoln's head pop up to make sure that no one else could hear and then, in the time it took to deliver a punch line, the laughter rang out from behind the stove.[13]

A few people did recall Lincoln taking a sip of wine or spirits, under rare circumstances. Ben McQueston, a young man in Springfield in the mid-1850s, served on a bucket brigade with Lincoln. When a building was on fire, Lincoln would often be among those passing containers of water along a line to the flames. "If he became exhausted at a fire," McQueston said, "he would go over to the whisky barrel and help himself as the others did, but I never heard him called a drinking man because of it."[14] Generally, Lincoln didn't like alcohol and hated the whole idea of drunkenness. In that, too, he was unlike many of his colleagues in law and politics. And in that, he was treading on yet another divisive issue in 1856: temperance. Many people who noticed that he didn't drink immediately wanted to know if he was a Prohibitionist. In the northeast, and in patches of the rest of the country, the effort to ban liquor was a full-fledged political movement. Lincoln was always careful to explain that his Prohibitionism extended to only one person.[15] As to licentious behavior, Lincoln did understand the temptation, according to Judge Davis. "Lincoln was a man of strong passion for women," Davis said, "his conscience kept him from seduction—this saved many—many a woman."[16] If that was true, then that inclination may explain why Lincoln was sometimes diffident in the presence of women—that, and the fact that women didn't vote. Women, for their part, didn't exhibit the same reticence, according to John Bunn, who was studying law in Springfield in 1856. "The impression has gone forth that Lincoln was always greatly embarrassed in the presence of ladies," he wrote later, "and indeed, that he seldom talked to ladies at all. Now, I have repeatedly seen Mr. Lincoln in social gatherings at Springfield, at the houses of prominent residents. At such places he was nearly always surrounded by ladies, who took special delight in talking to him. I did not observe his great embarrassment . . . They used to gather about him and make him talk."[17]

If Lincoln was in the right mood, it didn't take much to make him talk, and he was certainly feeling loquacious in the days leading up to the Convention. He was not the best listener at such times, which is why he was fortunate—or clever—to be in the midst of a group of young disciples. They would certainly listen. They might spar, but they would never bore.

J. O. Cunningham, an editor, was part of the group. As he recalled, the train schedule gave them all an afternoon with nothing to do in Decatur:

The company kept well together, strolling about town, and finally, at the suggestion of Mr. Lincoln, all went together to the then nearby Sangamon timber. Here, seated upon the trunk of a fallen tree, which lay in a thicket of spice brush, we spent most of the remaining afternoon. Lincoln talked freely, as he had during the afternoon, of his hopes and fears of the results of the coming convention, and of his earnest wish that the old Whig element from Southern Illinois might be well represented there. He well knew that the radical anti-slavery element from the North would be there in force and hoped for enough of the conservatives to give it, politically, a cosmopolitan character, he yet feared the effect upon the Whig element among the voters of any appearance of radicalism, and planned to avoid it.[18]

Lincoln was afraid that Owen Lovejoy and the more reckless element of abolitionists might overwhelm the meeting. He was hoping that old-line Whigs from the southern part of the state would support the meeting, too, and give it scope. Others from Lincoln's Whig background were even more leery of something else: that the renegade Democrats might take over the new party and make it a shadow of their old party.

Lincoln spent Tuesday night in Decatur's Cassell House hotel.[19] He and his band of Anti-Nebraskans left on the morning train for Bloomington. Cunningham remembered Lincoln roaming up and down the aisle during the trip. "Mr. Lincoln," he said, "seemed very solicitous to meet some of his old Whig friends from southern Illinois, whom he hoped to enlist in the new political movement, and searched the train to find such."[20] A fellow lawyer, Henry Whitney, was with Lincoln that day, too, and he also recalled Lincoln's anxiety to find other delegates, especially from the southern region.

The odds of finding a person from southern Illinois willing to attend a convention devoted to containing slavery weren't especially good in 1856. They were even worse on Lincoln's trip to Bloomington. As Whitney noted, they were sitting in the only car in which smoking wasn't allowed. Since Lincoln didn't smoke, that was probably his preference. But it was one he might have regretted, since the car was practically empty, with just one other gaggle of passengers at the opposite end.

Lincoln paced around the car, snooping as much as he could. "I really would like to know if any of those men are from down south, going to the convention," he said to Whitney. Finally, he gave in to curiosity, and made his way down the aisle to see for himself.

"In fifteen or twenty minutes," Whitney recalled, "He came back, his face radiant with happiness; he had found two delegates from Marion County."[21] According to Cunningham's recollections, one of the men whom Lincoln met was, in fact, from Lawrence County: Jesse K. Dubois, a forty-six year-old land agent. In any case, both counties are in southern Illinois. Dubois was not listed as a delegate, but was nonetheless going to Bloomington to attend the Convention.

Bloomington was slightly smaller than Springfield in 1856, but it had grown even more quickly over the five preceding years, tripling its population to just over 5,000. That may have been a quaint number by the standards of the east, but on the prairie, it constituted a city nonetheless. Counting by the currency of the west, Bloomington was unusually rich, with two major rail lines.

Lincoln's train from Decatur arrived at the Illinois Central station in Bloomington in late morning. For Lincoln, bag and umbrella in hand, the first stop was Judge Davis' house, where he was to stay. He could easily walk there from the station, especially because the weather was fair and sunny. Davis himself was not going to be around, but he had invited Lincoln and three other lawyers, including Whitney, to enjoy the family hospitality. After lunch, Lincoln suggested to Whitney that they go down to the city's second train station, the Chicago, Alton & St. Louis, to see who might be arriving there on the afternoon train. The station was located farther away than the one for the Illinois Central, and required a fairly long walk from downtown Bloomington. In fact, it was such a long hike that the Chicago, Alton "Air Line," as the rail company called its service from the northern part of the state, ran horse-drawn buses to shuttle the arriving passengers downtown.

By that point on Wednesday afternoon, Bloomington's downtown streets were crowded with politicians: prominent and neophyte, reticent and restless. Rev. Owen Lovejoy, knowing full well that he was looked on as a wild abolitionist animal by many of the delegates, was toning down his message for the good of the party, if there was to be a party.[22] A solidly built man, with a ruddy complexion and shiny black hair, Lovejoy had a thin, wide mouth that could purse into a silent admonishment or bloom into the happiest of smiles. It was the latter that Lovejoy flashed on Wednesday. One person who was in Bloomington commented that he wandered around "making love to all the delegates." The delegates, numbering about two hundred and seventy, were not the only ones drawn to the city, however.

The Convention grew larger through the day, even as it filled the streets with all those drawn to a circus of portent. Shifting power and the prospect of publicity spiraled upward around one another, as ever. Whenever a dispatch regarding the violence in Kansas (where a pro-slavery militia had attacked the abolitionist settlement at Lawrence) was received at the telegraph office, it was read publicly. Likewise, men stood on steps, especially at the Pike House Hotel, and shouted the latest dispatch on the recovery of Senator Sumner.

One person who was not in Bloomington for the Convention was the man who nonetheless towered over it: Colonel Bissell, the favorite. Though he stayed home in Belleville, he sent a letter to be read at the Convention on Thursday, letting it be known that he had reached a decision about running for governor, if he were to be nominated. Of course, he knew he would be nominated. There were delegates wandering around the Courthouse Square in Bloomington who were quite literally finding it hard to wait a whole day before starting to chant his name.

Ezra Prince, a recent graduate of Harvard Law School, was associated with Leonard Swett, who was a successful lawyer in Bloomington and a particularly loyal friend to Abraham Lincoln. Through Swett, Prince had heard all about Lincoln. On the day before the Convention, he was standing in his office overlooking the square, watching for recognizable faces. Suddenly Swett's brother-in-law called him to another window, saying, "Come quick, Prince, here is Mr. Lincoln." Prince looked down and easily picked out the right man. "A tall gaunt man of sallow complexion," he said, recalling his first glimpse of Lincoln, "coarse dark hair, wearing an old battered stove pipe hat on the back of his head, coarse rough boots, innocent of blacking, baggy pants much too short for his long legs, and a rusty bombazine [twill] coat that hung loosely about his frame."[23]

Lincoln was a man without vanity regarding his appearance—but he was not a man without vanity. He encouraged a low opinion of his looks, taking apparent delight in telling stories that brought attention to them. Brash strangers were emboldened to call him "ugly"; polite ones said "homely." Lincoln wasn't anything like the ogre he made himself out to be, but it was a stance with practical benefits, as a way to warm any room to his side. Therein lay his vanity.

Lincoln didn't seem to have much to do in Bloomington on Wednesday, except—like any conventioneer anywhere—see who else had arrived. He was on his way to the train station with Whitney when he stopped at a small jewelry store to buy a pair of reading glasses. Whitney, who recalled the price as thirty-seven-and-a-half cents, later maintained that they were Lincoln's first pair: "He then remarked to me," Whitney said, "that he had got to be forty-seven years old, and 'kinder' needed them."[24] Lincoln bought the reading glasses when he finally had no choice but to admit that he was forty-seven and not twenty—but he didn't like to wear them in public. And with only one exception, whenever he had his picture taken, he whipped off the glasses first.

Lincoln and Whitney continued their hike to the Chicago, Alton & St. Louis station. "As we approached the depot," Whitney remembered, "we found ourselves to be late, and that the omnibuses were just starting away, full of passengers, several of whom at once recognized and called out to Lincoln."[25] For his part, Lincoln recognized some of them, too, including Norman Judd, a savvy Chicago lawyer who then held local office as a Democrat.

"As we turned to retrace our steps," Whitney said, "Lincoln said to me *sotto voice*, but enthusiastically: 'That's the best sign yet; Judd is there; and he's a trimmer.'"[26] A *trimmer* was a person ready to switch political allegiance according to the prevailing winds. Lincoln's description was true. It was also practically insulting, but he knew that Judd could do with a little teasing. Anyway, he was feeling oddly frisky. Seeing the faces invigorated him as the mere list of expected delegates had not. The new party was apparently a reality. Whether it would last or be effective was still a question, but the prospects were more exciting by the moment, as Lincoln surveyed the omnibus, filled with disparate politicians smiling on the outside and, on the inside, warily willing to unite. Lincoln and Whitney started back on foot to the people and chatter spilling out of the hotels downtown.

In Springfield, it was just a Wednesday, quiet and hot. Jane Anderson was walked from her jail cell into a waiting carriage on her way to court. She probably hadn't seen Theodore. The only people she had seen were lawyers. In addition to the ones working on her defense, James Matheny had been appointed as administrator of the estate.[27] Since George Anderson hadn't left a will, his estate had to be settled. The assets that he had in his name did not transfer to anyone, including a wife, unless the court authorized it. And the court typically didn't settle an estate unless it was satisfied that Anderson's other heirs—his four children—would be well cared for.

Matheny was responsible for the paperwork, and he was also expected to protect the assets. For the time being, all of the household bills had to be submitted to Matheny, including, for example, the charge on a parasol that Jane had had repaired on the previous Saturday. It was only twenty-five cents, but Matheny had to authorize it.[28]

Matheny, who was also the Sangamon Circuit Court Clerk, had been friends with Abraham Lincoln for twenty years. In fact, he was best man at the Lincolns' wedding. Slim and sharp-featured, he could be a busybody, and he became more and more interested in the Anderson case. With Mrs. Anderson's education lacking and her future uncertain, he began proceedings to be named guardian for the four Anderson children.

Theodore Anderson had been sent back to his jail cell, his hearing having been interrupted for the new development in the Jane Anderson case. The streets were quite empty as the police carriage made its way through town, the dirt-and-gravel pavement smoother than usual, thanks to the dry weather. The carriage pulled up to the Courthouse on the square, and Jane Anderson was escorted past the sand-textured pillars into the courtroom. Two new justices were hearing the case, in place of King and Adams. But after a discussion about the planned presentation of testimony with Amzi McWilliams and the two defense lawyers—John Stuart and Benjamin Edwards—the justices ruled that there was no new evidence to be brought forward against Mrs. Anderson. To the frustration of McWilliams, she was released again. McWilliams was well aware that there would be trouble about that. Every time he saw Mrs. Anderson walking away free, he saw his future as a prosecutor going with her. As she left, Theodore Anderson was summoned from jail to resume his hearing.

At midday, Mrs. Anderson was out in the world in a sun so bright that she needed her parasol. She only had a short walk, though, a scant two blocks south on Sixth Street toward Monroe Street, just beyond the American House Hotel. At just about the time that Mrs. Anderson passed the hotel, Orville Browning was coming out the front door.

Browning took a carriage north on Sixth Street, past the Courthouse toward the railroad station on Third near Madison. Boarding a train at one o'-clock, he arrived in Bloomington at about four. On checking in at the Pike House there, Browning was less than pleased with the state of affairs organizationally, noting dourly in his diary that, "No resolutions had been prepared for the Convention tomorrow, and no programme of Proceedings settled; and many discordant elements to be harmonized."[29] Unlike Lincoln, Browning was not content merely to wander around, working the crowd.

Somewhere in the outdoor lobby that downtown Bloomington had become, full of milling politicians, was James S. Emery, an abolitionist resident of Kansas. He'd been on a speaking tour in the east when he heard that his hometown, Lawrence, Kansas, had been laid to waste on May 21 by pro-slavery raiders. Emery was a lawyer and newspaper editor in Lawrence. Or at least he had been an editor—he had just learned that his printing press in Lawrence had been destroyed. Walking around downtown, he bumped into the former governor of Kansas Territory, Andrew Reeder, who had only escaped with his life by putting on workmen's clothes and adopting an Irish accent. At supper time, Reeder stood on the steps of one of the hotels and addressed a large crowd.

Lincoln didn't care what Reeder was saying; he avoided him and the speech. Reeder was known to have benefited from land speculation in the territory, which was just the sort of misuse of power that Lincoln reviled. Moreover, Reeder, a former pro-slavery Democrat, had swung around on the issue in a rather opportunist way. Every delegate at the Convention feared one faction or another. Some feared the Democrats, figuring that like the men inside the Trojan Horse, they would conquer the new party from the inside. Lincoln feared the radical abolitionists, who would drag the party down an impossible path. He considered Reeder an abolitionist of the worst, rabble-rousing kind. On the night before the Convention, though,

Reeder didn't employ his usual style. Either for the sake of added drama, or because he was in shock, he gave an eerily detached speech, merely reciting the atrocities he'd seen in Kansas over the past week.

Browning ignored the open-air speeches, but only because he had more important things to do. He always did. Taking over a room in one of the hotels, he gathered, according to his diary entry that night, "15 or 20 of the leading men of all shades of opinion" to work on an agenda for the meeting.[30] Lincoln was not invited to attend. Browning may have presumed that he could represent Lincoln's basic point-of-view, but it was still a stunning oversight, proving that while Lincoln was an important player in the Convention, he wasn't indispensable.

Browning's *ad hoc* group addressed a critical rift in the ranks of the delegates, between the Germans and the erstwhile Know Nothings, who were pledged against foreign-born Americans.[31] Though Lincoln was not present, his influence was in the room. According to George Schneider, a leader of the German community, Lincoln's advice had been critical to the inclusion of a resolution opposing Know-Nothingism at the original Decatur editors' meeting in February.[32] That led to the inclusion of a paragraph in the state party platform at Bloomington, as it was hammered out in Browning's hotel room.*

However Lincoln felt about Browning's meeting going on without him, he harbored ambitions for the Convention. He knew that he would be

---

* At Decatur, the relevant part of the editors' fourth resolution, approved by Lincoln, was strongly worded and read: "we shall maintain the naturalization laws AS THEY ARE, believing as we do, that we should welcome the exiles and emigrants from the old World, to homes of enterprise and of freedom in the New."

At Bloomington, the anti-Know Nothing plank was toned down a bit, running, "that the spirit of our institutions, as well as our constitution of our country, guarantees the liberty of conscience as well as political freedom and that we will proscribe no one by legislation or otherwise on account of religious opinion or in consequence of place of birth."

Eventually, the national convention in Philadelphia would retain the idea in the last line of its final resolution: "believing that the spirit of our institutions as well as the Constitution of our country guarantees liberty of conscience and equality of rights among citizens, we oppose all legislation impairing their security." The three resolutions were not identical, but Lincoln's initial support helped ensure that the intent was part of the new party's identity.

asked to give a speech, and that was the moment for which he was readying himself, as he walked around, holding sidewalk caucuses in the fading light. "Lincoln was active, alert, energetic and enthusiastic," Whitney remarked, "I never saw him more busily engaged, more energetically at work, or with his mind and heart so thoroughly enlisted."[33]

After dinner, the excitement in Bloomington only intensified. As George T. Brown, Lincoln's friend and the editor of the *Alton Courier* wrote, "The hotels were filled to overflowing. An immense crowd assembled in front of the Pike House was addressed by Hon. J. M. Palmer, Hon. Owen Lovejoy, 'Long John' Wentworth, and others."[34]

Among the others was Abraham Lincoln. A reporter unsympathetic to his point of view paid him the compliment of at least noticing him, which is more than Brown had done. "Lincoln . . . said he didn't expect to make a speech then," the reporter noted:

> that he had prepared himself for one, but 'twas not suitable at that time'; but that after a while he would make them a most excellent one. Notwithstanding, he kept on speaking, told his old story about the fence (meaning Missouri restriction) being torn down and the cattle eating up the crops; then talked about the outrages in Kansas, said a man couldn't think, dream or breathe of a free state there, but what he was kicked, cuffed, shot down and hung.[35]

Even allowing for the veil of disapproval that obscured the reporter's description, the speech was not Lincoln's finest effort. The people gathered in front of Pike House had been interrupted all day by dispatches from Kansas, ripped from telegraph desks and read on the streets. They wanted to hear their own outrage reflected and amplified through the speeches. Lincoln obliged, as did the others. He refrained, however, from doing much more. There was no point in it; the time to build the new party was still a day away. With the end of the speech, he went back to Davis' house and talked politics with his friends, Davis' other houseguests, long into the night.

A month before the Convention, twenty-three-year-old Reuben M. Benjamin had moved to Bloomington from his home in New York State.

With a degree from Amherst College and a year at Harvard Law School, he had arranged to study law in the firm of Asahel Gridley and John Wickhizer, two blunt-spoken and powerful lawyers in Bloomington. Benjamin regarded himself as a sophisticate, but he was stunned by something he saw on his first day at the firm. "On the wall of the office," he recalled, "I read in Mr. Wickhizer's handwriting: 'The repeal of the Missouri Compromise will lead to civil war.'"[36] There was nothing temporary about the sentiment. Wickhizer had made it part of the very building, the rock and dirt of Bloomington, where the Convention came to gather on a Thursday in late May.

CHAPTER 8

MAY 29

MAJOR'S HALL

E arly on Thursday, Will Porter, a rangy sixteen-year-old farmboy, was working on his parents' land near Bloomington. All morning, he watched people going toward the city on horseback or in carriages, and when they passed, as he later recalled, "I heard them saying they were going to hear what was going on; so I hitched up my team and went along to that meeting."[1]

William Kellogg, an enthusiastic delegate from western Illinois, was already there. "The Convention was held in Major's Hall, an unpretentious assembly room located over a store, capable of seating at the utmost not more than five or six hundred people," he said.[2] But that estimate didn't account for the ingenuity of the Bloomington farmboys.

"When I got there," Will Porter said, "I found the hall was crowded and all I could do was to tiptoe up and listen as best I could." Then he spotted a beam, jutting high across the back of the room. "Lou Iganna was a-sitting' up there and four or five others, but there was a little more room and Lou Iganna says, 'Come up here, Will, we can make room for ye' . . . and that way I got a good seat and heard it all."[3]

Outside Major's Hall, newspapers were selling as soon as they hit the street. Enterprising newsboys were even hawking out-of-town newspapers. Each edition provided the latest dispatches regarding the attack on Lawrence, Kansas. The hotel had been burned, James Emery's printing press had been thrown into a river, and so on. No one needed to buy a paper to learn about Kansas, though. A wiry man with a walrus mustache was standing at the entrance of the Pike House hotel reading the latest communications from Kansas "with almost tragic emphasis."[4] The delegates heard snatches of his news flashes, and then walked a little faster to the hall.

Just before the start of the meeting at 10 A.M., W. J. Usrey, the editor of a Decatur newspaper, sprinted to the telegraph office and sent a paragraph to his newsroom: "Over one thousand strangers and delegates are here. Delegates from all quarters are pouring in constantly . . . There is one universal 'shriek' against the recent outrages in Kansas—Col. Bissell will receive the nomination for Governor by acclamation."[5]

One of the people crowding into Major's Hall was Henry Hunt. He wasn't a delegate, just another local fellow interested in seeing what would happen, like the boys up on the beam. A typical old-line Whig, Hunt was balanced on the razor-thin line between his resistance to the extension of slavery and his conservative instinct to leave it as it was in the South. And, as an old-line Whig, he was sure the meeting would be destroyed by the presence of Owen Lovejoy and the other abolitionists. He looked around the room and spotted the famous figures of the day, Browning of Quincy, Gridley of Bloomington, Palmer of Western Illinois, and then his eye lingered on one of the abolitionist leaders, a close colleague of Lovejoy's. He resented him at first glance, and braced for him "to pronounce slave-holders the chief sinners and slavery the sum of all villainies." For Hunt, that kind of attitude was infuriating and he was hardly alone in thinking so.

Just as the meeting started, Hunt noticed Abraham Lincoln at the front of the room. "I saw Lincoln's long form stretched out near the rostrum," he wrote, "apparently at perfect ease, but observing every move sharply, as he knew the old line Whigs and Abolitionists would come in collision."[6] He was right—and it didn't take long.

Before the political business of the Convention could start, the delegates had to be identified. Illinois' counties were called in alphabetical order, and the respective delegates for each county, if there were any, presented their names. Thirty-five counties, all from the southern part of the state, failed to send anyone at all, and Lincoln noted each with regret. But he consoled himself with those few, such as Lawrence County, that he knew for certain to have a representative in the hall. Whitney recalled what happened next:

> When Lawrence County was called, no response came. The secretary was proceeding with the call when Lincoln arose and exclaimed, anxiously looking all around: "Mr. Chairman, let Lawrence be called again: there is a delegate in town from there, and a very good man he is, too." The call was repeated, but no reply came. The delegate, whose courage failed him at the last moment, in the presence of the Abolitionist contingent, was Jesse K. Dubois.[7]

Dubois was the man from southern Illinois that Lincoln had so delighted in meeting on the train, the day before. "He came, indeed, as a delegate," Whitney explained, "but, seeing Lovejoy and other Abolitionists there as cherished delegates, he, through indignation or timidity, stayed away for the time being."[8]

"The old line Whigs hated the Abolitionists intensely,"[9] Henry Hunt emphasized. Lincoln heard Dubois' stubborn silence speak to that point. He took his seat near the podium again. Just having enemies together in the same room was a far cry from launching a new party.

Before the business of the Convention opened, one of the delegates raised his hand and practically burst with excitement in nominating William Bissell for the governorship. He was entirely out of order. But if anyone on the rostrum tried to point out that it was too early to take nominations—as there wasn't yet a party—they were shouted down by the noisy approval of Bissell's nomination in what Cunningham called "a tornado of seconds from all parts of the floor."[10]

The one man who could unite any party in Illinois in 1856 was Bissell: Doctor-Colonel-Congressman William Bissell, Esquire. Selecting which one of his titles to use may have been optional, but in most circles in Illinois, it was very bad form to utter his name without saying either "dashing" or "gallant" first. If he had been willing, the Democrats would no doubt have made him their candidate. At the Anti-Nebraska Convention, George Brown, the editor from Alton, came forward with Bissell's letter and read it out loud as soon as the cheering faded. Bissell described his health at length, saying that overall, it was good, but that he could only walk with "a cane and the aid of a friendly arm." He concluded, however, with the promise that he would accept the nomination, if offered. He couldn't close the letter, however, without adding, that "in all candor, I prefer that the nomination should fall on another."[11] The delegates dismissed that line, as though it were just more of the Colonel's gallantry, and Bissell was nominated by acclamation, if not a near riot. Not all of his reservations had passed, but he was indeed a soldier who wouldn't shirk a fight, whatever the dangers.

From the dais, Lincoln could readily see that the Convention, for all of its schisms, wanted to unite. It just didn't know quite how, with no history behind it, and utter uncertainty in the future. As the meeting went about its business, committees retired one at a time to prepare suggestions on the organization or platform, and while they were gone, speeches kept the attention of the delegates.

Lincoln was busy to one extent or another with the committee work, but he was said to have heard the speech of James Emery, the editor from Kansas. Emery spoke about the violence in his territory, and repeated the prediction that if the Missouri Compromise was restored (and slavery denied further expansion), the South would secede.[12] He seemed to have no remorse about seeing the South go. His whole speech, in fact, was "severe and almost intemperate in his appeals for armed interference in Kansas."[13] That kind of talk made some of the delegates cheer, and others visibly uncomfortable. It was an incendiary speech, but it wasn't the voice of the party.

John Palmer, priding himself on being president of the Convention, spoke in a more reasonable tone about "a general desire to save the country."

Palmer tried hard, but his dullish words were not the voice of the party, either. While he was speaking, Lincoln was appointed as head of a committee to bring other nominations to the floor. He chose representatives of every faction and region, according to his own sense of proportion, in order to underscore the scope of the new party. For one office, he put forth the name of Jesse Dubois of Lawrence County: not even a delegate, but, in his eyes, a necessity nonetheless.

While Lincoln was in a back room listing nominations, President Palmer tried to adjourn for lunch, but he was shouted down.[14] Instead, the effortlessly popular Richard Yates was called upon for a speech. He was the sort of man who didn't have to do anything to be hailed and adored. And at Bloomington, he didn't do anything. Most of his speech consisted of an apology for not being ready. "He said it was hard work to make an appropriate speech," a reporter noted. Having made that point, Yates concluded by saying that he loved his party very much—it being all of two hours' old at that point. He added, however, that he loved the Union even more. Then it was lunchtime.

At three o'clock, during the lunch break, W. J. Usrey trotted back to the telegraph office and sent another report, just in time for his paper's afternoon edition back in Decatur. "Convention organized,"[15] he wrote. From the point of view of a man whittling down his words for a telegram, that was all that needed to be said. For the sake of detail, though, he also mentioned Palmer as president, the nomination of Bissell, the speeches by Emery and Yates, and the overwhelming enthusiasm.

After lunch, "Long" John Wentworth, a veteran of Illinois politics and a man who was, at six-foot-five, even taller than Lincoln, amused the Convention with a speech on Senator Douglas' failings. He could have gone on all day, as far as the delegates were concerned, but he was soon followed by George Brown, the editor from Alton, presenting a serious resolution on the same theme. It passed unanimously. But the new party had to be more than just anti–Stephen Douglas.

The delegates made loud calls for a speech from Orville Browning, and after some consideration, he deigned to oblige. He "arose with great dignity," according to Hunt and "resembled an Episcopal minister in his faultless dress of black, with large white choker and spotless linen."[16] Browning spoke of the old-line Whigs, such as himself (and Lincoln). He had many examples to prove that the platform of resolutions just passed for the new party was entirely compatible with the thinking of the late Whig hero, Henry Clay. Be that as it may, Clay could not be the voice of the new party. He was old stuff. There had to be a fresh impetus. "He was an able man," Henry Hunt said of Browning, "but I thought at the time somewhat tedious."[17]

Owen Lovejoy was visibly uncomfortable during Browning's speech, wiggling around in his seat. He probably wanted to throttle the old Whig, with his Kentucky accent and fussy Southern clothes. Lovejoy waited his turn and then "sprang to his feet." Fortunately, he remembered who he was and where he was, for the sake of the party, and delivered a speech against slavery, but not against the South or its friends. No one walked out, and Lovejoy was admired long afterward for his restraint.

The party had practically everything it required: a well-attended convention, a popular nominee in Bissell, speeches by eminent politicians, and enthusiasm. It didn't have a name, though. And it didn't yet have a spirit, a feeling much deeper than the enthusiasm measured by cheering. The Convention was far from over, but as its formal business came to a close late in the afternoon, the most compelling emotion in the room was relief that the day had come off without a rift. That was the sort of accomplishment that dissolved as soon as the delegates boarded their homebound trains, however. Without a feeling to which the delegates could return in the worst of days to come, it might as well remain without a name.

As the hour drew late and the sun drooped down, the delegates began to shout for Abraham Lincoln. Cunningham called it a "wild yell," attributing the forcefulness of the cries to the "expectations on the part of some that he would fan the flame of acrimony and discontent aroused by the remarks of some of the preceding speakers."[18] Lincoln was by then sitting in the audience. He made his way to the platform "amid deafening applause," George Brown wrote.[19]

"Mr. Lincoln arose quite cool, but very earnest in manner," Hunt said.[20]

"Mr. Lincoln began very slowly," Kellogg concurred, "holding in his left hand a card upon which he had evidently jotted down some of his leading thoughts."[21]

Lincoln asked the clerk to read the original notice for the Convention, the one that ended with a call to those "who are in favor of restoring the administration to the Policy of Washington and Jefferson..."[22] Will Porter said that eased Lincoln into an introduction, "by way of preamble, that if Washington and his fellow patriots had a hard seven years' war to prove the Declaration of Independence meant what it said, it would be a great mistake—or a great pity, I can't remember his exact words—it would be a calamity to have the union broken up now."[23]

According to Hunt's retelling, Lincoln then made the point that the call to form a party, "included all opposed to the extension of slavery in the Territories—not men who wanted to air their prejudices or grievances."[24]

"He enumerated the pressing reasons of the present movement," George Brown reported, "He was here ready to fuse with any one who would unite with him to oppose slave power."[25] Lincoln wanted the dimension of the party to be wide in the kind of people attracted to it, but not in the lengths to which it would go in the slavery crisis. In order to pull the Convention back from the rabble-rousing that the delegates had heard outside, he had to make sure that it was a political party, not an army.

"Seeming to know that there had been wild talk about people going to Kansas armed with Sharpe's rifles, with which to settle the contentions there," Cunningham said, "he began most gently with a rebuke for such appeals to violence. In words he deprecated the use of force as a means of settling the issue, and concluded this part of his speech with these words as nearly as I remember them: 'Now, my friends, I'll tell you what we will do, we will wait until November, and then we will shoot paper ballots at them.'"[26]

"From time to time," Kellogg said, "as he reached some climax in his argument, he would advance to the front of the platform as he spoke, and with a peculiar gesture hurl the point, so to speak, at his audience; then as the audience rose to their feet to cheer, he would walk slowly backward, bowing and glancing at the card he held in his hand, again he would resume his speech, making his points in the same manner and with like effect."[27]

"From this pleasant disposition of the war talk," Cunningham continued, "he then turned his remarks to a logical discussion of the legislation set on foot by Judge [Senator Stephen] Douglas, and illustrated its unwisdom by citing the then condition of Kansas, as a necessary result of the competition, invited by the law, between freedom and slavery."[28]

"Declaring that Douglas' position upon the question of unfriendly legislation was rank sophistry," Kellogg said, "Lincoln used the epigram, 'You can fool all the people some of the time, you can fool some of the people all the time, but you can't fool all the people all the time.'"[29]

Dispensing with Douglas, Lincoln then "spoke of the bugbear disunion, which was so vaguely threatened." Cunningham recalled that "Mr. Lincoln devoted much of his discourse to the threats and insinuation of a dissolution of the Union of the United States, made by southern men and published broadcast in the North."[30]

Whenever Southerners threatened secession, most Northerners shrank back and searched for some form of appeasement. As Lincoln built his thoughts, the audience began to realize for the first time just how incensed he was by that old, familiar parry. Brown recorded his words, and his point:

> It [is] to be remembered that the *Union must be preserved in the purity of its principles as well as in the integrity of its territorial parts.* It must be Liberty *and* Union, now and forever, one and inseparable.[31]

"He argued and reasoned as if the South in person then stood before him and was listening to him," Cunningham explained, "To this supposititious audience he argued the unwisdom of disunion and the direful consequences to the country of an attempt of any party at dissolution. He assured his audience that northern men had no desire for a separation and would never consent to it. Warming up with his topic and still using the pronoun of the second person, he closed this part of his speech with these remarkable words—"[32]

Will Porter heard them just as well up on the beam. He remembered Lincoln's resolve, speaking as the North to the South: "We WILL not go out and you SHALL not."[33]

"This was said with great deliberation," Cunningham said, "when he had raised his figure to its greatest height, his eyes, usually so mild and playful, now flashing wild determination, and with vehement gestures with his head and arms."[34]

"At that moment," said John Scott, the unflappable lawyer from Bloomington, "he was the handsomest man I ever saw."[35]

Lincoln's speech lasted about an hour-and-a-half. It delved into other aspects of the slavery crisis, but the points that were recalled long afterward pertained to two themes: Union and dedication to the government. That was the consensus among the many people asked to recollect the speech later. And they remembered the tone, the emotion in Lincoln that would not be denied.

Lincoln's address at the Convention became known as the "Lost Speech" long afterward, because a written record wasn't made of it at the time. No mention of the speech has ever been found in a contemporary letter, though, of course, most of the correspondence of that day has been lost or destroyed through the years. Orville Browning's diary entry for May 29 is the only private acknowledgment that there had even been such a speech. One passage near the end of the entry noted, "I was called out and made two speeches in the afternoon. Convention also addressed by Lovejoy, Lincoln, Cook & others."[36]

George Brown did make a disjointed one-paragraph summary of the speech for the *Alton Weekly Courier,* and the Chicago *Democratic Press* sang its praises,[37] but neither went into detail. The legend that came down in later years was that the reporters who were supposed to write it down became so caught up that they dropped their pencils. More likely, they were there to cover the Convention as a whole, rather than any particular speech. By the time they realized that Lincoln's speech *was* the Convention, the opportunity was already gone. Perhaps that's just as well. The greatness of the speech was in the effect on those who heard it, and it is best recorded in their memories.

In later years, those who were at the Convention spoke of the "Lost Speech" in hallowed terms, and recited points that still remained with them ten years, forty years, and even seventy years later. It wasn't a speech that defined Lincoln for the state or for the nation, or even for future generations. It was for the audience at hand: politicians who had known Lincoln for decades, who thought they knew him still. The speech was for them; Lincoln crystallized the motivations common to all in that difficult moment of frayed opinions and blurred allegiances. It was a speech for the politicians in the seats, and for Lincoln himself: a declaration of a newly realized commitment to the course of the nation.

"Men that day were hardly able to take the true gauge of Mr. Lincoln," wrote James Emery, "He had not yet been recognized as a great man, and so we were not a little puzzled to know where his power came from."[38]

"His mode of speaking was new," agreed George Schneider, a Chicago delegate at the Convention who had known Lincoln for years, "He was full of philosophy, and got into the souls of men. He produced a new manner of politics."[39]

With the formation of the party, Lincoln was relieved of the only politics he had ever known: accommodating himself to the Whigs, who had themselves been increasingly mismatched. That frustrating exercise was over. He could help to shape the new party and, with it, the times. He had to have been inspired when he looked out at the array of powerful politicians gathered in Major's Hall, because he delivered a speech unlike any he'd given before. "There was not so much a feeling in the body of the Convention that he was discussing a momentous question," said Kellogg, "as a kind of delirious enthusiasm which found voice in the feeling, here is a man whom we will follow to the end."[40]

Hunt felt the same sensation. "I saw at once he was the leader to whom all submitted," he wrote.[41] William Herndon looked back on the speech ten years later and wrote the most emphatic assessment of all, in regard to its importance in Lincoln's career. "I have heard or read all of Mr. Lincoln's great speeches, and I give it as my opinion that the Bloomington speech was the grand effort of his life. Heretofore he had simply argued the slavery question on grounds of policy—the statesman's grounds—never reaching the question of the radical and the eternal right. Now he was newly baptized and freshly born . . ."[42]

Herndon framed Lincoln's inspiration in Bloomington in terms of his anti-slavery position. That was in keeping with the delineation of the day:

abolitionist versus slavocrat, with other positions by degrees in between. Lincoln's emphatic stance against slave power was part of his new impetus. That was one aspect of his new-found, or newly displayed, passion.

Even more profound was his identification with the signers of the Declaration of Independence. That connection was noted in Brown's summary, and given even greater importance by him, and by many of those who left reminiscences of the speech. The *Union must be preserved in the purity of its principles as well as in the integrity of its territorial parts.* If the legacy of the Founding Fathers was in jeopardy, Lincoln was adopting their cause. All those who cheered him that day, in the nascent moments of the Republican Party, and who recalled later that they looked to him as leader from then on, were sharing that sense of a crisis even greater than the slave question.

As soon as the Convention ended, delegates poured out of the meeting hall; Henry Whitney made his way downstairs with Jesse Dubois. Lincoln was still upstairs, trapped by people congratulating him and asking to shake his hand. "Lincoln got disentangled from the applauding crowd at length,"[43] Whitney wrote, and the two of them left the building and ducked into a side street to recover from the overwhelming excitement— and to come down to earth. Lincoln couldn't stop talking. He was aware of that fact, though, and worked at keeping his voice low. When he asked Whitney something along the lines of "How do you think I did?" Whitney replied, "You know that my statements about your speeches are not good authority, so I will tell you what Dubois, who is not so enthusiastic as I am, said to me as we came out of the hall. He said: 'Whitney, that is the greatest speech ever made in Illinois and it puts Lincoln on the track for the Presidency.'"[44]

That quieted Lincoln down. "He walked along without straightening himself up for some thirty seconds, perhaps," Whitney remembered, "without saying a word; but with a thoughtful, abstracted look—then he straightened up and immediately made a remark about some commonplace subject, having no reference to the subject we had been considering."[45]

Lincoln had inspired the room in a way that surprised even him on the afternoon of the Lost Speech. Whether it would be an anomaly or the launch of a fresh start was yet to be seen, as Lincoln was all too aware. The Convention had appointed him an elector for the state-at-large, meaning in practical terms that he would be available to make speeches anywhere in Illinois on behalf of the party.

For Lincoln, the 1856 election would be a dual campaign. First, he was in the fray on behalf of the party. Likewise, he had a new start on behalf of himself and a chance to extend the influence of his Bloomington speech.

Herndon wrote of Abraham Lincoln at about this time, "The man who thinks Lincoln calmly sat down and gathered his robes about him, waiting for the people to call him, has a very erroneous knowledge of Lincoln. He was always calculating, and always planning ahead. His ambition was a little engine that knew no rest."[46] Lincoln might later reject the idea that any interest in "personal advancement," as he termed it,[47] was connected with his commitment to the new party. Even if it was, though, he couldn't help it. Righteousness in the face of the slave crisis was propelling him as never before, but ambition, as Herndon pointed out, was part of him, too.

(left) *Abraham Lincoln appeared frank and friendly in a portrait taken in Chicago in February 1857 by Alexander Hesler. Courtesy of the Abraham Lincoln Presidential Library & Museum.*

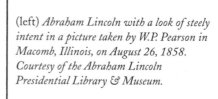

(above) *On May 7, 1858, Abraham Lincoln sat for A.B. Byers in Beardstown, Illinois. He is wearing a light-colored linen duster of the type he favored in warm weather. Courtesy of the Abraham Lincoln Presidential Library & Museum.*

(left) *Abraham Lincoln with a look of steely intent in a picture taken by W.P. Pearson in Macomb, Illinois, on August 26, 1858. Courtesy of the Abraham Lincoln Presidential Library & Museum.*

The Lincoln home as sketched by Xavier C. Meyer, to appear as it did before the expansion undertaken in 1856. The house was originally built in 1839, and the Lincolns bought it in 1844. Courtesy of the Abraham Lincoln Presidential Library & Museum.

The Lincoln house in 1858, when it was photographed by A.J. Whipple. Abraham Lincoln is in the front yard, with one of his sons, probably Willie judging by the boy's height. Courtesy of the Abraham Lincoln Presidential Library & Museum.

One of the downstairs rooms in the Lincoln home, as drawn in 1861. The decoration was comfortable and elegant, befitting an upper-middle-class family. Frank Leslie's Illustrated Newspaper, *March 9, 1861.*

William Bissell (1811–1860) was the most universally admired politician in Illinois in 1856. A former Congressman, he was a hero of the Mexican-American War, and was qualified as both a physician and attorney. Courtesy of the Abraham Lincoln Presidential Library & Museum.

John T. Stuart (1807–1885) was a powerful attorney based in Springfield. Abraham Lincoln counted him as a friend and colleague, though the two disagreed on the issue of slavery. Courtesy of the Abraham Lincoln Presidential Library & Museum.

Orville Browning (1806–1881) had the bearing and erudition to make a strong impression. An attorney from Quincy, Browning held many of the same views as Lincoln, yet never quite understood his rival's political appeal. Courtesy of the Abraham Lincoln Presidential Library & Museum.

William Herndon (1818–1891) practiced law as Lincoln's partner in Springfield. Courtesy of the Abraham Lincoln Presidential Library & Museum.

Mary Todd Lincoln with her sons, Tad (left) and Willie (right), in a photograph taken circa 1862. Courtesy of the Abraham Lincoln Presidential Library & Museum.

A notice for Lincoln & Herndon appears with those of other local lawyers in a Springfield newspaper column. In the mid-1800s, such columns were equivalent to the yellow pages of the telephone book. Attorneys and other professionals, including Lincoln & Herndon, typically placed ads on a daily basis. Springfield State Journal, *May 15, 1856.*

The law office of Lincoln & Herndon consisted of one room, depicted here in an 1860 drawing. Those seated are (left to right): a student or client, Herndon, and Lincoln. Frank Leslie's Illustrated Newspaper, *December 22, 1860.*

Lincoln wrote this bill for his work in Spink v. Chiniquy *on a tiny slip of paper, which was then signed by his client, Charles Chiniquy. Lincoln later wrote the agreement that concluded the case, also pictured. Illinois History and Lincoln Collections, University of Illinois Library at Urbana-Champaign.*

A view of Springfield's Washington Street in 1856, showing the air of spaciousness about the city. This would be a view from the State House Square to the west, just around the corner from the offices of Lincoln & Herndon. Note the Chicago, Alton & St. Louis locomotive running in the background. Ballou's Pictorial Drawing-Room Companion, *November 15, 1856.*

The Sangamon County Courthouse drawn in silhouette-style in 1856. The Courthouse, frequented by Lincoln for legal matters as well as political meetings, was the scene of the Anderson murder trial in late November, 1856. Note the children playing hoops on the sidewalk. Ballou's Pictorial Drawing-Room Companion, *November 15, 1856.*

CHAPTER 9

JUNE

SUMMER DAYS

After the Convention, Abraham Lincoln went home to Springfield, probably for the first time since late March.[1] The weather was cool but clear[2] and people were outside, doing chores or enjoying the air. Arriving on Eighth Street, Lincoln stopped rather theatrically in front of his house, newly remodeled, and looked around. He was no doubt aware that he'd been noticed. "Wilkie," he called out to Abner Wilkinson, the tailor who lived opposite, "Can you tell me where old Abe Lincoln lived around these parts?"[3] It wasn't the most piquant example of Lincoln's ready wit, but it lasted for years in the neighborhood lore.

While Lincoln was away, the house had expanded in size and certainly doubled in stature. The well-contained, one-and-a-half story house was transformed into a two-story house of relaxed proportions. When the original owner saw the remodeling, he grumbled about it. The house had indeed lost a measure of its character, in favor of a plainer, more common style, but it was finally big enough for a family of five. Thenceforth, they would have to be the source of the house's personality.

Abraham Lincoln was perfectly happy with the remodeling, according to the same neighborhood lore, saying, in tribute to Mary Lincoln's management of the project, that it showed how much a woman could accomplish, if she wanted. He was also supposed to have greeted his wife by saying, "Well, Mary, you remind me of the story of the fellow who went to California and left one baby at home, and when he returned three years after, found three. The fellow looked at his wife and said, 'Well, Lizzie, for a little woman and without any help, you have raised thunder amazingly.'"[4] The story smacked of the type of analogy of which Lincoln was master, but it is hard to think of him telling an off-color story such as that one to his well-bred wife.

Herndon, according to his own memoir, tried to organize a rally for the new political party "a few days" after he and Lincoln returned. "He could go out and get the gang in," said a Springfield man of Herndon, "Lincoln could dispose of them."[5] Apparently, it didn't always work out that way. Only one person showed up at the rally—the janitor in the Courthouse, where the rally was to be staged. If Herndon was recollecting correctly and the meeting was really the debacle he described, he must have rushed into it—and dragged Lincoln along. Herndon was said to have distributed handbills,[6] but he probably believed in the cause so much that he didn't think the meeting needed any publicity. Lincoln was unfazed. On the basis that he and Herndon were the only certain attendees, he said only that the meeting was "larger than he *knew* it would be."[7] In showing up for the poorly planned event, he may just have been humoring his excitable junior partner. It was probably just as well that the meeting was nothing more than a murmur. The first few days after the Convention offered time to gauge the response and forecast the lasting influence of all the noise and cheering. As in the case of others who found themselves at the center of transforming events, Lincoln had the luxury of reading the papers as they came in from around the state, corroborating what had actually happened. He could also catch up on the local news. In that regard, he took note that his old friend, Amzi McWilliams, was under attack.

The most conspicuous space in the Springfield *State Journal*—page two, column one, just under the masthead—had previously carried the call for the meeting in advance of the Bloomington Convention, the one with "A. Lincoln" first on the list of signers. Over the weekend following the Convention, a new petition was in that slot. It pointedly recommended a new prosecuting attorney to replace Amzi McWilliams. W. H. Herndon signed it, and so did all the powerful lawyers in Springfield: John Stuart, Benjamin Edwards, Stephen T. Logan, James Conkling, and eleven others.[8] Abraham Lincoln was the only one of the top dogs who declined. He was friends with Amzi McWilliams. More to the point, he had been out of town during the Anderson murder arraignments, and hadn't seen the muddle they'd become.

Theodore Anderson was in jail, as he had been since May 16, the day after George Anderson was bludgeoned in his backyard. Jane Anderson was free, living at home on Monroe Street. She'd been arrested twice for the crime, and released both times. Theodore's hearing had ended on Friday night, with the justices concluding that the crime was too serious and the case too full of intrigue for a decision in police court. The arraignment was referred to the Grand Jury. The case divided the city, with McWilliams pinned in between. Some believed that he wasn't doing enough in what seemed to be a simple case; others believed he was hounding Mrs. Anderson and Theodore with insufficient evidence.

In the charged atmosphere of Springfield and in the contentious year of 1856, the Anderson case had become another arena, a way to take sides. Inevitably, the contest spilled over into politics.

For the time being, Lincoln was only an observer. In fact, he had a light load at work during the first week of June.[9] A land case he represented came up in U.S. District Court and was continued to the next term. The big news of the week was the announcement of a ratification meeting for the new Anti-Nebraska party the following Tuesday. John Palmer was going to speak, along with Lincoln.[10] The organizers, including William Herndon, were busy promoting it all week, to ensure that more than one person would attend. Lincoln, however, had most of the week to himself, to work in the office. Or to not work.

Sometimes on sunny afternoons, such as those in early June, Ben McQueston, a clerk at J. W. Matheny's store, would call up the stairway to the law office, "Mr. Lincoln, we are going to play ball." Unless something very pressing was on the table, Lincoln gladly trotted down to a field with the others and played whatever game was on, often a version of "town ball" or rudimentary baseball. "Everybody played ball," McQueston said, "There was nothing incongruous about a leading lawyer like Lincoln joining in with tradesmen, clerks, and professional men for an afternoon's amusement. Everyone had time for recreation and business did not suffer."[11] Lincoln was also known around town as a willing competitor in impromptu hand-ball games downtown. In his younger days, he had regarded himself as an athlete; in his mid-forties, he couldn't be expected to work at a desk all day, every day.

With the easy schedule of early June, Lincoln could also fall back into his routine around the house. "He used to do his own marketing," recalled Page Eaton, who lived on Fifth Street in Springfield, "I used to see him at the baker's and butcher's every morning with his basket on his arm."[12] He was willing to help in the kitchen, as well, though Mary Lincoln was considered an excellent cook. "On coming from the office he would take off his coat," according to the recollections of a neighbor, "put on a large blue apron, and do whatever was needed."[13]

Henry Rankin, who was studying law in Springfield in 1856, met the Lincolns under various circumstances, including visiting their home. He recalled that Mrs. Lincoln had to be insistent if she wanted her husband to eat square meals. Lincoln preferred "browsing around," in his own words, absent-mindedly making a meal of cheese and crackers while he worked. His disinterest in food was more than just an indication of his focus on more important matters. It was probably related to his health problems. He was troubled by his digestion, including recurrent constipation, according to John Stuart, who once recommended a remedy in the form of a "little blue pill." His complexion was described in the mid-1850s as tending to be sallow, yet he often displayed inordinate energy. He may not have been the very picture of robust vigor—as was Lovejoy, for example—but he wasn't sickly, either. He was just careless of his own well-being, if not ascetic by nature; and so, for his wife, he was another of the boys to be worried about.

Known for making sharp remarks, Mary Lincoln had a habit of insulting maids and neighbors. Her husband wasn't immune from her barbs, either. Whether he took offense is impossible to say. Apparently he took it in stride, according to one of Mrs. Lincoln's sisters: "They understood each other thoroughly," Emily Todd Helm wrote, "and Mr. Lincoln looked beyond the impulsive words and manner, and knew that his wife was devoted to him and to his interests."[14]

For his part, Lincoln was not the easiest husband to have, for all the gentleness of his nature. Aside from going away for six months every year, he was a non-conformist in his habits and his attitudes. A measure of obliviousness to the norm helped to make him a brilliant political philosopher. It also might have handicapped his chances of being taken seriously. When Mrs. Lincoln berated him about some matters of appearances and society, she meant to help and probably did. She had a difficult job, pushing him to think about the details that matter to others, without clogging his mind with them. Her way was to be direct, and even pointed. For that reason, the sting of her comments could perhaps be shrugged off.

At home, Lincoln liked nothing better than to be one of the boys, wrestling on the parlor floor with his sons, and taking them with him wherever he went around town. He also made the house lively with pets of all sorts. Herndon observed that Lincoln was drawn to animals for a sense of renewal, especially when his mind was burdened, while Mrs. Lincoln said that her husband made a "hobby" of his cats, happily lying down on the carpet with one for a long, unhurried talk.[15]

The Lincoln boys and their friends liked to put on shows in the barn at the back of the house, charging admission in the neighborhood currency of pins and buttons. One day when Lincoln was at work in his office downtown, the backyard gang decided to train two large dogs for an exhibition in the barn. All morning, the boys tried to induce the dogs to stand on their rear legs and make a threatening sound—which seems more like a trick for a lion than one suited to a dog. Perhaps for that reason, they had no success. "We had to take hold of them and hold them up," recalled Hobart Graves, one of the young trainers, "which I know was hard work for they were heavy. So we concluded to put a rope around each dog's neck and throw the end over the rafter and then all hands pull them up."[16]

A man passing by heard the dogs howling and looked inside one of the windows. He then hurried down to Lincoln's office on the square, ran up the steps and interrupted Lincoln's work to say that, "a crowd of boys were hanging dogs in his barn."[17] He added that he thought two were already dead. Lincoln raced out of the office to his house. Graves described what happened next:

> Mrs. Lincoln had been making soap sometime before and had left the ash hopper standing. The hoops had bursted and staves on the barrel curled out [and] was still standing, held by the bottom hoops. Mr. Lincoln did not go in the house first but came in the side gate and started for the barn, grabbing one stave as he passed the ash barrel. We saw him coming but to get out a way from him was only through the little square hole made to throw the refuse of the stable out.[18]

The boys had tied the barn door shut to keep other kids out, but Lincoln snapped the ropes with a yank. By then, most of the boys had already scrambled out through the manure shoot, but Hobart recalled "Lincoln getting one crack at me as I was pretty near out, causing me to take my meals standing for sometime."[19] Lincoln untied the dogs and then went back to his office.

Later in the day, Mrs. Lincoln entered the story, according to Hobart. "I think simply to spite Mr. Lincoln," he recalled, she "sent Bob Lincoln around and invited us to her house, to a molasses candy pulling. Every boy was on his head to go but me. I did love candy but was not in fair condition to enjoy it—but I went and Mrs. Lincoln was awful nice."[20] Mary Lincoln sent a couple of the boys out to buy molasses and the rest helped her start a fire in the stove in the kitchen. Then the boys went in the backyard to play, while the molasses cooked. That's when Abraham Lincoln happened to come home from work. He showed that his anger, as rarely as it came to the surface, ran deep.

Lincoln siezed the pot of molasses from the stove and bolted out the back door with it, throwing the whole thing against a fence. With the candy for the party dripping down the wooden boards, Lincoln chased the boys

off the property. Hobart didn't record what he said at the time. It can probably be imagined. "We were a sad looking show company," Hobart admitted, "I don't think we held any more shows."[21]

Hobart Graves didn't think any less of Lincoln for the incident. It was
all part of the way of the world for him and his friends. Whenever the local
youngsters did something stupid or wrong (or both), the adults got mad.
When it involved cruelty of any sort, then even Lincoln, the most fun-
loving of all the kids, had to change sides.

During the first week of June, with the political world roiled by daily devel-
opments, Lincoln almost certainly stopped in each day at the office of the
Illinois State Journal newspaper. He had long regarded it as almost a second
home, since the editors enjoyed talking about politics almost as much as he
did. More important, though, Lincoln liked to read the out-of-town newspapers that the *Journal* received routinely.

The *Journal* had changed hands the year before. Then, early in 1856,
when the United States seemed headed toward a one-party system, the former Whig paper started leaning toward the Know Nothings and their effort
to emerge as a national force in politics. Herndon antagonized the new editors over the apparent shift. For their part, the editors had refused Herndon's contributions during the spring.[22] But with the success of the
Bloomington Convention, they were all coming back together under the
aegis of the new party. Abraham Lincoln had never broken ranks with the
Journal—or any other newspaper if he could possibly help it. Moreover, he
liked the new managing editor, twenty-seven year-old Edward L. Baker, a
Harvard graduate and the husband of one of Mary Lincoln's nieces.

In June, with the national political parties staging their conventions
back east and choosing candidates, the *Journal* office would have offered the
best way for Lincoln to obtain fresh information. "He was a frequent visitor
at the Journal Office," recalled J. D. Roper, a longtime employee of the
paper, "always greeting everyone with a pleasant word. Sometimes he had
with him his two small boys [Willie and Tad], who would often slip out

into the work room, just back of the editorial room; when Mr. Lincoln would find that the boys had gone, he would go and find them, leading them back by the hands; this would occur two or three times at each visit when the boys were with him. Most of these visits would occupy an hour or more, talking with Mr. Baker, the editor, and reading the New York *Tribune* and other eastern papers."[23]

During those first few days of June, Sen. Stephen Douglas was regarded as the frontrunner for the Democratic presidential nomination, though he lacked strong support in the northeast. For that reason, the Democratic Convention bypassed him on June 5 for James Buchanan of Pennsylvania. Buchanan, sixty-five, was a veteran politician who would be at least potentially electable in every state, north and south. The Know Nothing and Anti-Nebraska (Republican) Conventions would be held later in the month. It was a predetermined fact, though, that the Know Nothing nominee would be New York State's Millard Fillmore, who had been president of the United States from 1850 to 1853, as a Whig. The Anti-Nebraskans were looking at a handful of possible candidates, including John McLean, a Supreme Court Justice, and John Frémont, the Western explorer.

On Monday, June 9, Judge David Davis arrived in Springfield, ready to open Sangamon County's Circuit Court the next day. Six-feet tall, Davis had been a fine-looking, muscular young man, but at the age of forty-one, he was heading fast toward the three-hundred-and-fifty pounds he would eventually carry. A native of Maryland, Davis had graduated from Kenyon College and attended New Haven Law School (later Yale), before moving to Illinois in 1836 to set up his practice. His first impression of life on the prairie was astonishment at how little money he was able to earn. In truth, Davis was not particularly distinguished in his work as a lawyer, but he did grow prosperous starting in the mid-1840s, when he and a fellow lawyer, Clifton Moore, began speculating in land. It was a partnership that would make them both millionaires.[24] Professionally, Davis came into his own in 1848, when he was elected judge of the Eighth Judicial Circuit.

Judge Davis was conspicuously a self-assured man. "While he was not tyrannical," wrote John Palmer, "he forcibly exercised power to accomplish the ends of justice."[25] Davis knew the law well enough to preside in court, he was a deft ringmaster for the various personalities that came through, and whenever he made shortcuts or allowed them, he knew just how far to stray before inviting judicial review. For example, when he was indisposed or busy, he typically assigned Lincoln to preside over the court as judge.[26] That was improper, but because Lincoln was held in universal respect—and because Eighth Circuit lawyers were not as exacting as their counterparts elsewhere—the substitute was never questioned. Davis calculated correctly on that and all other matters pertaining to his court.

Outside of court, and sometimes even in it, Judge Davis loved a funny story, with his hearty laughter ringing out loudly. Lincoln was his favorite source of fun, a raconteur who could have made a career as a humorist, if he weren't a lawyer and politician. The two undoubtedly had a good time in their years together on the circuit, and they were well-suited colleagues. Whether or not they were actually friends was more of a mystery, their camaraderie being untouched by anything like affection.[27] In 1856, though, they were inseparably teacher and pet. The trouble they had lay in settling which one was which.

The fact that Lincoln occupied a special place in Davis' esteem was well-known on the circuit. "Such was the marked deference he showed to Mr. Lincoln," wrote the attorney Usher Linder, "that Lincoln threw the rest of us into the shade."[28] Linder suspected that the judge's preferential attitude was a factor in court. He went out of his way in his memoirs to remark that he himself was not at all "damaged by the friendship shown for him [Lincoln] by his honor"—but that, Linder added, was only because he and Lincoln were so often on the same side.[29] No other lawyers suspected any favoritism, however, and the statistics seem to support that impression. Lincoln actually chalked up a higher percentage of victories in Circuit Court when a jury was deciding a case than when the verdict fell to Davis.

On Tuesday, June 10, Judge Davis convened his court at the Sangamon County Court House in Springfield. Abraham Lincoln was on hand with a number of small matters. In one, Jacob Booth, a carriagemaker, had retained him in a suit to recover a debt of $122.50; Judge Davis found for Booth.[30] For Davis, though, the first priority on that Tuesday was straightening out the case of the Anderson murder.

The local magistrates had referred Theodore Anderson's arraignment to the Grand Jury. Unfortunately, no Grand Jury was scheduled to sit in Sangamon County until the fall term. Judge Davis responded to the imperative of the Anderson case, involving as it did a capital crime and a whipsaw of emotions in the city. He exercised his prerogative to order a special Grand Jury and, remarkably, it was sworn and ready to hear testimony that same afternoon. The foreman was William Hickman, a retired farmer who had recently moved to a house in Springfield, two blocks away from the Lincolns, on Eighth Street. Hickman was a responsible man, who took an active interest in municipal affairs.[31]

In the meantime, Abraham Lincoln finished his work at the Courthouse. He was learning a great deal about the Anderson murder from the proceedings, as well as from his colleagues. The case was still the talk of the Courthouse, even as witnesses arrived to tell their stories in court for the third or even the fourth time since the gruesome crime had been committed. At the end of the day on Tuesday, the Grand Jury was far from finished hearing testimony. Judge Davis ordered it to reconvene the next day.

As the court emptied, the janitor prepared the room for the Anti-Nebraska ratification meeting to be held later that evening. Even he was probably hoping that someone else would show, unlike the last time—and they did, about two hundred strong.[32] When the meeting started, every seat was taken, and those who weren't willing to stand in the aisles had to go home.

The audience consisted of people who were not necessarily friendly to the Anti-Nebraska message, a group even more mixed than the delegates to the Bloomington Convention. In addition, the meeting attracted people from the enemy camp: Democrats and Douglas supporters. It also pulled in those from other factions, curious as to what the new party offered.

Overall, the audience was representative of the Springfield population at large. And Springfield, along with the rest of Central Illinois, represented the country along the hot seam of the crisis over slavery. As a locale in which abolitionists and slavocrats were both loudly heard, it presented a puzzle for a politician. Farther north or south in the state (and likewise, in the country), opinions were much more homogeneous, and politicians knew what to say to win an audience. In Springfield, Lincoln's own hometown, even he wasn't sure. In the long term, it would make him a stronger politician in relation to the slavery crisis, but in mid-June, he was less certain there than he had been two weeks before at Major's Hall.

"Mr. Lincoln opened his speech," noted the reporter from the Springfield *Register*, "and for more than an hour he bored his audience with one of the weakest speeches that he ever perpetrated."[33] The *Register* being a newspaper with a Democratic slant, the criticism might be discounted. The opposing Springfield *State Journal* called the speech "logical" and Lincoln's delivery "calm and unimpassioned." Then it added the faintest of all praise for a speaker in a critical political battle: "We shall not mar its beauty by an attempt to give a synopsis of it."[34] Under the circumstances, that might be construed as a friendly reporter's euphemism for "bored his audience with one of the weakest speeches that he ever perpetrated."[35]

At least the report in the *Register* paid Lincoln the honor of engaging in a long discussion of the speech. Apparently, Lincoln spoke at length about the fusion of various elements into the new party, but he didn't make the memorable points he made at Bloomington regarding the sanctity of the Union and the responsibility of the pro-slavery elements for jeopardizing it. Although the *Register*'s reporter was critical of the platform of the new party, the article was also surprisingly sensitive to Lincoln's position that night in Springfield. "He was evidently laboring under much restraint," the reporter suggested,

conscious that he was doling out new doctrine to the old whigs about him, and fearful that in keeping within moderate bounds, he would so filter his discourse that it would not in any degree reach the end he desired. He would occasionally launch out and lead his hearers to think that the most ultra-abolitionism would follow, when, under the old whig eyes we have mentioned, he would soften his remarks to a supposed palatable texture. In this way, backing and filling, he frittered away anything of argument that he might have presented.[36]

The *Register* undoubtedly represented the opposition. It vehemently rejected Lincoln's opinions, his friends, and certainly his new party, yet it was never against Lincoln himself. In the pages of the *Register,* his name was always accorded friendly respect, even in the midst of the vitriol usually accorded to his colleagues in the Anti-Nebraska movement. Lincoln was apparently having his troubles finding a bearing in Springfield on the night of the ratification meeting. He had been so bold and so sure at Bloomington, apparently speaking from deep within himself, but that was nearly two weeks before.

Facing the cold eyes of the old Whigs and Democrats in front, his train of thought—the arguments that had come to him with stunning inevitability before—was hobbled by his inclination to be careful. "His timidity before the peculiar audience he addressed," wrote the reporter from the *Register,* "prevented its earnest advocacy with the power and ability he is known to possess."[37] Even a critic had to note that with a kind of regret.

CHAPTER 10

JULY AND AUGUST

THE MARCH OF THE WHAT-Y'A-CALL-EMS

On the day after the Springfield ratification meeting, Lincoln was back at the Courthouse, and so was William Herndon. In a room on the first floor, Theodore Anderson's hearing entered its second day before the Grand Jury, while in the main courtroom upstairs, Judge Davis continued to preside over Circuit Court cases. Lincoln and Herndon were both listed on the docket in a debt collection case for Presco Wright, the former crockery merchant, who was trying to settle an account from the days of his store. Wright was not only the plaintiff in the case, but the assistant court clerk.[1] He settled the case just before the trial, which no doubt pleased Lincoln, as well as Davis, who quickly granted a motion to dismiss. Nonetheless, Presco's future was still in the courtroom, or so he hoped, since he was running for office as a candidate for the chief clerk's job.

Lincoln was working on his own cases that day as well. And so was Herndon, who found himself representing Jane Anderson and her family. He became involved almost by accident, but then, he could barely avoid it on that Wednesday, when every room in the Courthouse was ringing with her name. Most of the lawyers in Springfield, it seemed, were in the process of trying to sink her, save her, or at least audit her. All except Lincoln. The highlight of his week was an interesting divorce case scheduled for the following day. He also nipped up to Decatur, to deliver a speech at an Anti-Nebraska meeting there.[2]

Herndon was not recruited into the effort to defend Jane Anderson, which was regarded as a prestige assignment, but rather, into the more commonplace job of protecting George Anderson's estate. William Talbott, George's former partner, regarded Jane Anderson with antipathy, at best. On May 29, less than two weeks after the murder, he filed a petition bringing her into court in response to his claim to half of the lot that he had owned with George Anderson. The timing was extremely inconsiderate of Mrs. Anderson, who was then still fighting the murder charge, but then, Talbott was entirely aware of that when he started the action.

Because Mrs. Anderson was illiterate and the children were minors, they looked to James Matheny, the court-appointed executor of George's estate, to handle the Talbott claim. Unfortunately, Matheny, an attorney, was then serving as chief clerk of the Sangamon County Court. Judge Davis may have overlooked the conflict of interest in Presco Wright's case—where the plaintiff was also the assistant clerk—but he didn't have to be in Springfield long to recognize that the Anderson case was quite different. With so much fury surrounding the widow, he couldn't allow any friendly shortcuts. Matheny's name was crossed out as executor, and Davis looked around for another guardian.

William Herndon agreed to take the job, but only as *guardian ad litem* (for the one case). He couldn't do much in that capacity anyway, except neaten the paperwork and submit it to Davis. Herndon was, however, exposed to the situation in the Anderson family and he typically would have discussed the case with Lincoln. In court, Judge Davis had little choice but to agree that half the lot belonged to Talbott, and order that it be sold as soon as possible, with the proceeds to be divided between the plaintiff and the estate.

All the while, the Grand Jury was continuing to hear testimony in the murder case. No one outside the hearing room knew what was happening, although Theodore Anderson, confined to his jail cell, was presumed to be in dire trouble. To some degree, that was due to the way the system naturally leaned. In any criminal case, a Grand Jury hears only from the witnesses brought forward by the prosecutor; the suspect isn't present and isn't even represented by counsel. Although the Grand Jury is entirely independent—and extremely powerful—it tends in practice to follow the prosecutor's cue.

Theodore's hearing was especially ominous, because a Grand Jury is not expected to assess guilt, but only "probable cause." That is enough to place any case in a gray area—and Theodore, with his supply of strychnine and his attentions to Mrs. Anderson, never appeared so clearly as when he was in a murky, gray area. Imagination filled in the details more neatly than even the most candid account of his actions would have done. Condemning him on that basis and in secret really wasn't hard; people were doing it all over the city. Even acknowledging that the case offered no hard evidence, as one resident reluctantly concluded, "It cannot but be admitted that some circumstances are very unfavorable to him."[3]

They were. The Grand Jury returned a murder indictment against Theodore Anderson—but that wasn't the shocker of the day, reverberating through the room, the Courthouse, the city, and eventually the region. The Grand Jury also indicted Jane Anderson. It was within its power to do so, but the whole fabric of the case was transformed with the double indictment. The question no longer concerned which of them committed the murder—the title of the indictment was *People versus Anderson and Anderson*. The new contention was that working together, they planned and accomplished George Anderson's death.

Jane Anderson was at home at the time of the verdict, oblivious to her fate. As of that moment, though, she was wanted by the police for the murder of her husband. The sheriff gathered the paperwork from Clerk Matheny and hurried off to Monroe Street to arrest her. It was the third time, and by far the most disturbing. As she packed her clothing in a bag and said goodbye to her children, she wasn't likely to see her freedom again for a long time. In her previous arrests, she was not indicted, but only waiting for the judicial system to make a decision; she could regard it all as a misunderstanding, a formality, or a very inconvenient insult. After the indictment, however, she changed from a suspect to a defendant, and with that, she belonged to the system of justice.

The sheriff explained to Mrs. Anderson that state law made no provision for bail in capital cases. She would be in jail until the trial. The same was true of Theodore. They were to be tried jointly at the next term of the Sangamon County Circuit Court, meaning that their trial would begin on the third Monday of November: more than five months in the future.

The excitement receded at the Courthouse much more quickly than it did in the rest of the city. Other matters were called and demanded attention, each one of them the case of the century in the eyes of the participants. James Matheny and Presco Wright pushed the cases before Judge Davis, who did his part to hasten them off the docket, through order, decree, verdict, or delay. The Circuit Court was scheduled to wrap up in Springfield on Friday, making it a busy day for everyone. Ordinarily, the adjournment there would conclude the spring term of the Eighth Circuit Court, but Judge Davis was obligated to return to Urbana, northeast of Springfield, the following Tuesday in order to tend some cases left unfinished during the regular session of the court there in May.

Naturally Lincoln went too, despite the fact that, as his fellow lawyer Henry Whitney recalled, the extra session in Urbana that spring "was extremely prosaic, having trial cases meagre both in amount and incident."[4] The circuit was Lincoln's beat, integral to the life of a lawyer who was known and respected in the eight counties of central-eastern Illinois. The reach of Lincoln's name, though, was about to expand through an introduction, however fleeting, to the national scene. Though he didn't know it, he was in the waning days of the first epoch of his life, when it could be truthfully said that his "reputation was hardly more than local."[5]

A Springfield resident, writing a newspaper column in mid-June, described Abraham Lincoln at precisely that juncture. Though biased politically, the offhand profile gives a picture of just what Lincoln's local reputation was at the time and among those who knew him in central Illinois:

He is a native of Kentucky; came to this State when a stripling, and settled about twenty miles or more from here for the purpose of farming; came to the conclusion that he could make a lawyer of himself and so went at it, and thus far has succeeded in the profession well. In politics he has figured somewhat; being very ambitious he is desirous of climbing up the ladder of fame. At first he was a Whig of free-soil proclivities, until the Whig party was no more, then joined the Republicans, and is now working side by side with John Wentworth, Lovejoy & Co. During the last session of the Legislature he was a candidate for U.S. Senator to fill the place of Gen. Shields, but his Abolition friends deceived him and elected Trumbull. The defeat set hard upon him, for he confidently expected to have been Senator . . . Lincoln has been a member of the Legislature, and one term represented this district in Congress. He is a man of considerable talent; is a moderate stump speaker, and can tell a yarn better than any man living . . . In appearance, Lincoln is over six feet in his stockings; a raw boned, large sized man, and as awkward an one as ever was made. He is about forty seven years old. Is acknowledged to be the ugliest man in the State.[6]

With that, the writer took advantage of the opportunity to repeat one of Lincoln's own tall tales, reflecting on his appearance:

Tis said that in his younger days, he made a vow that if ever he should find a man uglier than himself, he would shoot him. One day while rambling over the hills with his rifle in his hand, in search of game, he met a man who was exceedingly ugly; immediately he cocked his gun and took aim, but upon being asked by the stranger what he was going to do, if he was going to murder him, Lincoln lowered his gun, told the stranger his vow and that he must prepare himself to meet his fate.

The stranger, after eyeing him for a while and scanning him from head to foot, exclaimed: "Well, if I am uglier than *you*, I don't want to live—so just shoot."

In conclusion, the writer added, "we will say that Lincoln is an affable, companionable man, and one whom very few would dislike personally, however much they might dislike him politically."[7] That was the impression left by Lincoln's public career as it had been since the beginning. In truth, his affability hadn't been enough, not for high office. But the political world was growing more grave, more complicated and, if he could manage to maneuver himself to the right position before it, a far fuller reflection of his character.

In Urbana for the special term, Davis, Lincoln, and Whitney were sharing a room at the American Hotel—though why Whitney needed to crowd into a guestroom when he owned a home in Urbana isn't clear. He was a young lawyer then, and may have considered his stay at the hotel as a chance to establish himself with the leading men of the circuit.

At the Courthouse, Lincoln was engaged in an appeal involving school taxes. He was also helping a man named Stillman Stevens collect a debt of $237.26 from his brother, Sylvanus. All of his work that week was monumentally *usual.* Professional boredom forced Lincoln to dwell closely with his own moody nature, which wasn't comfortable for him or those around him. At such times, he sometimes relied on his distinct need for fun—playing games with his sons, going to plays, telling stories with the other lawyers. But his sons were back in Springfield, there were no shows in Urbana, and the other lawyers, in that special term, consisted largely of Davis and Whitney. It was then that Lincoln went momentarily haywire.

He stole the dinner gong at the hotel. He snatched it from a sideboard outside the dining room, showed it to Whitney and Davis, and then hid it in a drawer in one of the tables in the lobby. As a minor act of larceny, it vexed the hotel owner for a day or so, until someone on the staff chanced to open the drawer, but it succeeded fully in the greater sense: giving Lincoln something else to think about, and Davis and Whitney, something else to talk about.

The other source of incident for the trio was the newspaper. Each day, Whitney brought a copy of the Chicago *Democratic Press* into the hotel room and read it out loud. On June 19, he presented the paper's report from the National Anti-Nebraska Convention in Philadelphia, revealing that the party's presidential nominee was to be the former explorer John C. Frémont. That came as a disappointment to Lincoln, who felt that Frémont leaned too far toward abolitionism to gain the support of the old Whigs, "men of conservative feelings, and slight pro-slavery proclivities,"[8] who were nonetheless against the expansion of the institution.

The next day, Whitney opened the *Press* and shared the results of the second day's business in Philadelphia. "The convention then proceeded to an informal ballot for Vice-President," he read, "which resulted as follows: Dayton 259; Lincoln 110; Ford 7; King 9 . . .." Although the same article affirmed that Dayton was ultimately chosen, the Lincoln delegates in New York, Pennsylvania, and Connecticut had remained loyal to the end. Their man had been taken up and taken seriously for the nation's second-highest office.

The votes, the national attention, and the pockets of enthusiasm in the Northeast were all new phenomenon for Abraham Lincoln. A few of his friends in the Illinois delegation, still propelled by the speech in Bloomington, had originated the idea of a Lincoln nomination and worked it into a reality, all without the knowledge of Lincoln himself. The master strategist was caught off-guard. And, though the news was good, he still didn't like the way it curved in unexpectedly. His mood wasn't steady to begin with during that trip to Urbana, and the big announcement only stilled his spirits altogether. "Davis and I were greatly excited," Whitney remembered, "but Lincoln was phlegmatic, listless and indifferent: his only remark was 'I reckon that ain't me; there's another great man in Massachusetts named Lincoln, and I reckon it's him.'"[9] One might read conceit into Lincoln's characterization of that Massachusetts Lincoln as *another* great man, but that was probably Whitney's slip in the retelling, and not Lincoln's.

The next day's papers affirmed that the nominee who drew the attention of the Convention was indeed Abraham Lincoln of Illinois or, as the Terre Haute, Indiana *Daily Express* got it, "Absolom Lincoln of Illinois."[10] Nobody ever said fame was easy on the nerves—but it was indeed a boost of fame that Lincoln received that day.

Even so, the nomination failed to cheer Lincoln up, according to Whitney's recollection. In an obtuse way, the reason may be contained in the only writing that Lincoln left from that interlude. It placed him a long, long way from Philadelphia, where his name came to the fore, however briefly, in national politics: "yet the said defendant," he wrote in his own hand, referring to Sylvanus Stevens, "(although often requested) has not paid said sum of money or any part of the sum, but . . . has hitherto wholly neglected and refused, and still does neglect and refuse—to the damage of the said plaintiff."[11]

With legal precision, Lincoln recorded the facts of the $237.26 dispute between the Stevens brothers, and in the end, won the judgment for Stillman Stevens. As days went by, that was his place a good deal of the time: a glorified bill collector. He gave a political speech while he was in Urbana, but for once, as Whitney recalled it, Lincoln couldn't wait to leave the circuit behind and just go home.

Charles Zane arrived in Springfield a few weeks after Lincoln's return. A twenty-five year-old college man from a farm village in Sangamon County, he was intent on becoming a lawyer. The usual method was to study with another lawyer, as Lincoln had done with Stuart, and so, since Zane had heard of Lincoln, he applied first at the office of Lincoln & Herndon. He was doubly disappointed there, though. Not only didn't the firm have space for him (already having a student in the office), he didn't even get to meet Abraham Lincoln, who was out at the time. Herndon was the only one around. Usually officious, if not icy, with strangers, he was kind enough that day to give Zane a letter of introduction to James Conkling, who ultimately agreed to take him on as a student.

"A day or two afterward," Zane wrote, "Mr. Lincoln happened to come in. Mr. Conkling introduced me to him, adding that I was a Republican. Mr. Lincoln shook hands with me in his kindly way." Though Lincoln was in the office only a short time, Zane remembered "the direct simplicity and naturalness of his bearing."[12]

After Lincoln left, Conkling turned to young Zane with a lawyerly assignment—to make a run to the post office. Out on the street, Zane spotted Lincoln. "Something seemed to attract his attention," he said, "He stopped and walked out to a self-raking reaping machine on exhibition. It was then a new invention, and quite intricate in its construction."[13] The implement was probably Rugg's Patent Square Draft Mower and Harvesting Machine, which was then being featured by a local agent.[14] Rugg's was one of a generation of machines that sought to reduce labor at harvest time, though many people were skeptical that such complex apparatus had any future on the farm. Under actual working conditions, models usually worked heroically for a row or two and then jammed.[15]

"It was the first self-raker that he had seen," Zane wrote of Lincoln, "He examined it with much interest, and then I listened to him explaining, in the fewest words but with great clearness, how power and motion were communicated to the different appliances, especially to the sickle, the revolving rake and the reel."[16]

Lincoln possessed the mind of an engineer, having even taken out a patent in 1849 for a means of easing riverboats over shoals. Though he never pursued his interest in mechanical inventions professionally, some of his characteristic traits were those of a scientific mind: his dependence on logic as a means of renewal, for example; his indifference to material comforts; and his ability to entirely lose himself in thought, as though in a different world.

Through the summer, Lincoln had only a few court dates requiring travel. The day hardly went by, though, that he didn't commit to a speaking engagement somewhere in the state on behalf of the Anti-Nebraska ticket. He wasn't unique in that respect. Yates, Trumbull, Conkling, Lovejoy, Herndon, Koerner, and a half-dozen others had just about as many political commitments. William Bissell was the only exception; being housebound much of the time, he wasn't making any promises to appear. That put even more pressure on the others, who were inundated with requests. Dr. Koerner, the Democratic lieutenant governor newly recruited to the Anti-Nebraskans, despaired that if he accepted every invitation, "I should have to double myself and speak every day from August to November."[17] He wouldn't have survived it, even if he had quadrupled himself. Giving a speech in the 1850s was a strenuous undertaking. A typical address at a campaign rally lasted for hours. When one of Lincoln's friends once expressed concern for his stamina after a comparatively short address of only an hour, Lincoln boasted, "No, I can speak three or four hours at a time without feeling weary."[18]

The question was whether anyone could listen for that long. In 1856, they could. Audiences then were not only prepared for long speeches, they looked forward to them. In the first place, the speakers, across the board, must have been on a high par: engaging, poised, and at least somewhat charismatic. Second, most of the political addresses during the campaign season were delivered at rallies, which bore no resemblance at all to dull lecture halls. On the contrary, they were as effervescent as the organizers could make them, by keeping to the reliable ingredients: girls, music, and free food.[19]

A rally usually started with a procession to draw audiences, in the manner of a circus parade, to whatever grove or field was going to come alive with politics that day. The procession would include a brass band and banners, followed by horse-drawn wagons arrayed with women dressed to represent the themes of the election. At a rally in Peoria, thirty-one young ladies all in white represented the states, but another, who was dressed in black, was supposed to be Kansas Territory, and she wore a sash reading "Give Me Justice."[20] In another diversion that was taken with the utmost seriousness, at least by the participants, the most eye-catching of the women in the float, the one in the most regal dress of the day, would represent "the adored Jesse," wife of John Frémont, the presidential candidate.

When Lincoln took the stage, he was expected to acknowledge the gaggle of local beauties. Eventually, he came up with a line that suited him—and them, and their proud parents: "I want to thank you especially," he would say, as he gestured to the girls in their finery, "for this beautiful bouquet." The procession and its accoutrements were all show business. Some people coming in from the hollow reaches of the countryside would expect nothing less, being veterans of political hullabaloo, but at every rally, there were those who would gawk as though frozen, never having seen anything like it before.

At most rallies, a picnic was also included. The organizers of a medium-sized rally in Urbana provided nine hundred pounds of cooked beef, along with other meats, and all the side dishes of a feast.[21]

Grand rallies could accommodate as many as thirty thousand people. How many of those people did anything but eat barbecue wasn't as carefully recorded. At a more standard event, the number in the audience could easily reach five thousand.

At the larger rallies—or when the organizers had an embarrassment of orators—more than one would speak at once. Sometimes, separate stands were set up all over the field; sometimes, a single square platform was erected in the middle, with each of four speakers facing out from the various sides. Members of the audience were free to roam from one to another, the way people change television channels today. It turned the speakers into carnival barkers, as much as campaign orators, though, forcing them to do anything necessary to keep the pigeons from getting away, while simultaneously presenting brilliant points in political philosophy.

As an elector-at-large for the Anti-Nebraska ticket, Lincoln received invitations as a matter of course. He was loath to turn anyone down, but even he strained his voice and became hoarse if he made too many appearances in a week. In addition, he was well aware that he was sacrificing part of his income by devoting so much time to the campaign.[22] That being the case, he thought it only fair that someone else help with the expenses, and to that end he approached a rich political supporter named Alexander Campbell, who quietly agreed to underwrite Lincoln's trips up to an amount of $500.[23]

At the beginning of the summer, most of the state's Anti-Nebraska leaders were looking to Senator Trumbull to coordinate the campaign. He hadn't even attended the state Convention, but he was a U.S. Senator, meaning that he could frank copies of Congressional publications for use as free campaign material. In a campaign without a central source of funding, such pamphlets represented a kind of political tender. Most of those active in the campaign kept in contact with Trumbull early in the summer. Herndon wrote to him on July 12, with a report on the political situation. "As for Mr. Lincoln and myself, we intend to do all the good we can, and as you suggest, go into the Southern part of our state."[24]

Just at that time, however, Lincoln was planning to go north to Chicago, "to attend a little business in court," as he wrote in a letter of his own that same day, July 12.[25] The letter was addressed to the governor of Iowa, who had asked him to speak on behalf of Frémont. The invitation was an indication of Lincoln's rising fame, thanks largely to the Bloomington speech. Lincoln declined the invitation to go to Iowa, first because he was busy, and second because he claimed to be superstitious about campaigns getting help from out-of-staters. Outsiders stirred up "more enemies than friends," he insisted, and then, according to his superstition, the candidate lost.[26] The national campaign organizations, such as they were in 1856, exerted very little influence over such matters as the scheduling of campaign appearances and the local strategies surrounding them.

Winning was left to the state leaders, but the national party leaders did have a role to play and something to occupy their time: they were responsible for spreading slander about the opposing candidates. The Republicans tried at first to make something out of the contention that the Democratic nominee, James Buchanan, was practically decrepit, at the age of sixty-five. "Buchanan looks old, old—very old," one newspaper observed.[27] He did seem rather great-grandfatherly, with his flowing white hair, but in fact, he wasn't all that much older than Millard Fillmore, the Know Nothing candidate, who was fifty-six. Buchanan was, however, old enough to be the father of John C. Frémont, the Anti-Nebraska nominee, who was forty-three. That brought up another fact about "old Buck," though, and one that became the theme of his enemies for the rest of the campaign. James Buchanan couldn't, for the public record, be anybody's father, because he had never been married. The Republicans tagged him relentlessly as an "old bachelor," and let people make of that what they would.

The Republicans were giving it a good try, but it was the Democrats who were the masters of the mud. In the first place, they focused on the goal: keeping the Know Nothings from folding into the Republican Party. Looking over the Know Nothing platform, they didn't note any animosity toward old bachelors, only toward foreigners and, especially, Catholics. With that, the country was drenched with the news that John Frémont was a Catholic—a lie that they managed to back up with facts. For instance, though Frémont was a practicing Episcopalian, his father had indeed been a Catholic. And Frémont had been married by a Catholic priest, due to his Protestant clergyman being indisposed at the last minute. In the campaign of 1856, that was more than enough to sustain a scandal that followed the Republican campaign all year. The majority of Know Nothing party members were against electing a president who was even possibly Catholic; the more resolute took just as dim a view of anyone who had been married by a priest. To them, that amounted to a kind of treason, too, and the Anti-Nebraskans undoubtedly lost votes because of it. Lincoln didn't acknowledge the accusations in his speeches, but he had to take them into account. From the first, he was acutely aware of the impact of the Know Nothing vote on the future of his new party.

In the first part of July, as Lincoln looked forward to his two-week trip to Chicago he could count on all sorts of political business there, most importantly, talks with others in the party, from those who were too impatient for abolition, such as the newspaper editor John ("Long John") Wentworth, to those who were slightly too careful about it, such as Norman B. Judd, a lawyer. The challenge of keeping the Republican fusion intact was Lincoln's first priority. Such machinations were as clear to him as the gearings of Rugg's Patent Square Draft Mower. The key to a national victory for Frémont was a defeat for Buchanan in Illinois. In that vein, Illinois wasn't the only consideration on the electoral map—Pennsylvania was another swing state—but it was critically important. If the Republicans couldn't effect a Buchanan defeat in Illinois all by themselves, an approach would have to be made to the Know Nothings.

The Know Nothing candidate, Millard Fillmore, was actually in the same position: he couldn't win the election, either, if Buchanan won Illinois. For Fillmore, it didn't even matter so much whether he or Frémont won the state, as long as Buchanan was shut out.

Lincoln thought about that frustrating situation. He probably thought about it too much, because he decided that the way to solve the problem was to take advantage of the essence of the Electoral College system: proxy voting. A few days before leaving for Chicago, he suggested in a letter to a political friend that "Fremont and Fillmore men unite on one entire ticket, with the understanding that that ticket, if elected, shall cast the vote of the State, for whichever of the two shall be known to have received the larger number of electoral votes, in the other states."[28]

The strategy was incisive, but it was founded on the creation of a peaceable kingdom, in which scrapping political parties join together and trust one another. The idea was brilliant, but unrealistic. Perhaps it was for the best that Lincoln's obsession with snatching the Know Nothing vote for the Republicans had to take a rest for a couple of weeks when he arrived in Chicago.

On the very day that Lincoln stepped off the train in Chicago, he could read about his own arrival in the *Democratic Press* newspaper. A short article on page two told readers that he was expected in the city during the day and added, "While here it is hoped he will consent to address the people upon the great political issues of the day."[29] Lincoln was more than happy to start working on arrangements for a speech—but first, he had legal business to tend.

Shortly after arriving in Chicago, Lincoln walked into the Saloon Building at the corner of Clark and Lake streets. It wasn't a barroom, but an office building that housed the U.S. Circuit Court. One of the cases Lincoln had to argue there was an eviction made interesting by the fact that it originated during the War of 1812, with the American attack on the French settlement at Peoria. Lincoln was helping defend the owner of several lots in the city against those who claimed to hold the original (pre-attack) deeds.[30] Despite the passage of forty-four years since the attack, the participants were true to their warring antecedents. They were as angry as hornets.

Elliott Anthony, an attorney in Chicago, was waiting for one of his cases to come before the judge at the same time that Lincoln was waiting for his trial to be called. Anthony later described the scene:

> Norman B. Judd and myself were sitting chatting together on one of the front benches in the court-room and Lincoln was walking backward and forward across the court-room, waiting for the call of a case in which he was interested. Robert S. Blackwell [another attorney] was making a most elaborate address to a jury, and was, it seemed to us, at times rather incoherent, as he talked of many things entirely foreign to the subject, and to illustrate some point in his discourse he proceeded to narrate at great length the habits of the storks in Holland, which lived, he said, among the dykes and destroyed insects, which would, if not disposed of, eat through and destroy the same. Lincoln stopped and listened for a few moments to what Blackwell was saying, and, coming to where we were sitting, hit Judd on the knee with his hand and said: "That beats me! Blackwell can concentrate more words into the fewest ideas of any man I ever knew. The storks of Holland! Why, they would eat him up before he began to get half through telling that story about them."[31]

Lincoln needn't have been so impatient for his moment. The 1812 land case didn't end that day; not that week, either. In fact, the matter eventually made its way to the U.S. Supreme Court, not once, but twice (by then, though, Lincoln was no longer involved).

Lincoln reverted to politics at the end of his first week in Chicago, making a trip to visit Dixon and Sterling, two towns west of the city. He spoke in each of them, before returning for a rally in Dearborn Park. The descriptions from the friendly and opposition papers were not essentially different, although, of course, each side colored its report. "The speaker was calm, clear and forcible," acknowledged the Chicago *Democratic Press,* which was, despite its name, entirely Anti-Nebraska in its leanings. That was about all that the paper said about the speech, but at least it was positive. "Very dry and prosy," reported a Democrat in the audience.[32]

"I was around in a number of circles on yesterday," added the Democrat, "and heard no one speak of it, and do not believe that there was even among their own party any one who cared enough about it, to talk of it to others." Judging from the perfunctory coverage that the speech received in the *Democratic Press,* the paper that had practically begged Lincoln for an address at the beginning of the week, it can be surmised that he didn't light the audience on fire, the way he could—the way he had, in Bloomington.

After Chicago on the seventeenth, Lincoln's next important appointment was the twenty-third, in Galena, a small city in the very northwest corner of Illinois. Galena became famous later as the hometown of Ulysses Grant. Having left the Army a few years before, Grant was working a farm near St. Louis in 1856, so there was no chance for him to see Lincoln in Galena that July day. Yet Grant, who briefly belonged to a Know Nothing lodge, was typical of the former Whigs Lincoln was courting hardest: he was against slavery, but not at any cost. Grant followed the presidential election avidly, and in his *Personal Memoirs* he recalled his conviction that in the South, the Republicans, or Anti-Nebraskans, were regarded without exception as abolitionists. "It was evident to my mind," he wrote, "that the election of a Republican president in 1856 meant the secession of all the Slave States, and rebellion."[33]

Lincoln was attuned to that kind of thinking. Around the time of his Galena trip, he was answering the same exact charge in his speeches. "It is constantly objected to Fremont & Dayton," Lincoln would say, "that they are supported by a sectional party, who, by their sectionalism, endanger the National Union. This objection, more than all others, causes men, really opposed to slavery extension, to hesitate. Practically, it is the most difficult objection we have to meet."[34]

In the speech at Galena, Lincoln went on the offensive on that same theme. And he sounded again as he had at Bloomington, both in his message and his emphatic insistence upon it. He was deeply annoyed by the Southern ability to threaten secession while simultaneously accusing the Anti-Nebraskans of being the disunionists.

Lincoln dissected the logic behind that attitude and found it wanting, but he allowed his emotions to rise much further as he concluded by assuring all present that secession wouldn't work, if the South decided to try it. He returned to his Bloomington refrain, that the North "won't" destroy the Union and the South "shan't,"[35] emphasizing withal that the North had the means necessary to enforce that promise. In delineating a national ethic with which to answer Southern agitation, he was back on the leading edge of the party.

The Galena speech was Lincoln's most influential since the campaign began in earnest. A local reporter wrote down enough of it to fill one whole column, and it was reprinted in newspapers around the state. In truth, the space devoted to Lincoln's own words was more significant than the most glowing review from a friendly paper, indicating by deed and not just word that Lincoln was making fresh arguments. The critic back in Chicago who had said of Lincoln's speech there that no one "cared enough about it, to talk of it to others" could not have said the same of the Galena speech. On the contrary, the two opposition newspapers in Springfield each devoted a full column to refuting the Galena speech. It was talked about, all right, and Lincoln repeated the argument and much of the same sense of urgency at other Republican rallies. Lincoln was offering themes that could give definition to the new party. He was openly refusing to allow Democrats and Southerners to push his new party into the position of tiptoeing around, or else being accused of trying to break up the nation. Politically, Lincoln was taking his argument forward. Audiences liked it and, what is more, the new party needed it.

The new party also happened to need a name. On the national level, the word "Republican" was in official use by early summer, but in some states, it was still a liability. In Indiana, the name was anathema and would be for years. In Illinois, it was coming on very slowly. When the organizers of a rally advertised their event as *Republican,* many people refused to attend on that basis alone. Lincoln himself shied away from a word so obviously burdened.[36]

In fact, Lincoln was still being identified as a "Henry Clay Whig," which was a little quaint, considering the way that his very modern new party was spinning ahead. Meanwhile, Democrats joyously used the name "Republican," knowing, as Grant had said, that it was taken as a euphemism for abolitionism in many quarters. Still, the members of the new party dithered so long that jokesters took to calling them the "What-y'a-call-ems."[37]

Lincoln returned to Springfield at the end of July. For a week or so, he was at home in that life he led when there weren't 10,000 people in attendance. He was back in the house, back in the family, back on Eighth and Jackson.

"Mr. Lincoln always took a thoroughly kind and human interest in all his neighbors," said a man whose family, the Wheelocks, lived across Eighth Street from the Lincolns. "My grandfather was for several years an invalid. On returning from a trip Mr. Lincoln did not fail to 'drop in for a chat with Mr. Wheelock.' Sitting on the edge of the high porch, with his feet resting on the ground, he would talk over the political news of the day."[38] All of the neighbors seemed to think well of Lincoln, but according to some theories, he was only campaigning, even with them. Davis, Stuart, and others later accused Lincoln of having a cold heart, devoid of emotion, and governed only by the calculation of what he wanted of people, including his neighbors. If some friends did later accuse Lincoln of merely putting on a kind and caring facade, then they also paid him the compliment of being an actor *par excellence,* because the people who knew him in a neighborly way in Springfield uniformly described him as a kind fellow. Perhaps that is all that he was capable of being: a friend to practically everyone, a best friend to no one. Men such as Davis, Stuart, and even Herndon ultimately found that frustrating.

"I am one of the trustees of the First Baptist Church," said one of the Lincolns' neighbors, "and although Mr. Lincoln was not an attendant with our congregation, he would always give $15, $20 or $25 every year to help support the minister. He was sure to give something to every charitable and benevolent purpose that came along. 'Well, how much do you want that I should give,' he would say, drawing his purse, 'You must leave me a little to feed the babies with.'"[39] That—now that was campaigning. But it had come from both sides of the conversation, after all.

On Saturday, August 2, Richard Yates, the popular orator from the town of Jacksonville, just west of Springfield, was in the capital for a Frémont Club organizational meeting. That afternoon, a tornado hit Springfield. "During its continuance," said a resident, "the sky was as black as midnight and the streets filled with dust."[40] Two people were hurt, but the politics of the day didn't pause. Sometime before the meeting, but after everyone had emerged from cover, Yates was anxious to talk with Lincoln, Herndon, and Dr. William Jayne, another staunch Republican.* The consensus of their discussion was that fully one-third of the voters were still undecided, and that Illinois needed visits from out-of-staters, especially former Whigs, speaking on behalf of Frémont. Since the Democrats were already infusing the state with big names from the East, the way was clear, according to Lincoln's superstition, for the Republicans to do the same.

To that end, Yates wrote to Trumbull requesting his help in "securing efficient speakers from other States." Efficient speakers would be the ones who zeroed in on the undecided vote: the old Whigs. "Lincoln feels confident Fremont will carry the State," Yates added, not necessarily because Lincoln said precisely that, but because efficient speakers were also the ones who didn't bother with states that were hopeless. Yates admitted as much in his letter.[41] In fact, though, Lincoln was feeling much more desperate than Yates indicated.

Without the benefit of polls, Lincoln had his own method of projecting election results. In early August, he boasted, "I think I now understand the relative strength of the three parties in this state, as well as any other one

---

* Since the name "Republican" gradually caught on and was in general use by the end of the campaign, it will be used hereinafter in this narrative, in place of "Anti-Nebraska."

man does and my opinion is that to-day, Buchanan has about 85,000—Fremont 78,000 and Fillmore 21,000."[42]

To an old friend in Massachusetts, Lincoln observed that the majority of voters in Illinois were against the Democrat, James Buchanan, but unfortunately, that same majority was divided between his man, Frémont, and the Know Nothing candidate, Fillmore. The Fillmore voters had no power, he wrote, except "bettering the chances of Buchanan. They know this; and I still hope the bulk of them will think better than to throw away their votes for such an object."[43] If 8,000 likely Fillmore voters switched to Frémont, that would be bulk enough to suffice.

"The little engine," as Herndon had put it,[44] that was Lincoln's political compulsion could not rest at such a moment. During the summer, he advised a young candidate for office in Springfield to walk right up to voters and ask for their support. Faced with frustrations in the presidential election, Lincoln took his own advice, picking up a pen to write a letter to an acquaintance:

> I understand you are a Fillmore man. If, as between Fremont and Buchanan, you *really* prefer the election of Buchanan, then burn this without reading a line further.
>
> But if you would like to defeat Buchanan, and his gang, allow me a word with you. Does anyone pretend that Fillmore can carry the vote of this state? I have not heared [sic] a single man pretend so. Every vote taken from Fremont and given to Fillmore, is just so much in favor of Buchanan. The Buchanan men see this; and hence their great anxiety in favor of the Fillmore movement. They know where the shoe pinches. They now greatly prefer having a man of your character go for Fillmore than for Buchanan, because they expect several to go with you, who would go for Fremont, if you were to go directly for Buchanan.[45]

The scenario could not be too complicated to suit Abraham Lincoln. Not every voter could or would try to follow his reverse reasoning, though. In courting the Know Nothing votes, he did have an even stronger drawing card, and one that was far easier to understand: the hero worship of Colonel

Bissell. He was a veritable magnifier for a point that Lincoln was fond of making: "You who hate slavery and love freedom, why not, as Fillmore and Buchanan are on the same ground, vote for Fremont? Why not vote for the man who takes your side of the question?"[46]

Illinoisans would find it far easier to vote for Bissell along that line of thought than for Frémont. While Bissell was against the extension of slavery, Frémont was more openly opposed to the institution itself, a position that discouraged many voters in the state. Bissell's position was more palatable and so, in Illinois, the coattails would flap upward, with the candidate for governor helping the presidential nominee. Lincoln didn't press that point, though, or use Bissell's name to bolster the Frémont cause. Whether he knew it or not, Bissell's candidacy was not at all the bulwark it appeared. On the contrary, it was critically dangerous for the Republican Party, and all of Lincoln's plans.

Colonel Bissell was Catholic. He had secretly joined the Church three years before. In any other year, it would not have mattered much, if at all, but in 1856, that personal religious conviction was the kind of news that Democrats, even nationally, hunted out fervently. The question is whether anyone else knew. Bissell ought to have told Senator Trumbull, Abraham Lincoln, or Dr. Koerner, his neighbor in Belleville, asking their approval before he accepted the nomination. There is no record that he did. It was all Bissell's gamble.

In the second week of August, Lincoln left on a swing through the southeast part of Illinois, taking the first part of the trip in the company of Henry P. H. Bromwell, a serious young lawyer and Frémont elector from Vandalia. After a rally in the town of Paris, almost on the Indiana border, Lincoln and Bromwell took the Terre Haute & Alton railroad to the picturesque town of Grand View. Interestingly enough, especially for Lincoln and Bromwell, the Terre Haute & Alton didn't have passenger cars.

Climbing down from a freight car, the two campaigners were met by a local supporter, Richard Sutherland, who took them by carriage into the town itself. Lincoln had agreed to the engagement as a personal favor to

Sutherland, a well-traveled former Whig who believed, as few did at that time, that Abraham Lincoln was a man of destiny. Unfortunately, Sutherland was one of only six Frémonters in town, so the rally didn't promise much. Sutherland gave his visitors a good lunch and then, at one o'clock, the speaking was to begin in an enclosed grove, covered in luxuriant, deep grass. Only about two hundred people were present, but they were going to be treated to a show.

Lincoln knew his audience. He took a jovial, lighthearted tone, but made it clear to those in the audience that "the slave-holders absolutely controlled both Whigs and Democrats, and that if they wanted to be free men themselves, they must fight slavery."[47] When both Lincoln and Bromwell were finished with their speeches, they left the platform. Bromwell laid down on the grass, sometimes sitting with his back against a walnut tree. "Mr. Lincoln lay at full length," Bromwell said, "and his head supported at times on his hand, his elbow on the ground."[48]

The next speaker was a strange choice at a Republican rally: a local physician named Dr. Goodell, who was against everything the Republicans stood for. It didn't really matter, though, because his act—and it was a beloved act—had nothing to do with what he said. It was how he said it. Stocky in build and leaning on a thick cane, he used syntax the way a snake charmer uses his pipe, fascinating the audience with statements such as "The new Republican party is composed of the essence of the quintessence of the putrescence of purulent matter . . ."[49] As the syllables danced off his lips, people were cheering and throwing their hats in the air every time he managed to find the end of a sentence.

The only man who could match wits with Dr. Goodell and his unconquerable vocabulary was a local lawyer named Cooper, who leapt on the stage as soon as the doctor was through. "Fellow citizens," he said, "I'm going home and when I get there I'm going to take down my dictionary and if I find one word in it of the damned rot you have just listened to, I'll burn the dashed thing in the cook stove so that none of it can escape."[50] People laughed for five minutes straight.

"That's more than any lawyer around here has seen lately," cried Dr. Goodell, "a vision of anything homogeneous with a dictionary would throw their whole systems into spasms."[51] The audience roared. "If a lawyer or anybody else should take spasms," Cooper replied, facing the audience, "or get foundered on any kind of valuable knowledge, a Democratic speech would work it all out of him in time to save his life."[52] The wit escalated, or seemed to, and the people listening were convulsed, holding their laughter and then gasping for breath, just long enough to hear each trumping insult. Cooper and Goodell traded them back and forth for almost an hour.

Lincoln had long since forgotten about politics. He was holding his sides, just like everyone else—rocking around in the glen—part of a sensation of hilarity that he had, in fact, helped to start. But he was caught up as he rarely ever was. Many people commented on the fact that while Lincoln frequently told funny stories, he didn't often let go himself. "Mr. Lincoln," Bromwell said, "laughed until he was worn out. Several who were near us found it impossible to stop. For my part, it was the first and only time in my life that I laughed till I became alarmed."[53]

When the doctor and lawyer finally showed mercy and left the stage, Lincoln and Bromwell climbed into a carriage for the ride back to Sutherland's for the night. Along the way, they heard laughter ringing out sporadically across the fields. It couldn't stop. "We rode back to Mr. Sutherland's," Bromwell said, "and nobody thought of going to bed before midnight; yet even then the laughter would break out somewhere about the house and all hands would join in, and so it went on for hours."[54]

CHAPTER 11

SEPTEMBER

BOARDING MEN

From Grand View, Lincoln went on alone to Shelbyville, another town where the Republicans were in the minority. But then, there were counties even farther to the south where they didn't exist at all. In Shelbyville, it would be futile to stage a Republican rally—only a handful of people would have been motivated to attend—and so the event was organized as a debate. Lincoln was to take the Republican side against an old friend and fellow attorney, Anthony Thornton. From a distance, Thornton could be mistaken for Lincoln: they were about the same height and build, with the same type of rugged face, though Thornton's black hair was receding. Likewise, they were both thoughtful in demeanor and careful in their reactions. Thornton had even been a Whig, on the same lines as Lincoln, but when the party dissolved, he chose to join the Democrats.

The day of the debate was hot. Lincoln was dressed neatly but very casually in a long, white linen duster and no vest. When he arrived in Shelbyville he went directly to the County Courthouse, the site of the debate. He was an hour early, but he wanted to get out of the sun. Thornton was already there, and the two of them, according to a local Republican named DeWitt Smith, "spent the time in telling anecdotes and in reminiscing, much to the enjoyment of the goodly number of men gathered around."[1] When it was time for the joint debate, they went to the front of the courtroom, where Lincoln had often argued legal cases before. During the preliminary speeches, he made himself at home, sitting in a hickory chair tipped back against the judge's desk, with his thumbs hooked into his suspenders.

When his turn came, he started his remarks differently than usual:

Fellow citizens: I rarely arise to address my fellow countrymen on any question of importance without experiencing conflicting emotions within me. I experience such at this hour as I have never experienced before. It is a matter of great regret to me that I have so learned, so able, and so eloquent a man as my friend Antony [sic], here to reply to what I shall say. On the other hand, I take some comfort from the fact that there are but sixteen Republicans in Shelby county, and, therefore, however poorly I may defend my cause I can hardly harm it, if I do it no good.[2]

Lincoln then delivered his speech, which lasted three hours.[3] Afterward, in the format of the joint debate, people were free to interrupt him from the audience with questions. A man named George Mitchell, who was sitting in the Republican seats, recalled that "In our section, men in the audience would yell 'Right you are!' 'That's true!' and give similar vocal support, but an equal number seemed intent on asking him what he meant by equality—the right of the Negro to vote, and such questions. Mr. Lincoln never became perturbed at all this. He towered above the crowd, looked down on them calmly and spoke to them always with ease."

"I remember," Mitchell continued, "that he inevitably went back to his statement that all men are created equal, and he explained that everybody, of whatever color, should have the right of life, liberty and the pursuit of happiness."[4] Lincoln was the only Republican to give a speech in Shelby County during the whole campaign, but in the end, hundreds voted Republican in the election.[5]

After the debate in Shelbyville, Lincoln went back to Springfield for a few days. The campaign was wearing, even for a man with his reserves of strength. His stature was rising in the state, and even the nation, but he was anything but the returning hero—just a traveling man, home for a rest. The reality of his profession was that other politicians, even the honest ones, moved effortlessly into a life of luxury as their reputation swelled, guided by worldly advice and a crash course in savoir faire. Lincoln came home from his speaking tours with no sense of aggrandizement. The same man who moved the minds of thousands with his addresses, and who probed the slave crisis more deeply than anyone, went right back to buying the groceries and mucking out the stall of his horse, Old Bob. If he had wanted to change, he would have.

William Bennett, a teenager who lived farther north on Eighth Street, remembered seeing Lincoln outside at about the time of the midsummer break. "Walking up the street by the old Lincoln residence, I saw Mr. Lincoln come out of the alleyway in the rear of the building in an antique one-horse vehicle," Bennett said, "To the old, mud-splashed spring-wagon was hitched the owner's old, rat-tailed, bay horse."

That wasn't just any rat-tailed horse, it was Old Bob. As Bennett continued, however, he remembered Lincoln "stretched out leisurely in the rig, his ample feet on the dash-board. Mrs. Lincoln was standing just inside the fence, in every-day costume of that day and with [an] animated face. It seemed that Mr. and Mrs. Lincoln were discussing some private domestic affairs. The words of the two, at my distance from them of several yards, were indistinct but very emphatic on both sides." Abraham Lincoln, Bennett recalled, "only smiled as the dialogue closed." As the vignette ended, Bennett said, "she remained standing in the yard and he drove his rat-tailed bay away and down the street."[6]

On Sundays, Mary Lincoln attended the First Presbyterian Church. Her husband sometimes joined her.[7] More usually, he went into the office and took the children along. Herndon wrote with special vigor about the Lincoln boys at the office, and the remarkable way that they got right down to business. "They pulled down all the books from the shelves, bent the points of all the pens, overturned ink-stands, scattered law-papers over the floor . . . threw the pencils into the spittoon," Herndon remarked, "it never disturbed the serenity of their father's good nature."[8]

Lincoln did have things to teach his sons. Office decorum just wasn't on the list. On one occasion at about the time of the campaign, another lawyer met Lincoln downtown with Bob, the oldest, and Tad, the youngest, in tow. Lincoln asked Tad to show the gentleman his new knife, but Tad explained that he had traded it to Bob for two pieces of penny candy. Lincoln had only to look at Bob, who immediately handed the knife back to Tad. With that, Lincoln gave each of the boys a nickel for a fresh round of candy.

The four Anderson children, Mary, Martha, Catherine, and George Junior, were in the care of one of Jane's sisters. For them, the summer was unhappy from the start, darkened as it was by the death of their father. Being separated from their mother, too, must have made it even more frightening, especially in view of the air of uncertainty that hung over her future. The family closed ranks in the aftermath of the arrest, and offered the children a busy, familiar home. They were probably cloistered on the property. Neighbors and other children were likely to have a lot to say to the youngsters regarding their mother.

While the Anderson murder couldn't remain the sizzling topic it had been in May and June, the story didn't fade away completely. The gossip about it may have made room for other tempests around town, but the anger remained. Most of the vitriol was directed against Jane Anderson. "A feeling had sprung up against the woman," affirmed Thomas Lewis, one of her lawyers.[9] She was probably despised more for the alleged adultery than even for the murder.

A murder was an aberration, to which a sympathetic motive might even be attached. Infidelity was neither as remote nor as unimaginable. Nor as forgivable. It was threatening, frightening, immoral, and—because a double standard on the subject was pronounced in the mid-nineteenth century— particularly despicable when it was perpetrated by the wife. Yet in Springfield in the mid-1850s, there was another aspect of the issue, one with its own separate morality.

The fury directed at Mrs. Anderson painted her as a housewife and mother up from poverty and content merely to dress herself up in fancy clothes . . . until her nephew arrived in the house. Part of the reason that that scenario was so incendiary in Springfield was the familiarity of its basic framework. Many families took in boarders, very commonly young men who were not yet prepared to settle down. Mary Lincoln was open to the practice, too: Stephen Smith, the twenty-seven-year-old brother of one of her brothers-in-law, would be living in the house by the end of the year, as a boarder.[10]

Young women at the time did not commonly board, but tended to remain with their families until they were themselves ready to settle down. Maids might be around, living with a family to help with the housekeeping, but the husbands were not, by and large, home alone with the maid all day long. A wife might well be with the boarder.

In the case of Springfield and other Western cities, the morality where adultery was concerned had that extra nuance: If the wives had opportunity, it was the home which would constitute the vehicle of their actions.

Not that every married woman with four children was ripe for the attentions and the passions of a young man—yet according to the prevailing suspicion, that was exactly the situation of Mrs. Anderson. If people believed it was true that she had given in to an affair, then it might be taken as a reflection of the inner desires of wives across the city with their boarders. It was a disturbing train of thought, but one that actually said less about Mrs. Anderson than about those who were so enraged by it. Still, there weren't many in the city who didn't see her that way: at fault for whatever happened between her and Theodore, and everything that happened as a result. The less the children heard of that kind of talk, the better, during the summer that their mother was locked in jail.

In mid-August, Lincoln left again, heading to a Saturday rally in the town of Oregon, in the friendlier, Republican turf of the northern part of the state. The same day, three of the party's big guns, Colonel Bissell, John M. Palmer, and Dr. Koerner, were set to hold forth at a rally in Alton.[11] Bissell, however, canceled at the last moment.

In the field at Oregon, Lincoln was second in the lineup, scheduled to speak after Long John Wentworth and before two very popular—and ribald—local favorites. He and Wentworth marched up to the grove with the procession, following behind a brass band. Tom Ferguson, a twenty-year-old, watched it go by with a kind of awe. He had never heard brass instruments before.

Lincoln was not very well-known in the northern part of the state, but Noah Brooks, an editor from a nearby town, was anxious to hear him. Brooks had been in the audience when Lincoln spoke at the ratification meeting in Dixon a month earlier. Back then, Brooks had met an old Democrat in the audience who was, Brooks said, "striking the earth with his cane as he stumped along and exclaiming, 'He's a dangerous man, sir, a d-d-dangerous man! He makes you believe what he says in spite of yourself!'"[12]

Wentworth's speech lasted for an hour-and-a-half. Those in the audience who were waiting for the ribald speakers were happy when he finished. And aghast when he bounced right back up, saying that he needed to speak for just a few more minutes. An hour later, he sat down again. "By this time," Tom Ferguson said, "I was pretty tired standing on that beautiful lawn and thought I would get out and hunt up my best girl . . . Well, I thought I would hear Lincoln a few minutes before I went in search of my girl, but those few minutes lasted all through his speech, which was about two and a half hours. We became so interested and fascinated by his wonderful talk that we forgot about our tired legs and for a time, at least, even about our best girls."[13]

After Lincoln spoke at the Oregon rally, he retreated to a spot on the lawn where he could rest. Brooks, the reporter, tagged along. Lincoln didn't mind. As Herndon once pointed out, "He never overlooked a newspaper man who had it in his power to say a good or bad thing of him."[14] Brooks was a committed Republican man—and it was a good thing that he was, if Lincoln actually said the things Brooks later claimed.

The two found a shady tree, just out of earshot of others. "Lincoln," Brooks recalled "lying flat on the ground, with his chin in his hands, talked on rather gloomily as to the present."[15] Despite the fact that Lincoln had just spoken for hours in the effort to elect John Frémont, he had apparently omitted just one thing. "He had no hope that Fremont would be elected," Brooks said.[16] Having wholeheartedly believed everything in the speech, Brooks was openly dismayed to hear the prediction of defeat in November. "As if half pitying my youthful ignorance," Brooks said of Lincoln, "but admiring my enthusiasm, he said, 'Don't be discouraged if we don't carry the day this year. We can't do it, that's certain. We can't carry Pennsylvania . . . But we shall, sooner or later, elect our president.'"[17]

Abraham Lincoln had only met Brooks that morning, just before the rally began. He couldn't have been certain that the editor could be trusted with unguarded comments. At just that time, the fashion among the newspapers was to accuse opposing party leaders of losing faith in their own candidates. "The Fremonters are disheartened," revealed an Illinois correspondent of a Democratic newspaper in St. Louis.[18] He might have been surprised to overhear Lincoln that afternoon in Oregon and learn that it was actually true.

It was true temporarily, anyway. Lincoln soldiered on in the campaign, even traveling to Michigan to deliver a speech in Kalamazoo. Although he had previously turned down the invitation to travel to Iowa for a speech, Michigan met his test: it had already been visited by out-of-state Know Nothing and Democratic speakers.

In Illinois, Lincoln couldn't always include his strongest anti-slavery remarks in his speeches, for fear of alienating old Whigs and Southern sympathizers who were stepping trepidaciously into the Republican ranks. In Michigan, he could be more direct, openly suggesting that he wasn't the only one ducking behind the expansion question, to avoid confronting the real issue:

The question is simply this:—Shall slavery be spread into the new Territories, or not? This is the naked question. If we should support Fremont successfully in this, it may be charged that we will not be content with restricting slavery in the new territories. If we should charge that James Buchanan, by his platform, is bound to extend slavery into the territories, and that he is in favor of its being thus spread, we should be puzzled to prove it. We believe it, nevertheless. By taking the issue as I present it, whether it shall be permitted as an issue, is made up between the parties. Each takes its own stand. This is the question: Shall the government of the United States prohibit slavery in the United States.[19]

As Lincoln suggested, the parties were not ready for that question, and neither was Illinois, and so he returned there to the fight that he had and the rules it imposed. His state, for its part, was attracting its own roster of guest speakers. Lincoln was probably looking forward most of all to a scheduled appearance in Springfield by Cassius Clay, a burly Kentucky Whig who had come out strongly against slavery. Clay, who was nationally famous, might hold some influence over that segment that Lincoln had himself targeted: voters who were quietly anti-slavery, though otherwise gently disposed toward the South; many of them were landing in the Know Nothing Party. In early September, Lincoln went after them yet again.

Abraham Lincoln was rarely as stealthy as he was that September, when the end of the campaign was in sight. First, he consulted with a printer, all on the sly. Next, he neatly wrote out a one-page letter of advice on the campaign, leaving blank spaces near the top for the salutation and the date. At the bottom, he wrote "(Confidential)." When he was satisfied with his workmanship, he brought the sheet to the printer, who made lithograph copies so true to the original that Lincoln could later write in the date and the name of the addressee without leaving any discernible difference between the printer's ink and his own. No one in Illinois politics had tried anything like it before. Lincoln may have invented junk mail.

Had Abraham Lincoln actually given up hope on the election of Frémont, as he told Brooks in the low moment at Oregon, he wouldn't have bothered carrying out his secret scheme with the form letters. But as he had explained in his letter to John Bennett in early August, his theory was that the only way to beat Buchanan in Illinois was for the voters in the other two parties to combine their strength. His suggestion at that time was for Mr. Bennett to see the light and take his Fillmore vote over to Frémont. In the printed letter, however, he had a far more complex scheme.

Calculating the probable electoral tally, Lincoln concluded that if Buchanan failed to win Illinois, none of the three candidates would have the majority of electoral votes necessary to win the overall election. It would be thrown to the House of Representatives, where, he said, Fillmore "may be made President by a compromise." For that reason, it followed that anyone who wanted Fillmore to be president had to block Buchanan in Illinois. According to Lincoln, however, Fillmore had no chance to win Illinois, while Frémont was close in the running, and so therefore—to come to the point—anyone truly interested in electing Fillmore would vote for Frémont:

> As Mr. Fillmore has no possible chance to carry Illinois *for himself*, it is plainly to his interest to let Fremont take it, and thus keep it out of the hands of Buchanan, Be not deceived. *Buchanan* is the hard horse to beat in this race. Let him have Illinois, and nothing can beat him; *and he will get Illinois*, if men persist in throwing away votes upon Mr. Fillmore.[20]

"This is as plain as adding up the weight of three small pigs," as Lincoln said in his form letter.[21]

The Eighth Circuit Court's fall term had begun on September 1 at the Courthouse in the town of Lincoln. For once, Abraham Lincoln's attendance on the Circuit Court was sporadic. He was making at least two political speeches per week. Having devoted much of the summer to an epic campaign, he may have been having a little trouble slowing down to the relatively tiny world of the Circuit Court. "I shall now have to get down to the practice," he said on an earlier occasion, when his dual careers clashed, "It is an easy matter to adjust a harvester to tall or short grain by raising or lowering the sickle, but it is not so easy to change our feelings and modes of expression to suit the stump or the bar."[22] He soon proved, though, that his mind wasn't entirely given over to politics, to county pluralities, and electoral stratagems.

Dr. George M. Angell, true to his word, was in the town of Lincoln, awaiting the return of the Logan County Circuit Court. The doctor from

Rhode Island still owed Abraham Lincoln money, borrowed on the April night his convoluted land deal was straightened out in the jurisprudence of the hotel room. "I found Lincoln in a barber shop," Angell said, speaking of the first week of September,

> and when the barber was through with him I told him that I was ready to pay off the note. I told him I thought it was about $15. He said he had the note in his grip [valise] at the hotel and started off almost on a run in that direction. When he had found the note he pushed it toward me and ejaculated, 'It's $16, by jingo.'"[23]

Dr. Angell didn't share Lincoln's delight. He paused and asked him if he wanted to calculate the interest. Lincoln probably caught the implication that he was a cheapskate, but he merely declined the interest without awaiting any show of gratitude. He not only remembered the debt, he was beginning to remember Dr. Angell.[24]

On September 8, a Monday, Lincoln missed the opening of the Circuit Court in Bloomington, in favor of a speaking engagement that night in Springfield. He would have to be in court the next day, though; he had a case in which he was representing his best client, the Illinois Central Railroad. Before he left Springfield, he set about mailing the first batch of the personalized form letters he had had printed, filling in the names, and then sending the sheets off to likely Know Nothing voters. One can imagine that he might have had two hundred letters printed, and intended to mail twenty-five per week until they were gone. In any case, it was his own campaign within the campaign, an effort in the later style of public relations to target trendsetters and let them spread the idea. The following weekend, Lincoln was back in Springfield, finding time to address more letters.

A good many of the letters could have been addressed to Lincoln's own friends and relatives. Many of them were anti-Nebraska, yet rejected the Republican Party. Joseph Gillespie, the exceptionally personable lawyer (and former lead miner) who had been at the Bloomington Convention, was known to have fallen away to the Know Nothings, as had John Stuart.

Benjamin Edwards, Lincoln's brother-in-law, was the most frustrating of all. Because Edwards was a prominent man and, as no one could forget, the son of a respected governor, his disposition in the election was considered news. "Mr. Edwards has hitherto been understood to be a Whig, but has for some time past," reported one paper, "been in the anxious seat."[25] It was true. In late July, Edwards wrote to Senator Trumbull, who had asked him to identify his political affiliation. Edwards returned four pages of tightly packed writing, all of it on the theme that he didn't know the answer to the question.[26] Whenever Lincoln was in town, he was sure to run into Benjamin Edwards, over whom he seemed to have the least influence of all.

Lincoln went to Bloomington and caught up with the Circuit Court. Of course, there was an ulterior motive, in the double life he was living that autumn. He was scheduled to make a speech in Bloomington at the end of the week, making a triumphant return to Major's Hall in an appearance with his rugged old friend Judge T. Lyle Dickey.

Forty-five miles to the east, a pair of horse wranglers was passing through the town of Champaign, taking a herd to the north. One of them, an eighteen year-old named Thomas Johnson, had a physical disability, but he could move around well enough, and when they stopped for the night, he made his way to a small watch shop owned by a family named Green. On his way out, he stole a solid-gold watch. He left town with it the next day. As a getaway, it left something to be desired: Johnson may have been able to hide the watch in his vest pocket, but not the small herd of horses with which he was traveling. The lawmen investigating the theft found him easily. He was arrested at noon and returned to Champaign, where he was charged the next day with larceny.[27]

The Justice of the Peace happened to be the father of Henry Whitney, Lincoln's friend on the circuit. Because Johnson couldn't afford bail, he was remanded to sit in jail until the Circuit Court arrived in nearby Urbana the following month. Before he was led away, he made a surprising request. "He was committed," Henry Whitney said, "but the boy had requested that the case be held open, till he could send for his uncle, Abraham Lincoln, to defend him."[28] Whitney's father ignored the request. With three witnesses to Johnson's presence in the shop, and the watch being found on his person,

Justice Whitney didn't figure there was anything that a lawyer could do until the Circuit Court convened.

Lincoln couldn't have come anyway. He was scheduled to give his speech that night in Major's Hall. He pleased his audience, but apparently offended his fellow speaker. At the Pike House Hotel after the speech, Judge Dickey said that he had been pained to hear Lincoln make the point that for the Union to survive, slavery would have to be either abolished or legalized everywhere. "What in God's name could induce you to promulgate such an opinion?" Dickey asked.

"Upon my soul, Dickey, I think it is true," Lincoln replied.

They argued some more, according to Dickey's account. "Suppose you are right in this opinion," Dickey said in a final attempt to make his point, "and that our government cannot last part free and part slave—what good is to be accomplished by inculcating that opinion (or truth, if you please) in the minds of the people." Lincoln began to see the point, according to Dickey. "You convince the whole people of this," Dickey continued, "and you necessarily make Abolitionists of all the people of the North and slavery proponents of all [those in the] South—and you precipitate a struggle which may end in disunion—The teaching of the opinion, it seems to me, tends to hasten the calamity."

In Dickey's recollection, Lincoln acquiesced, shaking Dickey's hand, as he admitted, "I don't see any necessity for teaching this doctrine—and I don't know but it might do harm. At all events, from respect for your judgment, Dickey, I'll promise you I won't say so again during this campaign."[29] Whether or not Lincoln was quite so thoroughly humbled, he would be inclined to take note of Dickey's point of view. As he nurtured the new party, he didn't want to lose the block of anti-expansion (yet Southern-sympathizing) voters represented by Judge Dickey if he could possibly help it.

On Saturday, Lincoln returned home. While he was at the house, he almost certainly found a message from one of his relatives about the dismaying arrest of Tom Johnson, the son of his step-brother, John. He and John were only one year apart in age, and had been raised together. John lived in Coles County, almost a hundred miles east of Springfield. Sadly,

Lincoln already knew a lot about Tom; he was in the process of defending him on a charge of stealing a gun in Coles County.

As summer was about to turn to fall, a man named Herring Chrisman arrived in Springfield with three of his friends from Chicago—and a scheme for relieving the state of some of its best land. Chrisman didn't much care about the politics swirling around his head; he was a business-man, a little sharp and very aggressive, all in a cheerful way that made him fit easily into the stampede that was Chicago. He had made a fortune trad-ing lots there, but he decided that the pace had to slow eventually, and he wanted to put his money into open lands, near Springfield. Three of his fel-low businessmen were of the same mind. "We all began to love the prairie grass and the wild flowers and the innocent joys of the quiet country life," he wrote.[30]

Only an operator such as Chrisman could, with a straight face, awaken to the innocent joys of the country life by finding a loophole in the state swamp laws that would allow him to buy prime property at wetland prices. According to his plan, he and each of his friends were to obtain 4,000 acres for the absurdly low price of $5,000. "We cast about for a lawyer to put the 'job' through,"[31] Chrisman wrote, finally settling on Abraham Lincoln since he lived in the right town and had experience in land deals.

"So down we rushed to Springfield," Chrisman recalled, "and upstairs to his office, never doubting that we virtually had four of the finest farms in our clutches to be found in the round world . . . We found the office dark and dingy, as was the fashion in those primitive days everywhere west, and very plainly furnished. A man was 'scrooched' low in a chair with his elbows on his knees and a book in his hands reading law for dear life. After quite a while he looked up and said, 'howdy.'"[32] Having found Lincoln, Chrisman explained the case and then magnanimously encouraged him to take his time, to go ahead and study the problem thoroughly. Lincoln listened po-litely and told the men to return in two weeks. By then, he would have ad-vice for them.[33]

Lincoln didn't have much of a chance to consider his opinion during the following week. Starting on Tuesday, September 16, he had to make speeches in three different cities in three days. On Wednesday, it was an all-day event in Urbana. Lincoln was one of the headline speakers in the late afternoon, but he had something other than politics on his mind. Before he was scheduled to begin, he spotted Henry Whitney wandering around and told him that he had to see him alone. "There is a boy in your jail I want to see," Lincoln said when they couldn't be overheard, "and I don't want anyone to know it, except us. I wish you would arrange with the jailer to go there, on the sly, after the meeting, and let us in."

A few hours later, Lincoln and Whitney were outside the jail, a rough-hewn monstrosity of a building considered very clever at the time. Designed to be escape-proof, the building didn't have any entrance—or exit, more important—except for a trap door in the roof. Prisoners had to use a ladder leading from the roof to the floor, a process that must have been especially difficult for Johnson. (It didn't present any problems, however, for the men who escaped through the years.) To pay Tom a visit, Lincoln and Whitney were led to the window of Johnson's cell. Whitney described the scene:

> He heard us and set up a hypocritical wailing, and thrust out toward us a very dirty Bible, which Lincoln took and turned over the leaves mechanically. He then said: "Where was you going, Tom?" The boy attempted to reply, but his wailing made it incoherent, so Lincoln cut him short by saying: "Now you do just what they tell you—behave yourself—don't talk to any one, and when court comes, I will be here and see what I can do. Now stop crying and behave yourself": and with a few more words we left, Lincoln being very sad: in fact, I never saw him more so.[34]

Over the course of the rest of the month, Lincoln divided his time between the Circuit Court and campaign appearances, though the division was not quite equal, with perhaps two days in court and the rest given over to rallies and politicking. He was beginning to stand out as the most dedicated of all the Republican speakers. And people were calling the 1856 campaign the most exciting in Illinois in sixteen years, and maybe the best of all time for shifting prospects, high stakes, and determined participants.

Lincoln was assuming greater visibility statewide than he ever had before, yet his own hometown of Springfield was far from certain for the Republicans. To improve their chances, he took part in organizing a rally in a grove in the city, on the afternoon of September 25, a Thursday. It was to be a full day for Springfield's Republicans. During the morning, the state party was meeting in an interim Convention. Then the rally in the afternoon, and finally, in the evening, a public meeting at the Courthouse.

The rally started with a procession, boasting a brass band from Chicago and a slew of banners sporting slogans such as "No Slavery in the Territories," "Illinois 20,000 for Bissell," and "Free Speech, Free Labor and Fremont."[35] The last was a shorter version of the full campaign slogan, "Free Speech, Free Press, Free Men, Free Labor, and Fremont." It was irresistibly catchy, unless, of course, one pronounced the candidate's name correctly (*Fray-mon*), according to the French.

Because party leaders were in town for the Convention, the rally featured a rare slate of political stars. Senator Trumbull himself was there as the first of the afternoon's speakers, and he was followed by the equally celebrated, though sometimes denigrated, Owen Lovejoy. Lincoln was not scheduled to speak until the evening meeting, along with Yates, Palmer, and others. At the grove, he was sitting in the audience.

Lovejoy may have been encouraged by the fact that he received three loud cheers on being introduced. On that day, he was unrestrained in his abolitionism, delivering a speech that a Democratic newspaper dismissed as "freedom shrieking."[36] It was apparently more than just shrieking. Lovejoy was a strong man physically, a Congregationalist minister with the abilities of a tent-show Evangelical, and he was hard to resist when he was at work on a platform. That may be why opponents disparaged him as something wild, as though they were, in part, a little afraid of coming under his spell. In one section of his speech at Springfield, he described the atrocities in Kansas, relating in ribbons of color how John Brown and his followers "had been killed, butchered, chopped up and thrown into their houses before their families."[37] He may have been a bit previous in describing the death of Brown (who stayed alive and whole for another three years), but it was incendiary material nonetheless.

As Lovejoy wound up his speech, there was a commotion near the plat-form. Lincoln tried to see what was going on, along with everyone else. Benjamin Edwards, middle-aged but energetic, was climbing up on the stage. Everyone knew he hated Lovejoy. Striding over to the thickset minis-ter, he put out his hand. Lovejoy, still exhilarated from the effort of speak-ing, clasped it. When Edwards realized that the audience had fallen silent at the sight, he turned and shouted, "Shake hands with Lovejoy?—I'd shake hands with the devil if he were opposed to slavery!"[38]

A tidal wave of cheering greeted Edwards' long-awaited commitment. According to a friend, Lincoln watched what happened and then "He completely broke down."[39] If Lincoln was weeping, as that friend recalled, he wasn't the only one. Rallies were designed to be stirring events. Politics was raggedly emotional in that particular election year. And the dramatic way in which Edwards came to a decision was the highpoint of the state Republican campaign up to that point. Lincoln may well have grown teary at the relief that exploded over all of Springfield's Republicans with Ed-wards' announcement.

But it was 1856. The opposition was always at the ready. The Demo-cratic newspaper in St. Louis reported the quote and delighted in "so ques-tionable a compliment" to Reverend Lovejoy, who had been, after all, equated with the devil. The paper fervently hoped that it hurt his feelings.[40]

Though Lincoln wasn't the hero of the day at the grove, his place in the party was continually growing. The perception that it was Trumbull's party was shifting. In mid-September, Reverend Julian Sturtavant, a well-mean-ing admirer from Jacksonville, Illinois, had written to Lincoln, suggesting that in return for his leadership in the party, he should be rewarded with a nomination for a Congressional seat. As it happened, it still wasn't too late for Lincoln to throw his hat into the ring. "I thank you for your good opin-ion of me personally," he wrote in a reply September 27, "and still more for the deep interest you take in the cause of our common country. It pains me a little that you have deemed it necessary to point out to me how I may be compensated for throwing myself in the breach now. This assumes that I am merely calculating the chances of personal advancement."[41] He added that if he were to run for Congress, it would hurt the party; in that, he was prob-

ably figuring that the race needed more of a Southern-leaning sort, someone anti-expansion but not necessarily anti-slavery, in order to balance the
top of the ticket.

Lincoln has to be taken at his word, regarding his attitude about personal advancement and the campaign at hand. However, he was not above
burnishing his own public image. On the night of the Springfield rally he
was to address an audience dotted with party leaders who were no less impressed than Reverend Sturtavant with all he had done to position the party
as a realistic, well-grounded alternative to the Democrats in Illinois. Anyway, he couldn't give his usual stump speech. Practically everyone in the audience had heard it before, either at the Bloomington Convention or at one
of the previous party meetings in Springfield.

Taking a new tack, Lincoln honored the record of Senator Trumbull, and
then took a detour to recall the vote in the legislature the previous year, which
put Trumbull in office. "He said that he himself would have loved to have
been elected," a reporter noted, "and that there were several of his friends who
would have voted for him till doomsday, if he had said so, but that rather than
his opponents should succeed he told them to go for Trumbull."[42] That had,
indeed, been a noble moment. And apparently, he didn't want it to be forgotten. Legends, as Lincoln knew full well, have to be helped along.

Herring Chrisman returned to Springfield from Chicago, as Lincoln had
requested, two weeks to the day after their first meeting. "By that time,"
Chrisman recalled, "I had come to fairly dote on country life and prairie
grass and 4,000 acres in a farm."[43] He had sold out his interests in Chicago,
and was ready to move. Feeling fine, he asked Lincoln how they were going
to proceed with his idea for buying farmland from the government at
swampland prices. "You can't do it," Lincoln said bluntly. Chrisman was
stunned. Had Lincoln been willing at least to try, the fee would have been
in the neighborhood of one thousand dollars.

"Who ever heard of an attorney refusing a fat case before?" Chrisman
later wrote, "I could not have done that myself."[44] As he stood in the office,

however, he didn't waste time erasing the blue sky and prairie grass from his mind's eye; instead, he was immediately suspicious that Lincoln intended to demand a huge fee for the advice rendered. Chrisman decided in his mind that fifty dollars was absolutely the most he would pay without a fight. He asked Lincoln to name the fee. "When he said it was $5," Chrisman said, "I paid it and went out. When I reached the street I began to feel ashamed of myself for accepting his work for so mere a pittance."[45] A few weeks later, Chrisman bought a large tract elsewhere in the state, at the normal prices.

Near the end of the month, Abraham Lincoln returned to the circuit, juggling cases with appearances as best he could. On Monday, he was in Pekin, arguing John Scates' appeal of the $25 judgment against him the previous year. It was the case that started when Scates' cattle broke into Philip Davin's barnyard. Lincoln and a local lawyer had argued the appeal once before, the previous May, but the jury then was unable to reach a decision. Scates, Lincoln's client, didn't think he should have to pay the $25. In the re-trial on Monday, ten witnesses came to Pekin from their homes twenty miles away. Since it took all day to travel that far, even in good weather, the trial represented a three-day effort for each of them, involving expenses for meals and hotel rooms as well.

Scates and Davin must have been a cantankerous pair. The court fees alone added up to over fifty dollars for the three trials—far more than the judgment itself. Lincoln's usual method would have been to bring them to a settlement before the trial; if he tried, though, he failed. Lincoln and his co-counsel ultimately won the appeal, and Philip Davin—the unwilling host to the wayward cattle—ended up receiving nothing and owing the court money.[46]

The very next evening, Lincoln was scheduled to address two thousand people in a rally in the town of Lacon, about thirty-five miles up the Illinois River from Pekin. The easiest and quickest way to get there was by boat. During the hectic campaign season, so inconveniently scheduled during the Circuit Court fall term, there was no means of transportation that Lincoln did not employ. It was trying, hour after hour, day after day, but ultimately, it was for the good. Lincoln may have craved the stimulation of the exciting campaign, but his mind seemed to require its own form of exercise, a kind of reordering through the logic upon which he depended. The benefit of long rides on road, water, or the rails was that he had the chance to think things all the way through, and then start again and rethink them from some other point of view. The hectic events of the campaign of 1856 alternated in a balanced way with long spans of silence, *en route,* a combination that likely contributed to Lincoln's performance.

On the first of October, the day after Lincoln's address at Lacon, people throughout the state focused their attention on Alton, located on the Mississippi River near St. Louis. All the roads leading to Alton were clogged with vehicles, from carts to commercial wagons.[47] The people were going to the state fair.

Despite the fact that the air was cold and raw, it was still the first day of the fair and Illinoisans wanted to see the giant pears, the championship-caliber Durham cows, and rare dahlias entered in the judging. There was a pavilion for artwork and an extensive show of farm machinery.[48] Politicians were going to be on display, too, across the five days of the fair, ready to be judged along with the rest of the state's produce.

As soon as Senator Douglas scheduled a speech for Wednesday night, he was the headline attraction of what was billed as a "Democratic celebration." Alton was in the southern part of the state, which had become Douglas' most solid source of support. Overall, though, the people in those carts and wagons waiting to get into the grounds included a healthy proportion of those Douglas-hating former Whigs that Lincoln wanted desperately to snatch from the Know Nothing grasp.

The Republicans had their celebration scheduled for Thursday night at the fair, but Lincoln couldn't be present. He had legal papers to file in a paternity suit in Springfield the next day. He couldn't skip the State Fair. Yet he couldn't miss the court filing. The best he could do was to try to arrange to speak on Thursday afternoon. So it was that on Thursday morning, he was jammed into an over-crowded train on the way down from Springfield. He was lucky to get into a car at all. When there wasn't any more room, a lot of people were left behind, watching the train leave with long faces that had once been looking forward to a day at the fair.[49]

Senator Douglas had his own problems getting to Alton, and he missed the Democratic celebration altogether on Wednesday night. As a result, on Thursday morning, he and Lincoln were both heading toward the grounds, hoping to salvage something there out of the confusion left by their ruinous schedules. The best that could be done for Lincoln was "an impromptu meeting assembled in front of the Presbyterian Church."[50] In other words, he was just supposed to climb up on the steps and start talking to the street until people stopped to listen. Another party member, in a gallant gesture, volunteered to go first.

Meanwhile, Senator Douglas was relegated to a far corner of the fair grounds, waiting to speak while a forlorn man circulated through the crowds in the pavilions, announcing the appearance. About five hundred people straggled along after him. Lincoln and Douglas, 1856: standing on street corners and trying to steal attention away from the Durhams and giant pears. But they were used to it; humiliation being one part of the trade they both knew well.

George T. Brown, the editor of the *Alton Courier*, was running himself ragged during fair week, but he managed to file a long article on Thursday's Republican activities. Brown was part of the inner circle of the party. He had been at the Decatur meeting that launched it in February, and at the Bloomington Convention as a delegate. He knew that his article on the party's day at the fair would be read by every person who participated in it.

A respectable number of people were standing in front of the Presbyterian Church by the time Lincoln looked out and began to speak. It grew quickly after that and over the course of his talk, he won the attention of a large crowd. Then he hustled to catch the evening train home to Springfield. The next morning, he was in his office on the square, writing an affidavit and preparing to go to court in the paternity suit. Back in Alton, people were opening the *Courier*, and reading the description it contained of Lincoln and the "old line whigs, who acknowledge him as their leader in this State."[51]

That may have come as news to some of the other politicians at the meeting, but no one could deny that a great many people, Whig and otherwise, were going along with Lincoln. It was an exciting time for a politician in any of the parties, and daunting, with the threat of disunion hanging over every vote. But it had been a glorious summer for Abraham Lincoln. The Republican Party in Illinois had before it only a narrow track to success, not much more than a tightrope, really, and Lincoln had taken the largest role in keeping the party well-balanced and on that track.

It was noticed. A speaker at a Peoria rally who just mentioned Lincoln's name had to pause for several minutes of spontaneous cheering. Lincoln hadn't yet even been to Peoria during the campaign.[52] People were referring to the state's Republican party as "Lincoln & Company." Physically, Lincoln was thriving in the midst of the progress, however pressured it was. "Old Abe," noted a reporter, "looks as hearty as a bull—and feels doubtless much heartier than a certain buck we know of.* He seems to be growing younger and taller and—we positively believe it—handsomer."[53] Others made the same observation. "When Lincoln was on the stump, in 1856," recalled the editor Noah Brooks, "his face, though naturally sallow, had a rosy flush. His eyes were full and bright, and he was in the fullness of health and vigor."[54] The only problem Lincoln had was that he had made so many speeches, which is to say, shouted so many speeches, that he began to lose his voice.

In early October, however, the glorious momentum that he'd orchestrated for himself and the party seemed to get tangled up. Someone showed one of Lincoln's confidential form letters to a Know Nothing newspaper. *The Conservative,* a newspaper in Springfield, soon reprinted it.

The Conservative had been launched earlier that year, ostensibly as a Know Nothing paper, to complement Springfield's other two papers, the *State Journal* (Republican) and the *Register* (Democratic). Lincoln privately contended, though, that the *Conservative* was funded by rich Democrats, only to keep Know Nothing votes from going to the Republicans. Yet the *Conservative* had always treated Lincoln kindly—until October 9, when it printed his lithographed letter, with an introduction calling it a "contemptible subterfuge."[55] The matter didn't end there. Papers around the state picked up the story and aired that copy of the letter, or others that suddenly

---

* James Buchanan was known as "Buck."

came out of desk drawers once the word "confidential" at the bottom had been breached. One friendly editor went out of his way in the midst of it all to defend Lincoln against charges that he had lied in the letter, in a ploy to get votes; "One of Mr. Lincoln's distinguishing traits is his honesty," admonished the editor, "He never says, public or private, what he does not himself believe."[56]

Lincoln was called a lot of names amid the firestorm. One man (one of the kinder ones) even looked to the 1840s, when Lincoln spoke in favor of Henry Clay for the presidency: "In those times," he wrote, "you never hoped to carry Illinois, but did you desert your leader and go over to the strong side? No sir!"[57] Everyone who wrote such things missed Lincoln's point: a Know Nothing who sincerely wanted Fillmore would vote for Frémont. Nobody grasped it. For that reason, Lincoln may have ignored the criticism and been glad that in the end the controversy gave the letter an even wider circulation than he'd originally hoped. He certainly stood by his reasoning. Unabashed, he kept sending out his letter, right up to the election.

Not all of the derision aimed at Lincoln could be traced to the controversy over the letter, but it did seem to escalate in the aftermath. Perhaps the fact that he inspired detractors was a sign of his growing fame. In mid-October, Lincoln visited the town of Eureka, sixty miles north of Springfield. A college of the same name had opened its doors the year before, and Lincoln was invited to deliver a speech in the chapel. The evening was mild, lit by clear moonlight, and the windows of the chapel were open. A group of about twenty-five men and boys were outside on the lawn, waiting to hear what was happening inside. They were sitting comfortably enough and those entering the crowded chapel assumed that they hadn't been able to find seats inside that they liked.

As soon as Lincoln was introduced and began to speak, the little crowd outside began to chant, "Hurray for Fillmore! Hurray for Fillmore!" One of the people in the audience described what happened next:

Lincoln paid no attention to them. In a few minutes, he put those of us who filed into the room into a tumult of laughter and cheering, by an anecdote. In a few minutes it happened again, and the rowdies outside began to gather about the open windows to see what was going on. Soon they were all looking in at the windows and listening as interestedly as the rest of us.[58]

Eureka was a triumph, but Lincoln had other kinds of luck with audiences, too. A correspondent for the *Missouri Republican* saw him appear at an event where the audience was largely Democratic. Most of the spectators were milling around without listening. Lincoln made a start, but then, "throwing up his hands in disgust and despair, said—'Oh, I can't interest this crowd,' and left the stand."[59] The story is off-putting, reflecting Lincoln in a bilious frame of mind, and it is tempting to dismiss it as nothing more than the work of an opposition paper, yet the *Missouri Republican,* though Democratic in its leanings, normally did a creditable job in reporting. And after all, even in a great season, there are those days.

CHAPTER 12

OCTOBER AND NOVEMBER

A MOTIVE EQUAL TO MURDER

As October wound down, only a few of the big rallies were left. Lincoln was undoubtedly tired, but he was still trying to appear at as many of the smaller events as possible. Of the smattering of letters that survive from his hand during the last weeks of the campaign, one in particular gives an impression of his effort to scrape together every last pocket of support for the party. The note, written to a state senator who had invited him to speak in a small town, ran, in its entirety, "I write this to apologize for not being with you to-day. I was forced off to Pike County, where I spoke yesterday, and I have just returned. *Be assured I could not help it.*"[1]

In the muddier, meaner trenches of the campaign, the slanderous attacks were escalating, especially against Colonel Bissell. He was still considered the frontrunner for the governorship, despite the fact that he had made only one or two public appearances, one of which was from the seat of a buggy. He apparently had the support of a majority of Know Nothings, who didn't have their own candidate running against him. That helped pull the Know Nothings closer to the Republicans. The Democrats, for their part, were aghast at the prospect of losing the governorship to the upstart party. They accused Bissell of owning slaves, but to no avail. And they started the rumor that at any minute Colonel Bissell was going to quit the race and leave it to Abraham Lincoln, as part of Bissell's plan to make a run for the Senate in 1858. When that rumor withered, the Democrats even helped a group of willing Know Nothings put up a gubernatorial candidate of their own. All of it to no avail.

Finally, as October was winding down, the Democrats left the gentleman's code behind. They called Colonel Bissell an invalid, who hadn't energy enough to speak at a rally. They openly questioned how he could hope to run a government in his condition. On that point, they finally succeeded, and people started to wonder about Colonel Bissell.

One of the last of the big rallies of the campaign was staged in Belleville, in the very southern part of the state. Lincoln would be there, as a keynote speaker. Colonel Bissell was also scheduled to speak,[2] but then that was not unique; he had been slated for major speeches in the past. He just canceled at the last minute.

Although Belleville was only ten miles from the slave state of Missouri across the Mississippi River, it was an anti-slavery stronghold, due to its large German population. Germans in the 1850s tended to bring a liberal cast to the communities in which they settled, many of them having left their native country because of the rise of reactionary elements there. Dr. Koerner, the German-born lieutenant governor, lived in Belleville, and so did Senator Trumbull, when he wasn't in Washington. And so did Colonel Bissell.

When Lincoln arrived, Dr. Koerner served as his host, taking him from home to home, introducing him to Republican families in town. In the early evening, a torchlight procession led them both to the site of the rally, in company with about five thousand other people. That was more than the population of Belleville.

Voters were not the only ones at the Belleville rally. "A great many ladies, a novelty thus far at a political meeting in this region, had turned out," recalled Dr. Koerner in his memoir, "and we had provided for them long benches in front of the speaker."[3] Women had become actively involved in the campaign up in Chicago, but in the more rural, southern part of the state, politics was generally regarded as a male domain.

Colonel Bissell managed to make his speech, reclining on a sofa brought onto the stage for his benefit, and he was robust enough verbally, if not physically, to turn back all doubts. Lincoln delivered the mature incarnation of his campaign address, unveiled at the Bloomington Convention, and tempered by at least fifty renditions since. An editor who had heard Lincoln at Bloomington and at other meetings since said that he had only grown stronger. One of the points Lincoln had added along the way underscored the differences between the Democrats and Republicans. "He showed that there are only two parties,"[4] summarized one account. It was a further means of establishing the new party permanently in the minds of the voters, and shunting the Know Nothings completely off the field.

Dr. Koerner was as impressed by Lincoln's speech that day as was a certain local editor, who called it "one of the most thrilling bursts of eloquence ever uttered in behalf of Liberty and the roiling millions."[5] Koerner, however, was not that effusive by nature. Perhaps no one was. In his restrained way, Koerner described how Lincoln "spoke in an almost conversational tone, but with such earnestness and such deep feeling upon the question of the day that he struck the hearts of all his hearers."[6] The audience must have loved him, in view of what happened next.

Aware that the speech was going well, Lincoln looked over the audience and felt inspired to "call down the blessings of the Almighty on their heads," in the words of the reporter for the *Belleville Weekly Advocate*.[7] Dr. Koerner picked up the story: "Referring to the fact that here, as well as in other places where he had spoken, he had found the Germans more enthusiastic for the cause of freedom than all other nationalities, he, almost with tears in his eyes, broke out in the words: 'God bless the Dutch!'"[8]

Unfortunately, they weren't Dutch. By and large, Germans took umbrage at the nineteenth-century American habit of calling everyone from the Austrians to the Bavarians to the Swiss—to the Dutch—by the same umbrella name.

The people in the audience loved Lincoln after the speech he'd delivered, and "no one took offense," according to Dr. Koerner, who added, however, that "a smart politician would not have failed to say 'Germans.'"[9]

In that, the erudite Dr. Koerner made his own misstep. Abraham Lincoln was a smart politician. He made a slip, easily forgotten by everyone (save a fellow politician), but that was nothing. He was banking everything he knew and everything he was on the 1856 campaign. And to that end, he was aware as October came to a close that he was within a few weeks of finding find out just how smart he was.

On October 20, Lincoln was in Urbana for the opening of the Circuit Court's fall term there. The town was already crowded, if only because *Spink v. Chiniquy* was on the docket. Father Chiniquy, the priest accused of slander by Peter Spink, was to be tried the next day. "All came to our county," groaned Henry Whitney, who lived in Urbana, "camp-outfits, musicians, parrots, pet dogs and all."[10] Lincoln was probably dreading *Spink,* a case that had gone much further than it ought to have. A lot had happened to Chiniquy since May, when Lincoln had first defended him (only to have the proceeding end in a mistrial before the eleven-man jury). In the first place, Chiniquy wasn't a priest anymore, having been dismissed in August by his bishop. In the second place, he wasn't a Roman Catholic anymore. He had been excommunicated in September. Church officials wouldn't disclose their reasons, though they implied that his morality where women were concerned was less than pure. For his part, he contended that they were just trumping up charges in retaliation for his righteous independence.

Lincoln had other business with the court as well, and a veritable assault of invitations for speaking engagements. Yet neither that nor even *Spink v. Chiniquy* was his first thought as he strode into the courtroom on Monday. "I shall never forget," said William H. Somers, a newly elected official, "the time nor his kindly act when, sitting at my desk in the capacity of clerk of the court, on opening day, with judge and lawyers taking their accustomed places preparatory to commencing the day's business, he approached me with extended hand, and, grasping mine cordially, in a few pleasant words congratulated me on my election."[11] Lincoln's interest in Somers' success was typical; it was said that he knew the names of more people along the circuit than any other person. That might have been another example of his constant campaigning, according to his more cynical friends, but it was his way, nonetheless.

Judge Davis was at the front of the courtroom, preparing to open the fall term. Meanwhile, Amzi McWilliams, the state's attorney, had arrived with a full roster of cases for the day. Before the start of court, he went to the bench and conferred with Judge Davis. A little later he sought out Henry Whitney, the lawyer who made his home in Urbana. McWilliams brought up the case of Lincoln's step-nephew, Tom Johnson, the teenager who was charged with stealing a solid-gold watch from the Green family's shop. McWilliams said that he and Davis had discussed the circumstances under which the charges would be dropped and he, as state's attorney, would declare the case *nolle prosequi* if certain requirements were met. "They had agreed that if the Greens would come into court," Whitney said, "and state that they did not desire to prosecute further, he could *nol. pros.* the case."[12]

Whitney passed the information along to Lincoln, who was all too familiar with the procedure. The local judge in Coles County was making the same stipulation, regarding the gun that Johnson had stolen there. Lincoln absorbed the news from Henry Whitney, but that was about all he had time to do. Over the next few days, his schedule was simple: just about anytime that he wasn't in court, a crowd somewhere would be waiting for him to speak. One of them was in Quincy, all the way across the state on the Mississippi River. To travel there in time to speak on Thursday, he would have to finish all of his casework by Tuesday night, so that he could leave on Wednesday morning.

The slander charge against Father Chiniquy—Mr. Chiniquy, as of August—came up in court on Monday. After a jury was seated, the prosecution witnesses began to testify against him. Chiniquy's memoirs are only occasionally coincident with the facts, where the facts are otherwise known, but according to Chiniquy, the trial soon turned away from his allegedly slanderous sermon to his relations with women. A fellow priest took the stand

and charged that Chiniquy "had attempted to do the most infamous things with my own sister."[13] In cross-examination, Lincoln tried his best to call the testimony into question, but even so, he wasn't happy with the direction of the trial.

That evening, Lincoln addressed a rally at the Courthouse in Urbana.[14] The Chiniquy trial resumed the next day. Lincoln had probably arrived in Urbana hopeful of finding some compromise in the case, but on the contrary, it was only becoming more thickly crisscrossed with accusations. With the momentum going against his client, he had to give up hope of a simple resolution. He was faced with no choice but to send a slightly annoyed letter to the sponsor of the rally in Quincy: "I am here at court," he wrote, "and find myself so hobbled with a particular case, that I can not leave & consequently can not be with you on the 23rd, I regret this exceedingly, but there is no help for it."[15] After another day in court, trying the Chiniquy case, Lincoln went with his friend Henry Whitney to a political meeting at a church in the town of Champaign.

Very few people in 1856 had heard more words on the subjects of Kansas, John Frémont, and the extension of slavery than Abraham Lincoln. Sitting through at least two speeches for every one that he gave, he had heard literally millions of words over the course of the campaign. He no doubt learned to gauge at a glance the lasting power of every other speaker. On that basis, looking over his fellow speakers, he decided he had plenty of time to duck out of the Champaign rally in company with Whitney. He wouldn't have any other opportunity to speak with Mr. and Mrs. Green.

"Lincoln and I left the meeting," Whitney said, "and made our way to the humble residence of these people. They were a venerable old couple and we found them seated in their humble kitchen, greatly astonished at our visit." The couple may not have been quite as wizened as he made out; Mrs. Green was only fifty-six and her husband sixty-eight. Whitney told them the reason for the visit and then, as he said, he "introduced Lincoln, who stated his position and wishes in the matter in a homely, plain way."[16] The watch that Johnson had stolen was worth $125, perhaps a month's profit for the watch store. Lincoln knew that he was asking a lot in hoping that the couple would waive the charge. The Greens had a teenager of their own, though, and they tried to understand that Tom Johnson had made a boyish mistake. After a further discussion, they agreed to go to the Circuit Court the next day to testify in favor of dropping the charges.

Lincoln left the Greens' house and returned to the church, where he had yet to be missed. When it was his turn, he arose and gave a well-received address. Afterward, he had a slow trip over dark roads back to Urbana and his hotel. By any standards, he had put in a long day.

According to Chiniquy, however, Lincoln's day wasn't over. Long after midnight, Chiniquy was lying awake in his room at the hotel, in a state of wretched anguish. That was not, by itself, unusual for him. "At 3 A.M.," he wrote, "I heard three knocks at my door and I quickly went to open it. Who was there? Abraham Lincoln, with a face beaming with joy!" In Chiniquy's version, someone had arrived from Chicago with evidence that the testimony against him was suborned, that women were being bribed with "eighties," or eighty-acre tracts of land, to accuse him of philandering. Lincoln learned of the new evidence in the middle of the night and told Chiniquy that the case against him was crumbling.[17]

The story may contain a glimmer of truth, though one would expect that if Chiniquy had any such hard evidence against his accusers, he'd have filed a counter suit with glee. Instead, he and Spink allowed Lincoln to write an agreement by which Spink dropped the slander charges and Chiniquy renounced any impression he may have left that Spink was a perjurer. With that, the case was dismissed and the city of Urbana emptied out, as Chiniquy's followers gathered their musical instruments and their pets, and returned to Kankakee.

Tom Johnson's case ended just about the same way. The Greens presented themselves in court, as promised. Amzi McWilliams filed a motion to dismiss the case, and with that Tom Johnson was freed: hauled up bodily from the doorless jailhouse. He may have presented a pitiable picture, pulled up from the dark like a kitten from a well, but Lincoln probably thought he needed more warning than sympathy, telling him roughly the same thing he'd said to Whitney when the case first arose, in the wake of the gun-stealing charge: "I shall do what I can for him in these two cases, but that's the last. After that, if he wants to be a thief, I shan't help him any more."[18]

The three overstuffed days in Urbana weren't typical of the whole autumn of 1856 for Lincoln, but they did reflect the juggling he had to do to stay in two careers at once. On the last weekend before election day, he was winding up the campaign by speaking at his last big rally. He wasn't far from home, only in the city of Jacksonville, in the next county to the west from Sangamon. Herndon was along, too. Lincoln probably traveled home with him that evening, weary in the satisfaction that he had left nothing undone for the sake of the party.

People in Springfield weren't sorry to see the campaigns ending with October; November promised to be even more exciting. First, there was Election Day, on the fourth, which would have the air of a holiday, although the drama of the whole thing wouldn't end until the results rolled in toward the end of the week. For real suspense, though, the city was awaiting the fall term of the Circuit Court and the trial of the Anderson murder case. Mrs. Anderson and Theodore had been in jail since June. Amzi McWilliams had been continuing his investigation, with success in finding new witnesses. He was a lame duck, though, even before the election; his own Democratic Party had declined to re-nominate him. Everyone knew that he had been, in effect, fired by his own party. His natural irritability was therefore easier than ever to trip, as he pushed through a palpable lack of confidence wherever he went.

Emotions over the Anderson murder case were running high, even among people who hadn't known the victim. Strangers, including some very influential ones, had already tried the case in their own minds, and were incensed at the prospect of two adulterers getting away with murder. The challenge lay in coaxing the court to try it with the same result, and as a means to that end, a collection was taken to pay for the engagement of another prosecutor. In Central Illinois at the time, one hundred dollars was considered a good fee for a single trial; the collection for the new prosecutor was such a success, it endowed a fee of two hundred. Since Amzi McWilliams was still the official state's attorney, he was given the choice of his "assistant." He decided to ask Abraham Lincoln, his only remaining friend in the Springfield bar.

On Election Day, Tuesday, November 4, some men went to the polls believing that the national election was a contest over the potential expansion of slavery into the West. That described Lincoln. He cast his vote early in the day, for Frémont. Others believed the election was about the races in America. John Stuart was in that category, and he cast his vote for Fill, the Know Nothing candidate. According to his good friend, Joe Gillespie, he "profoundly believed in the superiority of the Caucasian family, and would rather endure the evils of slavery than what [he] thought would be the ruin of the white race."[19] Stuart wasn't, of course, among those who had to endure the evils of slavery, but in terms of political strategy for 1856, voters with his point of view were entirely lost to the new Republican Party.

"Many educated and, otherwise, sensible persons appeared to believe that emancipation meant social equality,"[20] scoffed Ulysses Grant, as though answering the likes of John Stuart—and as though he himself was far too reasonable to conclude anything so absurd. Yet Grant was an enlightened man, compared to many others. And while he agreed with the Republicans, he nonetheless voted with the Democrats. "With a Democrat elected by the unanimous vote of the Slave States, there could be no pretext for secession for four years," he wrote, "I very much hoped that the passions of the people would subside in that time, and the catastrophe be averted altogether."[21] Grant and other voters of his ilk were a genuine loss to the Republicans. They believed in the platform, but were afraid of the party: afraid it would tear the country apart.

The 1856 election was all about slavery, ultimately subsuming the anti-Catholic movement. Yet it was the peripheral issues that sorted voters into different categories. The electorate shied from a clash over the real question, and politicians followed suit in focusing the debate on the side issues. Lincoln was as careful as any to avoid offending voters so easily frightened by the enormity of the passion behind the central issue. He was able to go fur-

ther than most, speaking to the morality of slavery, without quite impugn-
ing its legality in the South. More often, he concentrated instead on the an-
cillary issues, such as expansion into the West and the threat of disunion.

The Democrat Buchanan ultimately won the presidential election and
gave those who yearned for it a little hope—for a miracle, perhaps, or anything else that might obviate the slavery crisis and remove the specter of
secession. Anyway, he gave them four years in which to be "better prepared to receive the shock and resist it," as Grant said.[22] Frémont, who
lost the race, won enough Northern states to establish the Republicans
there. A party member in Philadelphia even termed it a "victorious defeat" for the Republicans, adding "They have not got a President, but they
have what is better, a North."[23]

In the state of Illinois, Buchanan beat Frémont, but not badly. The final
outcome was astonishingly close to that which Lincoln had predicted in
August:

Illinois Presidential Voting, 1856

Candidate	Actual Result[24]	Lincoln's Prediction[25]
Buchanan (Democrat)	105,528 (44.1 percent)	85,000 (46.2 percent)
Frémont (Republican)	96,278 (40.2 percent)	78,000 (42.4 percent)
Fillmore (Know Nothing)	37,531 (15.7 percent)	21,000 (11.4 percent)

The scenario over which Lincoln had fretted since July came to pass, in that
the combined votes of Frémont and Fillmore would have defeated
Buchanan. Had Frémont received even half of Fillmore's Know Nothing
votes, he could have defeated Buchanan in Illinois. Lincoln certainly did his
best to wrest them away. But even if he had succeeded, Frémont still would
have lost the national election.

The Republicans in Illinois were jubilant, nonetheless, with the election
of Colonel Bissell as governor, and the concomitant defeat of Senator
Douglas' hand-picked Democratic candidate. For all of the attacks on Bissell—and the ones that could have been made had the secret of his religion
been known—his election boosted Republican fortunes in the state enormously. Lincoln was openly regarded as the man to take them even further;

without Bissell's victory, though, Lincoln would not have had the base of power that he required for 1858 and 1860.

"Well," wrote Theodore Parker, a Boston Republican, to William Herndon, "the cause of American democracy was in less terrible peril November 17, 1776 than November 17, 1856."[26] Lincoln probably would have agreed. During the span of his political career, slavery survived because no major party had had the will to fight it. Lincoln watched it survive in 1856 because the electorate was afraid of the future and in disarray as a result. "The repeal of the Missouri Compromise will lead to civil war"—the sign that was scrawled on Wickhizer's wall in Bloomington—was the single source of fear on all sides. Practically everyone had a different reaction, but it was the specter of disunion that made them scatter. With the establishment of the Republican Party, the disarray was set to subside. Lincoln could come in from the peripheries of the debate and then shape it along the lines that reflected his reasoning.

The fall term of the Sangamon County Circuit Court was due to open three weeks after the election. In mid-November, Benjamin S. Edwards, John Stuart's law partner, wrote a long letter to his daughter, and after describing the shenanigans revolving around various family birthday celebrations, he thought about his work, and commented, "Next week the session of the Circuit Court commences and I shall be very much engaged, possibly for four weeks. Mrs. Anderson will be tried on next week. All hope that she will be acquitted."[27] Certainly Edwards hoped she would be acquitted; he was one of her lawyers.

The defense team in *People v. Anderson and Anderson* was formidable, totaling six attorneys. Officially, Theodore had two lawyers, the tenacious Stephen Logan and John Rosette, fairly new to Springfield but known for his competence. Mrs. Anderson was represented by the two partners, John Stuart and Benjamin Edwards, along with Thomas Lewis, a lawyer with a sprightly intelligence, and the workmanlike William Campbell. As a team, it boasted just about all of Springfield's strongest lawyers.

Arrayed opposite them was Amzi McWilliams. He faced a number of cases before he left his job as state's attorney, but the Anderson murder was the only one that could make a difference to his reputation. Three years before, he had been a prominent lawyer in Bloomington.[28] In 1855, McWilliams had moved to Springfield. "The same success attended him here," said a Springfield resident, "and had it not been for an unfortunate temper he would have left a highly honorable and proud record."[29] As it was, he was a prosecutor down to his last few weeks of work in Springfield. McWilliams looked to Abraham Lincoln to augment his most important effort, the Anderson murder case.

Lincoln liked McWilliams and could handle his temper. Once, a witness was giving evidence in court that McWilliams considered inadmissible, and so he impatiently shouted, "No! No! No !!!" Lincoln, as opposing counsel, didn't lose a beat, interjecting, "Oh, Yes! YES! YES!!!" Henry Whitney, who was present in the courtroom, recalled that Lincoln was "looking daggers at McWilliams, who quailed under Lincoln's determined look."[30] The friendship survived the explosion, and McWilliams turned to Lincoln first when he needed help in the prosecution of the upcoming trial. In the Springfield crisis of the Anderson murder, the time had come for Lincoln to take one side or the other.

Lincoln had only prosecuted one case before. He happened to be in Tazewell County in 1853 when a little girl was raped. A mob captured the man who was apparently responsible and threatened to throw him in a river with a weight tied around his neck unless he confessed. He said he would, if he were assured of a fair trial. After the confession, a speedy trial was regarded as crucial, and so Lincoln was hastily recruited to serve as prosecutor. He won the conviction in that case,[31] but generally, he wasn't disposed by training or inclination to put people in jail. Lincoln turned McWilliams down.

As a lawyer, Lincoln had a quirk that might be looked upon as a professional failing. In a criminal trial, he couldn't represent a client in whom he didn't believe. Somers, the clerk in Urbana, was one of many who made the same assessment: "No counsel more able or advocate more eloquent ever espoused a just cause," Somers said, "On the wrong side of a case, it is true, he was weak, because he could not be forcible if he believed himself in the wrong—his head and his heart must go together . . . In a case tried in my county, after he had heard the evidence, he said to his associate, 'The man is guilty. You defend him. I cannot.'"[32]

Fifty years on, Thomas Lewis was fond of recalling his days in Illinois in the 1840s and 1850s. In his experience, so he said, the interest generated in the Anderson case was never equalled. Perhaps that is one of the reasons that Abraham Lincoln chose to remain home during the interim between Election Day and the start of the term in Springfield. A big train was coming.

As Lewis remembered those days leading up to the trial, he tended to mix up the lawyers on the defense team, but he can be forgiven that. There were so many of them. Overlooking Campbell altogether, Lewis said that Mrs. Anderson "employed Logan, Edwards & Lewis to defend. She raised $300 and gave each attorney $100. Conscious as [we] were of the innocence of the parties, we offered Abraham Lincoln $25 each, making the fees $75 each."

The gesture didn't necessarily reflect any sense of panic; recruitment of an attorney with only weeks to spare wasn't unique in Lincoln's era. The defense was bolstering itself with the qualities that distinguished Lincoln in trial work: his ease before a jury, his uncanny way with a witness, and his sense of strategy. His unrivalled understanding of Judge Davis presented a further asset. If the team wasn't precisely sure at the outset what Lincoln would contribute, it was a good bet that he would be useful at some point.

Lincoln set his rates according to the job, not the time expended, but overall, he seemed to aim for fees totalling five to ten dollars per hour. The Anderson case was likely to be a money-loser, according to that scale; with predictions of a three-week trial, he could look forward to earning a dollar an hour at best.

People v. Anderson & Anderson was a big case, though: big in every way. For infamy, Springfield had never seen anything like it—and wouldn't through the rest of the century.[33] For complexity, it was far more interesting than the average property case, at least to a student of human nature. For both of those reasons, the Anderson murder trial had developed into a kind of lawyer's showcase. It ought to have been appealing to Abraham Lincoln, but he had already turned it down once when the prosecution offered him a role. No one in the city was immune to the fascination of the incendiary case, though, and the demand it made for a passionate opinion, one way or the other. Even Lincoln, who had been away at the time of the crime itself and through most of the aftermath, had his own immutable feeling about it.

"Lincoln accepted," Lewis continued, "He said he would sooner defend the woman for nothing than prosecute her for $200."[34] Though Lewis' story turns on the fact that Mrs. Anderson paid Lincoln's salary, a newspaper report of the day listed him as counsel for Theodore. The lawyers apparently made no distinction among themselves, working as a team, and so it may have been difficult for the reporter to tell who was working for whom. The more significant aspect of the recruitment of Lincoln is that he believed that Mrs. Anderson and Theodore were innocent. That must have come as a breeze of good news for the defendants, in the stillness of their cells. Lincoln's place on the defense team wasn't to be overestimated, though, least of all by himself. Lincoln was, as usual in the legal sphere, in good company, but only as a star among even bigger stars.

On the first day of the Sangamon County fall term, November 17, Presco Wright was the assistant to the retiring clerk—James Matheny, with his undisciplined handwriting and tendency to drip ink. Presco had won election as the county court clerk in November's elections and his days as a mere assistant were numbered. John Cook, the former mayor, was employed again, too, having been elected sheriff. During the trial, he and his deputies would transfer the prisoners and take charge of the floor.

The term opened on Monday afternoon in the courtroom, a great hollow of a space with little in the way of decoration, located on the second story of the Courthouse. Three cases led the docket: one case of larceny, and two of failure to keep the peace. After that, there was the murder case.

Matheny called *People v. Anderson & Anderson* on Tuesday morning. Judge Davis was presiding from the bench; as he looked over the court, McWilliams was sitting at one table. At another, the defense lawyers crowded each other in a row: Rosette, looking younger than his thirty-three years; Lincoln; Stuart, ever animated; Lewis; Campbell, and Logan, looking like a fox with his long hair swept back from the small features of his face.

When John Cook escorted Theodore Anderson into court, he sat at one end of the same table; Jane Anderson took a place in the middle of the line.

The courtroom had seating for four hundred people, and it was crowded, not only with onlookers, but with prospective jurors. Normally, twenty-four jurors were summoned to court, in order to make a selection of twelve. In a capital case, such as the Anderson murder trial, the defense was allowed to dismiss twenty potential jurors without stating a reason (peremptory challenges), while the prosecution was allowed ten. Incredibly enough, two hundred and forty men were called and interviewed before twelve were selected to fill the panel for the Anderson trial.

Due to the publicity surrounding the crime, Judge Davis must have allowed unlimited challenges, and with seven lawyers evaluating each prospective juror, the motions to dismiss flew fast. In addition, some of those summoned may have done their best to be excused, since the trial was predicted to last at least two weeks. The mystery is how Sheriff Cook happened to have such a bottomless reserve of new faces. Judge Davis, intent on hearing the case in Springfield and wary of a motion for change of venue, undoubtedly warned Cook in advance to call in extras, lots of extras.

As it was, approximately two percent of the population of the county trooped past the lawyers on Tuesday, in the pursuit of a jury that was impartial—or at least, one that was not predictably disposed to vote with the opposition. Arrangements had already been made to sequester the jury at the American House Hotel, one block down Sixth Street from the Courthouse. Not all of the jurors lived in Springfield, and they couldn't travel back and forth to their homes every day. As it was, no one complained about staying at the American House: it was the best hotel in the city.

Most of the jurors were farmers, without much else to do in late November. The best-known members of the panel were Moses Horn, thirty-six, the superintendent of the County Alms House, and Philemon Stout, thirty-four, a widower who had re-married a few months before. Stout owned a small empire of a farm, self-sufficient and very prosperous.[35] The average age of the jurors was about thirty-seven, and they were predominantly family men. They were, in other words, a lot like the late George Anderson.

The first witness called by McWilliams was Thomas Connor, who didn't instill much confidence in the proceeding. In answer to the very first question as the testimony began on Thursday, he confirmed that he remembered the transactions of the case. In answer to the second question, he said that the murder happened "sometime in the first part of June." Or so: the date was actually May 15. McWilliams didn't pause to contradict him; it was his witness, after all.

Connor had been the first to go near the body on the night of the crime. McWilliams led him through a detailed description of the position and the state of the body. Conner said that Anderson, dressed in underclothes and an overcoat, was lying on his back in a very straight line, nestled in the impression in the ground caused by his own falling weight. Connor said there was no appearance of a struggle.

The cross-examination by the defense team tarried only briefly over the events on the night of the murder, and then hit on a theme that would be repeated with practically every witness. Connor was led back to the time when Anderson was still alive, though ill. He said that he had sometimes sat with Anderson at night. Under questioning, he attested to the fact that Mrs. Anderson had taken good care of her husband, and that he had never seen "a sick man have more confidence in his wife than deceased had in the accused."[36]

The Anderson trial was a local obsession. The Springfield *State Journal* newspaper did not merely send a reporter to cover it each day, but a stenographer. Illinois courts didn't employ court reporters or produce transcripts in the 1850s. Occasionally, a participant might hire a private secretary to record the proceedings in shorthand. That was rare, but the Anderson case marked the first time that a newspaper became involved by commissioning a transcript. The paper had tried out the technique in the arraignment hearings in May. The November trial, however, represented a greater commitment of space: as much as a full page in the four-page paper nearly every day. The editors were probably glad to allot that much room, the end of the political campaigns having left a void in their columns. The testimony was usually printed in tiny, agate type, the kind used for classified ads.

With that, the sale of magnifying glasses probably boomed in Springfield, but newspaper readers didn't learn much on the first day. McWilliams was most interested in the position of the body, while the defense seemed to be preparing Mrs. Anderson's case for sainthood. On Friday, however, the focus turned to Theodore. Frederick Dean, a clerk, had been at the Anderson residence on the night of the murder. In fact, he was one of those who lingered there all night, knowing perhaps that no place would ever be quite so exciting. He was asked by McWilliams whether Mrs. Anderson had offered any theories on her husband's death. Dean hadn't heard any.

Then Dean said that he met Theodore at the kitchen door. According to the third-person account of the transcript, he heard Theodore say, "he thought deceased must have fallen and hit his head on one of the steps; Theodore was at the house of deceased that night; witness first saw him in the kitchen door; witness had a conversation with Theodore Anderson that morning; and he still contended that George Anderson must have fallen and hit his head upon the steps."[37] McWilliams didn't pick up on the potential of that comment, moving immediately into a discussion of the loaded gun in Anderson's pocket. Finally, he seemed to do a mental double-take, and he rushed back to the image of Theodore volunteering his theories in the kitchen. "When conversing the next morning about the death of Mr. Anderson," Dean said, "Theodore remarked that George's hair was very thick and that probably his head bounced off before the blood had time to get through it." Dean suggested to Theodore that under those circumstances, some of the hair would have stuck to the step. Theodore replied, according to Dean, that "George's hair was very strong and would not pull out very easy."[38] Theodore didn't explain how Anderson went from bouncing his head off the steps to lying as straight as a rod in an impression in the earth five feet away. For that reason, Dean called the theory "improbable."

McWilliams next called a new witness to the stand, a man that had never been seen in Springfield before. As Matheny read the name, Dr. John L. White of the town of Jerseyville in southern Illinois, McWilliams made sure that the bottle of strychnine taken from Theodore's trunk was visible on the evidence table. White, a physician, said that he lived in a hotel in Jerseyville, with an office nearby. He recounted the way that he had met

Theodore at the hotel in April. Then he testified that Theodore had visited his office twice, although he didn't explain the purpose of the visits, whether they were professional or social. He did say that he had kept a bottle of strychnine in an unlocked bookcase in his office, a two-dram (or one-quarter ounce) bottle exactly like the one found in Theodore's trunk. The cork was different, though. In fact, as he looked at the bottle on the table before him, he said that he'd never seen a cork like that one in a standard pharmaceutical bottle.

Dr. White testified that his bottle of strychnine "was stolen." He didn't have cause to use strychnine very often, but he recalled seeing the bottle in mid-March, and he noticed it was missing in early May.

McWilliams handed him the bottle taken from Theodore's trunk. Dr. White looked at it and admitted that he couldn't swear that it was his, but he could say that the bottle itself and the label were the same as his. He noted that his bottle had been practically full, while the one taken from the trunk was only about half full. He estimated that the difference represented enough poison to "kill two or three hundred men."

One of the deputies testified next that he had visited Theodore at the jail on the Monday after the murder. Theodore asked him how things looked. The deputy replied that they looked very black; that something had been found in his trunk. Theodore knew immediately what he meant—the strychnine—but he wasn't concerned. He said that he'd purchased it in New Jersey to use on his hands, to prevent skin diseases. Medically, application to the skin was not an accepted use for strychnine and, in fact, the poison can be absorbed almost as efficiently that way as through ingestion. If Theodore had indeed used a strychnine hand wash, he might not have had to worry about skin diseases for very long.

The newspaper transcript didn't identify which of the defense lawyers was conducting the cross-examination at any particular time. Lincoln may have been content to listen. His style in trials was to allow the prosecution to make its best case; sometimes, he even helped to delineate the state's case. When he felt that everyone in court understood the opposing argument clearly, he could all the more easily break it apart and dispense with it. To some degree, he did the same thing in his speeches, when he explained opposing political opinions with perfect equanimity—and then obliterated them. Apparently, Lincoln was not particularly concerned with the testimony surrounding the crime, or crimes: the bludgeoning and the poisoning that apparently preceded it. He was more concerned with the introduction of the relationship between Theodore and Mrs. Anderson. He must have been listening intently when Mr. Smithers, the daguerreotype portrait artist, testified after the deputy was through.

Smithers took the stand to testify about the visits that Theodore and Mrs. Anderson had made to his studio. He had described the sessions at the hearings in May, how he had taken a picture of Mrs. Anderson in a light dress first, but that she had decided she didn't like it and had insisted on sitting again. The second portrait was the one found in Theodore's trunk. About those pictures, Smithers had something new to tell the court.

A short time after taking the portraits of Mrs. Anderson, Smithers happened to bump into George Anderson, who was then looking forward to moving his blacksmith business into new quarters. "He said," Smithers testified, "as soon as he got into his new shop he would come up and give me a call, and get some work done." In an expansive mood, Anderson announced that he wanted to have pictures taken of his wife and children. Smithers was not often called upon to be discreet in his profession, like a hotel clerk or a jewelry salesman, but he was suddenly facing a moral dilemma. He caught his breath and decided in that moment that he couldn't tell George Anderson that his wife had just had her picture taken as a present for his nephew.

CHAPTER 13

NOVEMBER AND EARLY DECEMBER

THE BEST HOPE
OF THE NATION

While the testimony was continuing on Friday, the attorney Usher Linder arrived in Springfield. Tall and angular, he was also known as "General" Linder in honor of his service in the Blackhawk War. Major John Stuart had likewise retained his title from that adventurous time, though he had the sense of humor to admit that he hadn't done much to earn it. Linder took himself a little more seriously than that. But then, he was a general. A high-strung man in private and quite theatrical in public, he caused a rustle of attention wherever he went. Around the state he was known for his personal charm and for his orations. Whitney called him "the most brilliant orator that ever lived in Illinois,"[1] but that was no slap at Lincoln. Lincoln spoke. Linder orated, following a more mannered tradition, and one that audiences found inspiring, in his charge.

In the courtroom, Linder was unyielding, especially when he was in the role of prosecutor. "I never felt that a defendant in a criminal case was safe from a verdict when Linder prosecuted," said his fellow lawyer, Joseph Gillespie, "no matter what the evidence might be in his favor."[2] A bulldog on the fine points of the law, and a master in addressing a jury, Linder was a fitting match for Abraham Lincoln, an expert strategist who was also masterful before a jury. He was the one man in the state who could balance the talents of the Anderson defense team all by himself. McWilliams must have looked on his sudden appearance in Springfield as a gift. If it was a gift: despite Linder's insistence that his arrival was a coincidence, the towering case cannot have escaped his notice, especially since it was in need of a prosecutor and he was a man who liked nothing more than winning a conviction, unless it was winning a conviction in a monumental trial.

"I went up to Springfield," Linder recalled twenty years later, "either on a visit or on some business or other when Judge Davis was holding his court there; and I had landed but about an hour when the prosecuting attorney hearing that I was in town, came and employed me to assist him in the prosecution of a woman and her paramour for the murder of her husband by the administration of poison."[3] When the news that Usher Linder was joining the prosecution reached the jail cells, Mrs. Anderson and Theodore were no doubt aware that they were in trouble. "I always believed that it was inhuman to confer the office of prosecuting attorney upon such men as Linder," reflected Gillespie.[4]

Usher Linder was a true free lance, willing to lend his talents practically anywhere. Unlike Lincoln, he wasn't swayed by the defendant's cause; he was mainly interested in the chances of winning. Linder had a reputation to preserve, and didn't waste his time on longshots. As word of his involvement in the trial leaked out, observers in Springfield could read the signs however they liked: Theodore and Mrs. Anderson must be doomed, because Linder had agreed to join the prosecution, or they had to be innocent, because Lincoln had chosen their side. On Saturday, the courtroom was full, and Judge Davis was ready to begin bright and early. Lincoln and the other attorneys were in their usual places at the defense table; Mrs. Anderson was seated near the middle, next to John Rosette. Theodore was on the other side of Rosette, at the end of the table. Amzi McWilliams was at the prosecution table, awaiting Linder, who arrived with his trademark fanfare.

"As I entered the court room," Linder recalled, "Judge Davis being on the bench and perceiving me enter the room with my pipe in my mouth, said in an audible voice, 'Mr. Sheriff, you will permit no one to smoke in this room while court is in session except General Linder.'"[5] Despite the fact that a murder was about to be tried, the line was well-received by the other lawyers and the gallery. "It created quite a laugh all over the house," Linder continued, "and you may rest assured I was not so modest or self-denying as to refuse to take advantage of the permission thus given me to smoke my pipe during the progress of the trial."[6]

The first prosecution witness on Saturday was John Armstrong, the carpenter whose shop faced the Anderson house across the alley. He answered two questions to that effect and then held up a map that he'd drawn himself, showing the shop, the house, and the sightlines between the two. The map must not have been quite as clear as Armstrong intended. All it did was kindle the idea that the jury would have to see the murder scene in person in order to understand the testimony, and so Judge Davis ordered a visit to Monroe Street. Sheriff Cook took charge of the jury and led them down the stairs at the Courthouse and out onto Sixth Street, trailed by McWilliams and Linder, Stuart, Edwards, Lincoln, Logan and the other defense attorneys. The prisoners were, meanwhile, returned to jail. Judge Davis stayed behind in the courtroom; he didn't have to see anybody's backyard to run a trial.

After looking at the outhouse and the place where Anderson fell, the group filed into the house, to see the bedroom shared by Mr. and Mrs. Anderson, and the dining room, where John Morgan slept. The tour was most beneficial to Usher Linder, who knew less about the murder than anyone in town.

When the trial resumed at midday, John Armstrong went back to the stand and told the court about Theodore's "peculiar" conduct, hanging around the door of the carpentry shop by the hour so that he could maintain his furtive surveillance over the Anderson's backyard. McWilliams was probably still doing the questioning, since Linder was so new to the case. John Armstrong recalled several occasions when Mrs. Anderson came out of the house into the backyard while Theodore was watching, or as he put it, while Theodore "was noticing Mrs. Anderson."[7] She didn't acknowledge him in any way. The looking was all on Theodore's part.

One of John Armstrong's employees took the stand and corroborated the description of Theodore's obsession with the Anderson's backyard. He added that the young man would play with the Anderson children when they were there, or just sit on the lumber pile and talk with them. One point that was made by Armstrong and several other witnesses concerned Mary Anderson, the thirteen-year-old in the family. As far as anyone knew, she was not involved with Theodore in any romantic way. She may well have had a crush on her cousin, been willing even to do anything that he asked, but her feelings were known only to her thirteen-year-old mind.

During the break for lunch, Sheriff Cook led the jurors to the American House and made sure that they didn't discuss the case. The attorneys, on the other hand, would go into conference and talk about nothing else. The prosecution case was coming together in an even stronger way than it had during the hearings in May. A certain imperative had been attached to possession of the strychnine, with Dr. White's implication that Theodore had stolen it in early April, after his domestic problems with the Andersons. Moreover, the jury had heard good testimony that Theodore had been behaving strangely toward the Andersons, and Mrs. Anderson in particular.

In the standard prosecution formula, means, motive, and opportunity must be addressed. McWilliams had succeeded in the first: Theodore had, it seems, willfully obtained the strychnine. McWilliams and Linder had yet to detail the opportunity, especially in Mrs. Anderson's ability to administer the poison. It remained after that to pull the means and opportunity together into an inevitable act, one that jumped from the first murder attempt, the strychnine, to the second, the clubbing. For that, the prosecution needed to supply a motive equal to murder: that Theodore and Mrs. Anderson had been involved with each other in an illicit relationship.

After the midday break, Judge Davis called the court to order. Everyone sat down, except a man named Joseph C. Woods, a carpenter who worked in John Armstrong's shop. After he was sworn in, he settled into the witness chair and gave a fairly bland version of his boss' previous testimony. Half the time he sounded like a defense witness, sheepishly saying that, actually,

Theodore hadn't done anything to attract attention while he was standing around the doorway. The image that John Armstrong had left of Theodore's acting with "conduct so peculiar that it caused remarks from the boys in the shop,"[8] was being superseded as Woods spoke. For that reason, McWilliams cut short his questioning and hurriedly concluded. The defense, which was largely handled by Abraham Lincoln that afternoon, was in no such hurry as Woods expressed his benign impression that Theodore "had nothing to do at the time and was there to pass the time . . . It was common for mechanics to come around the shops to talk to the hands," Woods elaborated.[9]

When Woods was finally through, McWilliams understandably decided to press on in a different direction. He called Samuel Harvey, a new witness, who described seeing Mrs. Anderson in front of her house on Monroe Street on the day of the murder, speaking to a man who was not her husband. Lincoln listened warily, but Harvey really didn't say anything, admitting even to McWilliams that he "couldn't recognize Theodore Anderson as the man."[10] Another witness told a similar story, that of seeing Mrs. Anderson standing in front of the house on the morning of May 15. According to the transcript, it was the most commonplace of tableaus: "Saw Mrs. Anderson and a man talking at the gate," recorded the *State Journal*, "when witness first saw them they were five or six feet apart . . . as witness saw them, Mrs. Anderson stepped off three or four steps as if to go away but continued talking to the man; as witness approached nearer, she again stepped back and stooped down and picked up something."[11] The witness could not identify the man.

The testimony was not to go any further on that subject. The murder trial was not going to be a repeat of the May testimony. At the earlier hearing, over a dozen witnesses took the stand to tell of seeing Mrs. Anderson and Theodore in compromising situations, being alone together in fields, laughing together in downtown stores, walking alone, conversing alone, and even ducking into an abandoned house together. The witnesses were available, but none who intended to describe those rendezvous were allowed to take the stand. "The prosecution attempted to show that there had been improper relations between the defendants," the legal historian John J. Duff explained, "In this they were blocked by objections on the part of Lincoln."[12] As a legal maneuver, keeping that testimony out of the trial was decisive, the type of bold, yet basic tactic that reflected Lincoln's work in court. Since adultery was itself against the law in Illinois,[13] allowing questioning on the potentially illegal relationship between Theodore and Mrs. Anderson could have been interpreted as trying them for a crime with which they were not charged. Lincoln changed the trial by drawing that line.

And in that, Lincoln was undoubtedly interrupted, countered, and generally tortured by Usher Linder. One of Linder's specialties was a meticulous knowledge of trial law and its precedents. Relying on a stubborn delight in technicality, he was known to preside over trials with even more authority than the judge. A battle certainly ensued when Lincoln objected to putting the defendants on trial for adultery. Linder knew what was at stake, and surely argued that the prosecution was seeking to establish a motive, but the testimony available to the trial was little more than innuendo. The witnesses lined up by the prosecution were strangers, passersby, people who saw things that were only of interest after the suggestion of adultery was introduced. When it came to eyewitness testimony, none of them saw anything. On its own, in fact, an indictment for adultery would be difficult, if not impossible to bring in.

Abraham Lincoln won the battle of the objections with Usher Linder, and the trial jury didn't hear about all of the time that Mrs. Anderson and Theodore spent together alone. Only one witness spoke of their relationship, but Lincoln couldn't stop him.

Cyrus Youst, a workman at the blacksmith shop, had boarded with the Anderson family early in the year, along with Theodore, and young John Morgan. At the May hearing, Youst didn't say much, primarily just that he "never saw Theodore and [Mrs. Anderson] together, only at the house."[14] In November, he opened up.

On the morning of the day that Theodore went away to Jerseyville, Youst said that he heard "a great fuss [argument] in the house . . . George and Theodore and Mrs. Anderson were all in the dining room at the time." Youst didn't know for certain what the argument was about, but he could give the court a good idea. "The evening before," he said, "Theodore had been complaining of being homesick, and said that if he had some one to comb his hair, he could go to sleep, and Mrs. Anderson said she could comb his hair, if that was all; she went into the room where he was . . . the next morning, there was a fuss; Theodore went to Jerseyville that evening."

That evening, just before Theodore left for Jerseyville, Youst saw him again, testifying that "as he and George were going toward the depot, in front of the Ball Alley, Theodore said to George he was 'very sorry he did it,' and George said: 'Oh well, I did the same thing when a boy.'"[15]

On cross-examination, Lincoln led Youst to emphasize that George was entirely amicable by the time he and his nephew were going to the train station, and the trial ended for the day on that note. Youst's testimony had flagged the fact that the relationship between Theodore and Mrs. Anderson was unusually friendly, even causing George to be jealous on one occasion, but no more could be made of it than that.

Lincoln had apparently used his objections to divide the trial into two very separate tracks: the adultery, which was easy to suggest, and the murder, which demanded, by its nature, a much heavier burden of proof. Each track made the other much more easy to believe, but once they were separated, the question of adultery could be put out-of-bounds. It was a strategy that Stuart, Edwards, Lewis, and Campbell had failed to employ in the arraignment hearing in May. At the trial, however, Lincoln could see that the outcome depended squarely on just such a separation. Lincoln wouldn't allow a murder conviction to slide in on the back of disgust over the affair. Without that separation, the case became too slippery, inviting the jurors to think about one crime while they were judging the defendants on another.

The trial lasted late into the afternoon on Saturday, when Judge Davis finally adjourned the court until Monday. The prosecution had yet to rest, and those people in the gallery who were determined not to miss a minute of the trial could figure on being in the same place the following Saturday, too.

On Sunday, Mary Lincoln worked on her correspondence. Her husband was probably relaxing in the house, or visiting with Senator Trumbull, who was in Springfield on his way to Washington. Through the years, Mary Lincoln did not appear to take as great an interest in her husband's legal work as in his political career. And, true to that form, a letter she wrote that day indicates that in the Lincoln household, the main topic hadn't changed, even in the midst of a *cause celèbre*. She wrote to her sister Emily:

> Your husband, like some of the rest of ours, has a great taste for politics and has taken much interest in the late contest which has resulted very much as I expected, not hoped.
>
> Although Mr. Lincoln is, or was, a Frémont man, you must not include him with so many of those who belong to that party,—an abolitionist. In principle, he is far from it. All he desires is that slavery shall not be extended,—Let it remain where it is . . . The Democrats have been defeated in our State in their governor, so there is a crumb of comfort for each and all. What day is so dark that there is no ray of sunshine to penetrate the gloom? . . . Now sit down, and write one of your agreeable missives, and do not wait for a return of each from a staid matron, the mother of three noisy boys.[16]

Mrs. Lincoln had described with basic accuracy the position her husband had taken in the 1856 campaign. She must have realized, though, that he was even then in motion, with the new political party as a vehicle.

When the trial reopened on Monday, the prosecution was about halfway through its testimony. At that juncture, someone who was present in the courtroom wrote, "The summing up of the prosecution is that poison was furnished the wife by the nephew, which was given to deceased, which accounts for his sickness and spasms; but that death not following as soon as anticipated, the nephew watched his opportunity and dealt the deadly blow."[17] Linder was taking a greater role in the prosecution, but McWilliams was probably still doing most of the interrogation, though he didn't always manage the witnesses deftly. He questioned the former sheriff, A. W. Coleman, honing in on Mrs. Anderson's behavior on the night of the murder. He evidently wanted the sheriff to describe her attempt to stop the autopsy.

Coleman started off well, from McWilliams' point of view, saying that when Mrs. Anderson found out what the doctors were doing, she "objected to their making a post mortem examination; she said they had no right to cut her husband all to pieces; that she would prosecute them for doing so."

That all sounded callous, and somewhat suspect, as though she were hiding something. The sheriff continued testifying, however, that "she said she could not bear to hear the grating of the saw while they were sawing his head."[18] No one could—except perhaps a murderer. The impression was reversed just that quickly: she would have seemed callous and suspect if she had been comfortable knowing her husband's skull was being sawn off, on a night that had begun so typically, and to be within earshot of the sound. Mrs. Anderson momentarily gained the sympathy of the courtroom.

In the afternoon, Linder called George Anderson's physicians, Lord and Fowler. Lord gave a detailed description of the course of Anderson's illness, much as he had previously. He did recount a pathetic moment, when Anderson said that he couldn't live through another spasm. "You're a hard man to kill," Dr. Lord remembered saying, "Don't be discouraged." Anderson may have taken that good word to heart, but generally he had come to distrust Lord, and formally requested that Fowler take over his treatment. Remarkably enough, Anderson began to improve right after that. The reason might have stemmed from the change in medicine Fowler prescribed. Or, the cure may have come from a conversation Dr. Fowler had at the Anderson house.

According to Dr. Fowler's testimony, he had a talk with George Anderson as soon as he took over management of the case. Mrs. Anderson was hovering in the background. The doctor told Anderson that he suspected that "something was wrong." That was about all he said; he didn't mention poisoning specifically, but that was what he meant. He then "gave them to understand that he would find out if there was." *If there was*, that is, something wrong—strychnine poisoning. Dr. Fowler testified that after he made that assertion, Anderson had an immediate recovery, suffering only one more isolated spasm up to the time of his murder.

When the prosecution rested at the end of Monday's testimony, Linder, for one, felt confident. Theodore procured the poison, Mrs. Anderson administered it, and when they thought that Dr. Fowler was onto them, the two frustrated poisoners backed off and found another way to kill George Anderson. Linder was confident that he and McWilliams had proven that much.

On Tuesday, the defense began to call its witnesses. The defense table, crowded throughout the trial, was a beehive of activity, with the lawyers conferring with each other and even with bystanders.One aspect of the defense strategy became apparent almost immediately: no defense witness would get off the stand without commenting on the marital bliss of Mr. and Mrs. Anderson. One or two of the consulting physicians at the end of the witness list may have been spared the duty, but throughout the rest of the testimony, the message was consistent.

The testimony began with a good friend of the Andersons, who made the same point that nine subsequent witnesses would make: "they had lived very happy together."

He went on to say that during George Anderson's last illness, the affection between the two increased: "it was so much so on the part of the deceased," he exclaimed, "that I thought he was foolish."[19] Other witnesses, more sentimental than he, perhaps, reinforced the fact that the Anderson marriage was contented, while several reiterated the assessment of a long-time friend who said that Mrs. Anderson's "character for integrity and virtue was as good as any one's."[20] A few praised Theodore's qualities as well. Several were induced to describe George's anxiety regarding a stranger on the property and the way he had secured a pistol for his protection, but the theory of the crime was distinctly secondary.

The majority of witnesses who leapt to defend the marriage—and Mrs. Anderson, and Theodore—were George Anderson's closest relatives. Ultimately, the star witnesses for the defense were George Anderson's sister, Phebe Todd, and his nephew, Charles Anderson. Mrs. Todd said that she had been staying with Charles on the night of the murder. Theodore boarded at the same house. She said that he came in at nine-thirty and went upstairs. Soon afterward, Mrs. Todd locked the door, presumably the only door in the house. The notable point about that door was that it led directly into the bedroom used by Charles Anderson. No one, she said, could go out without Charles knowing it. On that theme, the testimony of Mrs. Todd and Charles Anderson combined to give Theodore an alibi.

The defense called its last witness on Wednesday afternoon. The trial was far from over, though; the closing arguments alone would take three-and-a-half days. All of the leading attorneys addressed the jury with speeches lasting several hours each. Edwards' was first for the defense. Lincoln spoke on Friday, while Logan was accorded the honor of closing the argument on Saturday. The case for the defense was strong. Lincoln's colleagues had successfully brought forward character witnesses to counter the basic facts that placed Theodore and Mrs. Anderson closest to the crime. Lincoln had incisively defined the basis, the parameter of the questioning, and that being the case, he hadn't left very much room for Linder to work his own argument. Lincoln's old friend—and adversary—was hobbled even before he delivered his closing argument. For Linder, though, a closing argument was a performance, and no one could be certain what to expect.

Late on Saturday afternoon, Linder finally rose to deliver the last word for the prosecution. He had been waiting all week for his chance. In his *Reminiscences,* he explained why:

> Amongst those in the defense known to me at the time I was engaged in the prosecution, were Abraham Lincoln, his Honor Judge Stephen T. Logan, John T. Stewart [sic], Benjamin Edwards, and some younger lawyers who were not known to me. The woman on trial sat in the midst of her eminent counsel, and close by her a young and handsome man, whom I took to be her paramour and associate in crime. During the progress of the trial, he showed no contrition, but put on, as I thought, a bold and impudent look, and frisked about and got law books and pointed out pages to Lincoln and the rest of the lawyers in defense.
>
> Thinks I to myself, 'My young chap, when I come to conclude this case, I will not fail to pay my special respects to you . . . I had no intention to deal with the case but in a serious and solemn manner, summing up the evidence and showing how strongly it pointed to the guilt of the woman and her paramour.[21]

Linder executed his plan and just as he was rising to a peak of outrage, he turned to the defense table. "Gentlemen of the jury," he said dramatically, "notice the conduct of the prisoner; notice I say, his conduct, here he is at one moment reading the books, at another whispering to the members of the bar—Gentlemen of the jury, if you wanted any additional evidence of this man's guilt," Linder pointed an accusing finger, "it would only be necessary

for you to recur to his boldness and impudence on this trial."[22] It was a stunning point, typical of the great Linder's sense of drama. It would even have
been brilliant, if he hadn't had the wrong man. While Linder was still point-
ing, John Rosette stood up and made his first contribution to the trial.

"General Linder," he said respectfully, "you are mistaken; I am not the
criminal, but my name is Rosette; I am a lawyer."[23] For the first time in any
courtroom, General Linder was utterly speechless. Judge Davis, the members of the jury, the other lawyers, and the spectators "roared with laughter," according to a newspaper account.[24] No one noted whether Theodore
and Mrs. Anderson thought it was funny; they were still on trial for murder. The comic mistake may have worked to their advantage, though. Linder later recalled that he "limped lamely" through the rest of his closing
argument.

The trial finally ended at about nine o'clock on Saturday evening. After
a break, Judge Davis gave the jurors instructions, and then they were led
downstairs to a deliberation room. The lawyers probably remained in the
Courthouse; their offices were nearby, but in the chill of late November,
they would have had to light their stoves to stay warm. It must have seemed
easier just to do what they'd been doing through so many years: hanging
around together at the Courthouse, any Courthouse.

Some six hours later, at three o'clock in the morning, the jury was finished talking and finished voting. The lawyers assembled; Sheriff Cook
brought the prisoners back from their cells, and Judge Davis called the court
into session. Philemon Stout read the verdict: not guilty.

In the middle of the night, everyone could go home, even Theodore
and Jane Anderson.

Ever afterward, Linder blamed his blunder in the closing argument for
the prosecution's defeat. While the misidentification was embarrassing, it
could have been overcome and would have been understood, since Linder
was an out-of-towner. In truth, Linder lost in the maneuvering with Lincoln. After a man of his reputation fails in so celebrated a case, though, a
snappy story makes for an escape of sorts. To the degree that Lincoln had
set the ground rules with his objections, he gave the jury little choice but to
find the pair innocent. The evidence in the murder, just the murder, was cir-
cumstantial at best. Something had happened in the dark at the Anderson

house, someone had gotten out of control, but the court hadn't been able to carry the speculation as to why George Anderson had to die any further than it flew in the winds of Springfield.

The verdict wasn't popular in the community. The same newspaper that had devoted a full page every day to the transcripts of the trial carried the news of the verdict in an article of just one sentence. In its tight-lipped way, that little squib communicated the resentment of the people in the city more clearly than any long editorial might have done.

The Anderson trial became a legend, long remembered in Springfield. The case from its inception was the backdrop for a year of sweeping transition for Abraham Lincoln, a man who had always been respected, always liked. Something new was happening, though, with the establishment of the Republican Party in Illinois, and the direction of national politics. Lincoln was needed. As a sense of order receded, it revealed more clearly than ever a chaos of fear—and clear thinking, where it existed. The same sense of crisis gripped the Sangamon County Courthouse in the last week of November.

Lincoln played the dominant role in the Anderson verdict. Had he joined the prosecution, rather than the defense, the balance would have tipped at a sharp angle away from the defendants. The fact that both sides tried to recruit him, and that the trial, in effect, was not to start without him on either one side or the other, testified in a public way to his stature in the bar. He may not typically have been described as the leading lawyer of his generation, but when the best and the most powerful found themselves in a critically important situation, they admitted to needing Abraham Lincoln. The lawyers of Springfield wouldn't be the last to find themselves in that position.

Lincoln went back to court on the Monday after the verdict for his usual work, except that it was he and not Davis who convened the Circuit Court. Davis wanted a day off, and so he named Lincoln to take his place. Starting Tuesday, Lincoln was in his usual place, on the lawyers' side of the bench, working his way through minor cases for defendants unknown to the public.

Ten days later, on Wednesday, December 10, Abraham Lincoln was in Chicago, making his way to the Tremont House hotel for dinner. It was to be a very formal affair, a truly gala evening he wouldn't have wanted to miss. Since he was in Chicago, though, he had managed to have a case in court the day before.

On Wednesday night, he made his way to the Republican Party victory banquet, the first one ever in Illinois. The banquet room at the Tremont was ready for the state's celebrating Republicans. John B. Drake, Chicago's most renowned hotelier, personally catered the gourmet dinner.[25] The walls were decorated with the stars and stripes—very elegantly, of course; the victory dinner was no rally in a dusty grove. From behind the dais, the motto, "Illinois Redeemed" looked down on the room.

Lincoln was not a sentimental man, but the Republican Party had come to mean a great deal to him in a surprisingly short time. On that subject, he would write a paragraph, the only memoir he left of the year that had been, 1856. It read, in part:

> The party is newly formed, and in forming, old party ties had to be broken, and the attractions of party pride, and influential leaders were wholly wanting. In spite of old differences, prejudices, and animosities, it's members were drawn together by a paramount common danger. They formed and manouvered in the face of the deciplined enemy, and in the teeth of all his persistent misrepresentations. Of course, they fell far short of gathering in all of their own. And yet, a year ago, they stood up, an army over thirteen hundred thousand strong. That army is, to-day, the best hope of the nation, and of the world. Their work is before them; and from which they may not guiltlessly turn away.[26]

After the last course at the banquet was cleared, the Reception Committee attended to a few items of business, and then the speeches were to begin. At a little after nine, the chairman introduced Abraham Lincoln and the cheers were said to be deafening.[27]

AFTERWORD

Mrs. Jane Anderson returned to the house on Monroe Street after the trial. George's estate provided her with enough money to care for the children. As of 1860, two men were boarding at the house, including another of her husband's nephews. Theodore returned to New Jersey. Whatever had happened between the two of them, they carried away separately and secretly.[1]

Colonel Bissell was a successful governor, despite his weakened health. He investigated the corruption left by the administration of his predecessor, Joel Matteson, and was credited with cleaning up the state government. He died of pneumonia while in office, in March 1860.[2]

Richard Yates won election later in the year to succeed Bissell. When Senator Stephen Douglas died in 1861, Yates appointed Orville Browning to take his place in Washington. Browning wanted a Supreme Court appointment from President Lincoln, but to his lasting resentment, he didn't receive it. Owen Lovejoy won election to Congress in 1856, and was re-elected every term until his death in 1864. He was an ardent supporter of Lincoln.

Amzi McWilliams was not happy in Springfield, and moved away not long after the Anderson trial. John M. Palmer recalled in his memoir that McWilliams "died in 1862, near St. Louis."[3] John T. Stuart did not even vote for his friend Abraham Lincoln in the 1860 election, and as a newly elected Democratic Congressman in 1863, he opposed the Emancipation Proclamation as well.[4] The people of greater Springfield did not return him to Washington for a second term. His daughter, Betty, could not become a lawyer and emulate him (in those days the Illinois Bar still did not admit women), but she did marry a lawyer, who became his partner and eventually took over the firm. It still exists today.

Judge David Davis managed the effort to secure the Republican presidential nomination for Lincoln in 1860. Two years later, Lincoln nominated him to a seat on the Supreme Court; he resigned it in 1877, after he was elected Senator from Illinois. In 1862, Dr. Gustave Koerner also received a presidential appointment, serving as Lincoln's Ambassador to Spain.

William Herndon continued to practice law until the mid-1860s. Though he had very little money and a drinking problem, he dedicated himself to collecting notes, letters, and interviews on the subject of Lincoln's life. They formed the basis of his 1889 *Life of Lincoln* (written with Jesse W. Weik), and have proved invaluable to biographers since. Charles Zane was for a while his law partner. Zane was later a Justice of the Utah Supreme Court.

The Anderson case was still discussed generations later, as one of the major crimes in Springfield's history.[5] No one ever afterward could offer a theory that didn't leave as many questions as it answered. Even if one is ready to dismiss Theodore and Mrs. Anderson as nothing more than a pair of clumsy romantics (an obsessed young man, something of a stalker, and a woman vain enough to be delighted by his attention), there is the matter of the strychnine. If they didn't conspire to kill George Anderson, it is hard to see how the strychnine entered his system. But then, the conspiracy may not have included Mrs. Anderson: Theodore may have coerced young Mary, the thirteen-year-old daughter in the family—apparently a girl with a crush, at the very least, on her cousin Theodore—into sneaking the poison into her father's food. Any such conjecture is plausible. With the jury finding Theodore and Mrs. Anderson innocent, the sheriff failed to continue the investigation.

The mystery of who killed George Anderson was never solved.

NOTES

CHAPTER 1

1. Dr. George M. Angell, undated clipping, Lincoln Collection, Abraham Lincoln Presidential Library and Museum, Springfield, Ill. (hereinafter referred to as ALPLM), Reminiscences file.
2. Paul M. Angle, *"Here I Have Lived": A History of Lincoln's Springfield* (New Brunswick, N.J.: Rutgers, 1935), p. 165.
3. State of Illinois, *Illinois Public Land Purchase Records* [database on-line] (Provo, Utah: The Generations Network, Inc., 1999).
4. James Conkling, speech, Jan. 12, 1881, reprinted in Rufus Wilson, *Lincoln Among his Friends* (Caldwell, Idaho: Claxton Printers Ltd., 1942), p. 106.
5. Angell, undated clipping, Lincoln Collection, ALPLM, Reminiscences file.
6. Ibid.
7. Ibid.
8. *Springfield Directory 1857–58* (Springfield, Ill.: S.H. Jameson, 1857), p. 17.
9. Medicus, letter to the editor, Springfield *State Journal*, June 12, 1856, p. 3.
10. "Identifying Lincoln's Law Offices," *Lincoln Lore*, Aug. 25, 1952, p. 1.
11. George P. Floyd, article in *McClure's Magazine*, Jan. 1908, reprinted in Wilson, *Lincoln Among his Friends*, p. 175.
12. Opinion, Mar. 24, 1856, *Dillingham v. Fisher*, in Martha L. Benner, Cullom Davis, et al., eds., *The Law Practice of Abraham Lincoln: Complete Documentary Edition*, DVD-ROM (Urbana: University of Illinois Press, 2000); opinion, Mar. 6, 1856, case file: *Lincoln provided legal opinion*, in Benner, Davis, et al., *The Law Practice of Abraham Lincoln*. Both of these opinions are also reprinted in Roy Basler, Marion D. Pratt, and Lloyd A. Dunlap, eds., *The Collected Works of Abraham Lincoln* (New Brunswick, N.J.: Rutgers University, 1953), vol. II, pp. 333–339.
13. Ralph Emerson, and Adaline T. Emerson, *Mr. and Mrs. Ralph Emerson Personal Recollections of Abraham Lincoln* (Rockford, Ill.: Wilson, 1909), p. 8.
14. Angell, undated clipping, Lincoln Collection, ALPLM, Reminiscences file.
15. Linder, *Reminiscences of the Early Bench and Bar of Illinois* (Chicago: The Chicago Legal News Company, 1879*)*, p. 348.

16.   Ibid.
17.   Joseph Gillespie, writing in John M. Palmer, ed., *Bench and Bar of Illinois, Historical and Reminiscent* (Chicago: Lewis Publishing Company, 1899), p. 188.
18.   Linder, *Reminiscences,* p. 348.
19.   "The Artesian Well," Springfield *State Journal,* Mar. 15, 1856, p. 2.
20.   Angell, undated clipping, Lincoln Collection, ALPLM, Reminiscences file.

CHAPTER 2

1.   "Citizens' Mass Meeting," Springfield *State Journal,* March 19, 1856, p. 3.
2.   "Illinois Correspondence," *Missouri Republican,* May 24, 1856, p. 2.
3.   Advertisement, George Anderson, Springfield *State Journal,* Jan. 2, 1851, p. 4
4.   Advertisement, Anderson & Coflin, Springfield *State Journal,* Mar. 27, 1851, p. 4
5.   Advertisement, Anderson & Coflin, Springfield *State Journal,* Feb. 20, 1852, p. 3
6.   Advertisement, Wright & Brown, Springfield *State Journal,* Mar. 15, 1856, p. 3.
7.   "People's Mass Meeting," Springfield *State Journal,* May 20, 1856, p. 2.
8.   John Cook, "A Note From Mr. Cook," Springfield *State Journal,* March 31, 1856, p. 2.
9.   Joseph Wallace, quoted in John M. Palmer, ed., *The Bench and the Bar of Illinois,* p. 184.
10.   George W. Julian, "The First Republican National Convention," *American Historical Review,* vol. 4, no. 2, Jan. 1899, p. 314.
11.   Joseph R. Nightingale, "Joseph H. Barrett and John Locke Scripps, Shapers of Lincoln's Religious Image," *Journal of the Illinois Historical Society,* 92–3, Autumn 1999, pp. 239–40.
12.   Paul Selby, "The Editorial Convention, February 22, 1856," *Transactions of the McLean County Historical Society,* volume 3, 1900, p. 35.
13.   "Funny," Springfield *State Journal,* Apr. 11, 1856, p. 3.
14.   Paul Selby, letter, February 14, 1856, quoted in Reinhard H. Luthin, "Abraham Lincoln Becomes a Republican," *Political Science Quarterly,* vol. 59, no. 3, p. 429.
15.   O.P. Wharton, *Lincoln and the Beginning of the Republican Party* (Springfield, Ill.: Illinois State Journal Co., 1912), p. 4.
16.   William Herndon, "Letter from Wm. H. Herndon," Springfield *State Journal,* Mar. 19, 1856, p. 2.
17.   Peter Whitmer, letter, July 1, 1908, Lincoln Collection, ALPLM, Reminiscences file, folder 4.
18.   "Palmer on Lincoln," *Chicago Evening Post* (dated 1892?), Lincoln Collection, ALPLM, Reminiscences file.
19.   Gustave Koerner, *Memoirs,* T. McCormack, ed. (Cedar Rapids, Iowa: Torch Press, 1909), p. 445.

CHAPTER 3

1.   "The Second Story of the Lincoln Home," *Journal of the Illinois State Historical Society,* vol. 49, no. 2, Summer, 1956, p. 217.
2.   Richard S. Hagen, "'What a Pleasant Home Abe Lincoln Has,'" *Journal of the Illinois State Historical Society,* vol. 48, no. 1, Spring, 1955, pp. 11–12.

3. "Local Footprints of Abraham Lincoln," *Taylorville (Ill.) Semi-Weekly Breeze,* Feb. 11, 1909, p. 1.
4. "Review of the Trade and Improvements of Springfield for 1856," Springfield *State Journal,* Jan. 6, 1857, p. 2.
5. Emerson and Emerson, *Mr. and Mrs. Ralph Emerson's Personal Recollections,* pp. 7–9.
6. Ibid.
7. Lawrence Weldon, "Reminiscences of Lincoln as a Lawyer," in William Hayes Ward, *Abraham Lincoln: Tributes from His Associates* (New York: Thomas Y. Crowell, 1895), p. 246.
8. John W. Bunn, letter, Nov. 8, 1910, in Paul M. Angle, *Abraham Lincoln by Some Men Who Knew Him* (Chicago: Americana, 1950), p. 109.
9. Mrs. Mary Stuart, letter to Bettie Stuart, April 3, 1856, Stuart-Hay Collection, ALPLM, Manuscripts Department.
10. Lawrence Weldon, "Reminiscences of Lincoln as a Lawyer," in William Hayes Ward, *Abraham Lincoln: Tributes from His Associates* (New York: Thomas Y. Crowell, 1895), p. 246.
11. Ibid.
12. Dr. George M. Angell, undated clipping, Lincoln Collection, ALPLM, Reminiscences file.
13. Ibid.
14. Ibid.
15. Ibid.
16. Brief and account, April, 1856, *Webster v. Angell and Rhodes,* in Benner et al., *The Law Practice of Abraham Lincoln.*
17. Dr. George M. Angell, undated clipping, Lincoln Collection, ALPLM, Reminiscences file.

CHAPTER 4

1. "Anti-Nebraska Convention," Springfield *State Journal* Apr. 9, 1956, p. 2.
2. Harry E. Pratt, "The Famous 'Chicken Bone' Case," *Journal of the Illinois State Historical Society,* Summer, 1952, pp. 164–5.
3. Affidavit, April 9, 1856, *Fleming v. Rogers & Crothers,* in Benner et al., *The Law Practice of Abraham Lincoln.*
4. April 1857, *Fleming v. Rogers & Crothers,* in Benner et al., *The Law Practice of Abraham Lincoln.*
5. "The Governorship," Springfield *State Journal,* Apr. 21, 1856, p. 2.
6. William Bissell, letter, May 5, 1856, Library of Congress, Lyman Trumbull papers.
7. Ibid.
8. Lord & Fowler, account, June 13, 1856, Probate Record, no. 1245 George Anderson 15 May 1856, Illinois Regional Archive Depository, Springfield.
9. Anna Ridgely, letter, Feb. 4, 1861, quoted in Ruth Painter Randall, *Lincoln's Sons* (Boston: Little, Brown, 1955), pp. 84–5.
10. Abraham Lincoln, letter to Dr. Anson G. Henry, July 4, 1860, Basler, ed., *Collected Works,* vol. IV, p. 81.
11. Dr. Preston Ballaiche, typescript reprinted in *Journal of the Illinois Historical Society,* 47–1, Spring 1954, pp. 59–60.

12. J.P. Kent, letter, Jan. 23, 1909, Lincoln Collection, ALPLM, Reminiscences file.
13. John Stuart, letter, Jan. 13, 1856, quoted in Harry E. Pratt, *Personal Finances of Abraham Lincoln* (Springfield, Ill.: The Abraham Lincoln Association, 1943), p. 97.
14. James H. Matheny, "History of Springfield," *Springfield City Directory,* 1856–57, p. 14.
15. William Herndon, letter April 28, 1856, printed in Joseph Newton, *Lincoln and Herndon* (Cedar Rapids, Iowa: Torch Press, 1910), p. 92.
16. William E. Bennett, "This Man, Now 87, Saw Lincoln Plain," newspaper article, no citation [1926], Lincoln Collection, ALPLM, Reminiscences file.
17. Advertisement, Springfield *State Journal,* Mar. 19, 1956, p. 1.
18. R.S. Lord, "Testimony," Springfield *State Journal,* May 22, 1856, p. 2.
19. Palmer, *Bench and Bar of Illinois,* p. 186.
20. David Davis, interview, Douglas L. Wilson and Rodney O. Davis, eds., *Herndon's Informants: letters, interviews and statements about Abraham Lincoln* (Urbana: University of Illinois Press, 1998), p. 350.
21. Appeal bond, April, 1856, *Davin v. Scates,* in Benner et al., *The Law Practice of Abraham Lincoln.*
22. Justice of the Peace Transcript, September 29, 1855, *Davin v. Scates,* in Benner et al., *The Law Practice of Abraham Lincoln.*
23. Witness affidavits, April 1856, *Davin v. Scates,* in Benner et al., *The Law Practice of Abraham Lincoln.*
24. William H. Herndon and Jesse W. Weik, *Herndon's Life of Lincoln* (New York: Fawcett, 1965. Reprint of 1889 ed.), p. 310.
25. Ibid.
26. Ibid.
27. Fee book, May 10, 1856, *Roberts v. Harkness,* in Benner et al., *The Law Practice of Abraham Lincoln.*
28. Isaac N. Arnold, *Reminiscences of the Illinois Bar Forty Years Ago* (Illinois State Bar Association, 1881), p. 7.
29. Herndon and Weik, *Herndon's Life of Lincoln,* p. 311.
30. R. S. Lord, "Testimony," Springfield *State Journal,* May 22, 1856, p. 2.
31. "Strychnine," *St. Louis Republican* Dec. 1, 1856, p. 1.
32. "Illinois Correspondence," *Missouri Republican,* May 17, 1856, p. 1.

CHAPTER 5

1. "Illinois Correspondence," *Missouri Republican,* May 17, 1856, p. 1.
2. George Woods clothier, receipt, May 15, 1856, Probate Record, no. 1245, George Anderson, Illinois Regional Archive Depository, Springfield.
3. Testimony of Levi Conant from transcript, *Illinois State Journal,* May 22, 1856, p. 2.
4. Pratt, *Personal Finances of Abraham Lincoln,* p. 148.
5. Ward H. Lamon, *Life of Abraham Lincoln* (Boston: James R. Osgood, 1872), p. 323. Also *Springfield City Directory for 1855–56,* p. 16.
6. Wayne C. Temple, *By Square and Compass; Saga of the Lincoln Home* (Mahomet, Ill.: Mayhaven Publications, 2002), p. 103.

7. Hagen, "What a Pleasant Home Abe Lincoln Has," p. 14.
8. Lamon, *Life of Abraham Lincoln,* p. 326.
9. Affidavit, May 15, 1855, *Stout v. Stout,* in Benner et al., *The Law Practice of Abraham Lincoln.*
10. Testimony of Rebecca Law, from transcript, *Illinois State Journal,* May 22, 1856, p. 2; testimony of John Morgan, ibid.
11. U.S. Census, Year: 1860; Census Place: Springfield, Sangamon, Illinois; Roll: M653_226; Page: 252; Image: 251.
12. *Springfield City Directory,* 1855–56, p. 8.
13. Testimony of Edwin Fowler, transcript, *Illinois State Journal,* May 22, 1856, p. 3.
14. U.S. Census, Year: 1850; Census Place: Springfield, Sangamon, Illinois; Roll: M432_127; Page: 118; Image: 240.
15. *Springfield City Directory,* 1855–56, p. 10.
16. Testimony of Thomas Connor, transcript, *Illinois State Journal,* May 22, 1856, p. 2.
17. Testimony of F.I. Dean, transcript, *Illinois State Journal,* May 22, 1856, p. 2.
18. U.S. Census, Year: 1860; Census Place: Springfield, Sangamon, Illinois; Roll: M653_226; Page: 249; Image: 248.
19. Testimony of Sanford Bell, transcript, *Illinois State Journal,* May 22, 1856, p. 3
20. Testimony of John W. Priest, transcript, *Illinois State Journal,* May 22, 1856, p. 3.
21. Testimony of Edwin Fowler, transcript, *Illinois State Journal,* May 22, 1856, p. 2.
22. "Murder in Springfield," Springfield *Register,* May 17, 1856, p. 2.
23. Ibid.
24. Ibid.
25. Ibid.
26. "Foul Play," Springfield *State Journal* May 16, 1856, p. 3.
27. Ibid., p. 2.
28. U.S. Census, Year: 1850; Census Place: Springfield, Sangamon, Illinois; Roll: M432_127; Page: 125; Image: 253.
29. "Murder of Anderson," Springfield *State Journal,* May 17, 1856, p. 3.
30. Benjamin Edwards, letter, May 17, 1856, *People v. Anderson and Anderson,* in Benner et al., *The Law Practice of Abraham Lincoln.*
31. George Usher F. Linder, *Reminiscences of the Early Bench and Bar of Illinois* (Chicago: Chicago Legal News Company, 1879), p. 350.
32. William Herndon, notes on an interview with David Davis, Sept. 20, 1866, in Douglas L. Wilson and Rodney O. Davis, *Herndon's Informants* (Urbana, Ill.: University of Illinois, 1998), p. 349.

CHAPTER 6

1. John Stuart, letter, May 18, 1856, Stuart-Hay Collection, ALPLM, Correspondence file.
2. Lord & Fowler, account, Anderson family, 1856 Probate Record, no. 1245, George Anderson 15 May 1856, Illinois Regional Archive Depository, Springfield.
3. Testimony of E. Smithers, transcript, *Illinois State Journal,* May 22, 1856, p. 2.
4. Testimony of John Morgan, transcript, *Illinois State Journal,* May 22, 1856, p. 2.
5. Ibid. In the original transcript, the name of Dr. Jayne was misspelled, "Jane."

6.   Ibid.

7.   Testimony of Mr. Burkhardt, transcript, *Illinois State Journal,* May 22, 1856, p. 2.

8.   Testimony of Mr. Northerner, transcript, *Illinois State Journal,* May 22, 1856, p. 2.

9.   Testimony of Edwin Fowler, transcript, *Illinois State Journal,* May 22, 1856, p. 2.

10. Testimony of Mary Anderson, transcript, *Illinois State Journal,* May 22, 1856, p. 2.

11. Testimony of William Planck, from transcript, *Illinois State Journal,* May 22, 1856, p. 2.

12. "Murders in Springfield," *Illinois Chronicle,* May 22, 1856, p. 1.

13. Philip Worcester, petition for change of venue, Nov. 13, 1855 *Spink v. Chiniquy,* in Benner et al., *The Law Practice of Abraham Lincoln.*

14. Charles Chiniquy, *Fifty Years in the Church of Rome* (London: The Protestant Truth Society, 1948), pp. 345–6.

15. Fee Bill, May 1856, *Spink v. Chiniquy,* in Benner et al., eds., *The Law Practice of Abraham Lincoln.*

16. Henry C. Whitney, *Life on the Circuit with Lincoln* (Caldwell, Idaho: Claxton Printers Ltd., 1940), p. 74–5.

17. "Illinois Correspondence," *Missouri Republican,* May 24, 1856, p. 2.

18. Ibid.

19. John Stuart, letter, May 22, 1856, Stuart-Hay Collection, ALPLM, Manuscripts Department.

20. "The Anderson Murder," Springfield *Register,* May 22, 1856, p. 3.

21. "Murder of George Anderson," Springfield *State Journal,* May 22, 1856, p. 3.

22. Linder, *Reminiscences,* p. 227.

23. "The Fusion Meeting on Saturday," Springfield *Register,* May 26, 1856, p. 2.

24. Ibid.

25. George T. Allen, letter, Aug. 8, 1856, Library of Congress, Lyman Trumbull papers.

26. William Herndon, letter, Oct. 30, 1855, in Newton, *Lincoln and Herndon,* p. 82.

27. "Sangamon County anti-Nebraska Convention," Springfield *State Journal,* May 26, 1856, p. 2.

28. "The Fusion Meeting on Saturday," Springfield *Register,* May 26, 1856, p. 2

29. "Assault in the United States Senate Chamber," Springfield *Register,* May 26, 1856, p. 2

30. Untitled article, June 12, 1856, Decatur, *Illinois State Chronicle,* p. 1.

31. Joseph Gillespie, letter, May 29, 1856, Library of Congress, Lyman Trumbull Papers.

32. Congressional Globe, 33rd Congress, 2nd Session, Appendix 59, quoted in Nightingale, "Joseph H. Barrett and John Locke Scripps," p. 239.

33. B.F. Williams to Salmon Chase, Feb. 7 1856, Chase Papers, Library of Congress, quoted in Reinhard H. Luthin, *The First Lincoln Campaign* (Cambridge, Mass.: Harvard University Press, 1944), p. 3.

34. Charles Granville Hamilton, "Lincoln and the Know Nothing Movement," *Annals of American Research,* 1954, p. 3.

35. Abraham Lincoln, letter, Aug. 11, 1855, in Basler et al., eds., *The Collected Works,* vol. 2, p. 323.

36. Abraham Lincoln, letter, Aug. 24, 1855, in ibid.

CHAPTER 7

1. Basler et al., eds., *The Collected Works*, pp. 382–3.
2. Herring Chrisman, *Memoirs of Lincoln* (privately published, 1930), pp. 55–6.
3. Order, May 26, 1856, *Parris v. Littler*, in Benner et al., eds., *The Law Practice of Abraham Lincoln.*
4. William Herndon, letter to Lyman Trumbull, May 19, 1856, Library of Congress, Lyman Trumbull papers.
5. J. O. Cunningham, *Some Recollections of Abraham Lincoln; Delivered before the Firelands pioneer association at Norwalk, Ohio July 4, 1907 and reprinted from the Pioneer of December 1909* (Norwalk, Ohio: Am. Pub. Co., n.d.), p. 6.
6. Orville H. Browning, *Diary of Orville H. Browning* (Springfield, Ill.: Illinois State Historical Library, 1925), vol. 1, p. 237.
7. Maurice Baxter, *Orville Browning* (Bloomington, Ind.: Indiana University Press, 1957), p. 53.
8. Koerner, *Memoirs*, p. 479.
9. Orville Browning, letter, May 19, 1856, Library of Congress, Lyman Trumbull papers.
10. Ibid.
11. David W. Bartlett, *Life and Public Speeches of Hon. Abraham Lincoln* (Freeport, New York: Books for Libraries, 1969; originally pub. 1860), p. 105.
12. Lawrence Weldon, "Reminiscences of Lincoln as a Lawyer," in *Abraham Lincoln: Tributes from his Associates*, p. 243.
13. Milton H. Shutes, *Lincoln's Emotional Life* (Philadelphia: Dorrance, 1957), pp. 112–3.
14. "Fought Fires with Lincoln Sixty-Five Years Ago," *Weekly Kansas City Star*, Feb. 18, 1920, in Lincoln Collection, ALPLM, Reminiscences file.
15. Lawrence Weldon, "Reminiscences of Lincoln as a Lawyer," in *Abraham Lincoln: Tributes from his Associates*, p. 239.
16. William Herndon, notes on an interview with David Davis, Sept. 20, 1866, in Wilson and Davis, *Herndon's Informants*, p. 348. Herndon capitalized some words in his original notes, apparently without import.
17. John W. Bunn letter, Nov. 8, 1910, in Angle, *Abraham Lincoln by Some Men Who Knew Him*, p. 109.
18. J.O. Cunningham, *Some Recollections of Abraham Lincoln*, p. 6.
19. Cunningham refers to the hotel as "Oglesby House," which was a later name for Cassell House.
20. "Address by Honorable George Schneider," *Transactions of the McLean County Historical Society*, vol. 3, 1900, p. 92.
21. Whitney, *Life on the Circuit*, p. 91.
22. J.O. Cunningham, "The Bloomington Convention of 1856 and Those Who Participated In It," *Transactions of the McLean County Historical Society*, no. 10, 1905, p. 18.
23. Ezra M. Prince, Introduction, *Transactions of the McLean County Historical Society*, vol. 3, 1900.
24. Whitney, *Life on the Circuit*, p. 92.
25. Ibid.
26. Ibid.

27. Letter testamentary, May 14, 1856, Probate Record, no. 1245, George Anderson, May 15, 1856, Illinois Regional Archive Depository, Springfield branch.

28. Receipt W.D. Wood, May 24, 1856, Probate Record, no. 1245, George Anderson, May 15, 1856, Illinois Regional Archive Depository, Springfield branch.

29. Browning, *Diary*, vol. 1, p. 237.

30. Ibid.

31. Ibid.

32. George T. Schneider, "Lincoln and the Anti-Know Nothing Resolutions," *Transactions of the McLean County Historical Society*, vol. 3, p. 90.

33. Whitney, *Life on the Circuit*, p. 92.

34. "Bloomington Convention," *Alton Weekly Courier*, June, 5 1856, p. 1.

35. "Black Republican State Convention of Illinois," *Springfield Daily Register*, May 31, 1856, p. 2.

36. "Reflections of Lincoln," *St. Louis Globe-Democrat Magazine*, Mar. 7, 1909, p. 3.

CHAPTER 8

1. Orville Dwyer, "Lincoln's 'Lost Speech' Quoted After 73 Years," *Chicago Daily Tribune*, Feb. 11, 1929 (also available in Lincoln Collection, ALPLM, Reminiscences file).

2. William P. Kellogg, letter Feb. 8, 1909, Lincoln Collection, ALPLM, Reminiscences file.

3. Dwyer, "Lincoln's 'Lost Speech' Quoted After 73 Years."

4. Cunningham, "The Bloomington Convention of 1856 and Those Who Participated In It."

5. W.J. Usrey, "By Telegraph from Bloomington," *Illinois State Chronicle* (Decatur), May 29, 1856, p. 1.

6. Henry Hunt letter to the editor, *Newark Daily Advocate*, Oct. 27, 1895, p. 1.

7. Whitney, *Life on the Circuit*, p. 92.

8. Ibid.

9. Hunt letter to the editor, *Newark Daily Advocate*, Oct. 27, 1895, p. 1.

10. Cunningham, "The Bloomington Convention of 1856 and Those Who Participated In It."

11. William Bissell, letter, May 24, 1856 *Springfield State Journal*, May 30, 1856, p. 2.

12. "The Bloomington Convention," *Alton Weekly Courier*, June 5, 1856, p. 1.

13. Cunningham, "The Bloomington Convention of 1856 and Those Who Participated In It."

14. "The Anti-Nebraska Convention," *Peoria Weekly Republican*, June 6, 1856, p. 1.

15. "Later," Decatur, *Illinois State Chronicle*, May 29, 1856, p. 1

16. Henry Hunt, letter to the editor, *Newark Daily Advocate*, Oct. 27, 1895, p. 1.

17. Ibid.

18. Cunningham, "The Bloomington Convention of 1856 and Those Who Participated In It."

19. "The Bloomington Convention," *Alton Weekly Courier*, June 5, 1856, p. 1.

20. Henry Hunt, letter to the editor, *Newark Daily Advocate*, Oct. 27, 1895, p. 1.

21. William P. Kellogg, letter Feb. 8, 1909, Lincoln Collection, ALPLM, Reminiscences file.

22. "To the Citizens of Sangamon County," Springfield *State Journal,* May 15, 1856, p. 2.

23. Dwyer, "Lincoln's 'Lost Speech' Quoted After 73 Years."

24. Henry Hunt, letter to the editor, *Newark Daily Advocate,* Oct. 27, 1895, p. 1.

25. "The Bloomington Convention," *Alton Weekly Courier,* June 5, 1856, p. 1.

26. "Address by Honorable George Schneider," *Transactions of the McLean County Historical Society,* vol. 3, 1900, p. 92.

27. William P. Kellogg, letter, Feb. 8, 1909, Lincoln Collection, ALPLM, Reminiscences file.

28. Cunningham, "The Bloomington Convention of 1856 and Those Who Participated In It."

29. William P. Kellogg, letter Feb. 8, 1909, Lincoln Collection, ALPLM, Reminiscences file.

30. Cunningham, "The Bloomington Convention of 1856 and Those Who Participated In It."

31. Abraham Lincoln, as reported in "The Bloomington Convention," *Alton Weekly Courier* May 31, 1856 (article was published again on June 5, 1856, p. 1).

32. Cunningham, "The Bloomington Convention of 1856 and Those Who Participated In It."

33. Dwyer, "Lincoln's 'Lost Speech' Quoted After 73 Years."

34. Cunningham, "The Bloomington Convention of 1856 and Those Who Participated In It."

35. John Scott, quoted in Ida Tarbell, *Life of Abraham Lincoln* (New York: Lincoln Historical Society, 1909), p. 88.

36. Browning, *Diary,* p. 238.

37. "Hon. A. Lincoln," *Chicago Press,* June 3, 1856, p. 2.

38. James Emery, *Transactions of the McLean County Historical Society,* vol. 3, 1900, p. 94.

39. "Address by Honorable George Schneider," *Transactions of the McLean County Historical Society,* vol. 3, 1900, p. 92.

40. William P. Kellogg, letter Feb. 8, 1909, Lincoln Collection, ALPLM, Reminiscences file.

41. Henry Hunt, letter to the editor, *Newark Daily Advocate,* Oct. 27, 1895, p. 1

42. Herndon and Weik, *Herndon's Life of Lincoln,* p. 312.

43. Whitney, *Life on the Circuit,* p. 93.

44. Ibid., p. 94

45. Ibid.

46. Herndon and Weik, *Herndon's Life of Lincoln,* p. 304.

47. Abraham Lincoln, letter Sept. 27, 1856 in Basler et al., eds., *The Collected Works of Abraham Lincoln,* vol. 2, pp. 378–9.

CHAPTER 9

1. In a letter of May 20, Herndon mentioned a conversation with his law partner on the previous Sunday; it may have occurred in the home office, but then, they might also have met on the road. All that is known for certain of Lincoln's

whereabouts is that he was due in Urbana the next day. William Herndon, letter, May 20, 1856, Library of Congress, Lyman Trumbull papers.

2.   Browning, *Diary*, p. 238.

3.   "The Sylvester Interview," *Sangamon Monitor*, Apr. 5, 1893, p. 1.

4.   "The Sylvester Interview," *Sangamon Monitor*, Apr. 5, 1893; also in Temple, *By Square & Compass*, pp. 274–6.

5.   William E. Bennett, "This Man, Now 87, Saw Lincoln Plain," newspaper article, no citation [1926], ALPLM, Reminiscences file.

6.   Albert Beveridge, *Abraham Lincoln, 1809–1858* (Boston: Houghton Mifflin, 1928), p. 282.

7.   Herndon and Weik, *Herndon's Life of Lincoln*, p. 313.

8.   Advertisement, Springfield *State Journal*, May 28, 1856, p. 2.

9.   Iota [pen name], "Illinois Correspondence," *Missouri Republican* (St. Louis), June 9, 1856, p. 2.

10. "Sangamon County Ratification Meeting," Springfield *State Journal*, June 6, 1856, p. 2.

11. "Fought Fires with Lincoln Sixty-Five Years Ago," *Weekly Kansas City Star*, Feb. 18, 1920, in Lincoln Collection, ALPLM, Reminiscences file.

12. "Personal Habits and Manners of President Lincoln," *Belvidere Standard*, (Ill.), April 14, 1868, p. 1.

13. Philip Wheelock Ayres, "The Lincolns and their Neighbors," *Review of Reviews*, Feb. 1918.

14. Emily Todd Helm, quoted in Henry Rankin, *Personal Recollections of Abraham Lincoln* (New York: Putnam's Sons, 1916), p. 186.

15. Ruth Painter Randall, *Lincoln's Sons* (Boston: Little, Brown, 1955), p. 44.

16. Hobart Rankin, letter, Oct. 3, 1926, Lincoln Collection, ALPLM, Reminiscences file.

17. Ibid.

18. Ibid.

19. Ibid.

20. Ibid.

21. Ibid.

22. William Herndon, letter, April 28, 1856, printed in Newton, *Lincoln and Herndon*, p. 92.

23. A.W. Shipton, *Lincoln's Association with the Journal* (Springfield, Illinois: Copley Press, 1945), p. 10.

24. Maurice Baxter, *Portrait of a Prairie Lawyer: Clifton H. Moore, 1851–1861 and 1870–1880, a Comparative Study* (Thesis presented at University of Illinois Urbana-Champaign in 1960), p. 24.

25. Palmer, *Bench and Bar of Illinois*, p. 544.

26. J. W. Porter, letter, Jan. 14, 1887, in Wilson et al., *Herndon's Informants*, p. 600.

27. Wilson et al., *Herndon's Informants*, pp. 348, 626.

28. Linder, *Reminiscences*, pp. 182–3.

29. Ibid., p. 183.

30. Court order and writ of *fieri facias*, June 10, 1856, *Booth v. Lake*, Sangamon County Circuit Court, in Benner et al., *The Law Practice of Abraham Lincoln*.

31.   Order, June 12, 1856, *People v. Anderson & Anderson,* Sangamon County Circuit Court, in Benner et al., *The Law Practice of Abraham Lincoln.*

32.   "The Bissell-Hoffman Fizzle—Lincoln and Palmer's Speeches," Springfield *Register,* June 12, 1856, p. 2.

33.   Ibid.

34.   "The Meeting Last Night," *Springfield State Journal,* June 11, 1856, p. 2.

35.   "The Bissell-Hoffman Fizzle—Lincoln and Palmer's Speeches," Springfield *Register,* June 12, 1856, p. 2.

36.   Ibid.

37.   Ibid.

CHAPTER 10

1.   Court order, June 10, 1856, *Wright & Brown v. Allender,* Sangamon County Circuit Court, in Benner et al., *The Law Practice of Lincoln.*

2.   Untitled item, *Peoria Weekly Republican,* June 13, 1856, p. 2, col. 1.

3.   Iota [pen name], "Illinois Correspondence," *Missouri Republican* (St. Louis), June 9, 1856, p. 2.

4.   Whitney, *Life on the Circuit,* p. 95.

5.   Charles S. Zane, "Lincoln as I Knew Him," *Sunset,* Oct. 1912, p. 430.

6.   Iota [pen name], "Illinois Correspondence, *Missouri Republican,* June 25, 1856, p. 2; the archaic use of "an one" in the description of Lincoln was original to the article.

7.   Ibid.

8.   Abraham Lincoln, letter, June 7, 1856, Basler et al., eds., *The Collected Works of Abraham Lincoln,* vol. 2, p. 342.

9.   Whitney, *Life on the Circuit,* p. 96.

10.   "National Republican Convention," *Terre Haute Daily Express,* June 21, 1856, p. 2.

11.   Abraham Lincoln, declaration, June, 1856, *Stevens v. Stevens,* Champaign County Circuit Court, Law Practice of Lincoln.

12.   Charles S. Zane, "Lincoln as I Knew Him," *Sunset,* Oct. 1912, p. 430.

13.   Ibid.

14.   Advertisement, George L. Huntington, Springfield *Register,* May 15, 1856, p. 2.

15.   "Trial of Reapers," *Illinois State Journal* (Decatur), July 30, 1857, p. 2.

16.   Charles S. Zane, "Lincoln as I Knew Him," *Sunset,* Oct. 1912, pp. 432–3.

17.   Koerner, *Memoirs,* vol. 2, p. 21.

18.   Wilson, *Lincoln Among His Friends,* p. 133.

19.   *Origin of the Republican Party,* p. 148.

20.   J.A. Davies, letter dated September 8, 1856, *Alton Weekly Courier,* October 16, 1856, p. 1.

21.   "The Republican Demonstration on Thursday," Urbana *Our Constitution,* Sept. 20, 1856, p. 2.

22.   Abraham Lincoln, letter, May 9, 1857, in Basler et al., eds., *The Collected Works of Abraham Lincoln,* vol. 2, p. 395.

23.   Abraham Lincoln, letter, June 25, 1858, in Basler et al., eds., *The Collected Works of Abraham Lincoln,* vol. 2, p. 473.

24.   William Herndon, letter, July 12, 1856, Library of Congress, Lyman Trumbull Collection.

25. Basler et al., eds., *The Collected Works of Abraham Lincoln*, vol. 2, p. 348.

26. F.I. Herriott, *Iowa and Abraham Lincoln, being an account of the presidential discussion and party preliminaries in Iowa, 1856–1860* (Des Moines, 1911), pp. 6–7; also in Basler et al., eds., *The Collected Works of Abraham Lincoln*, vol. 2, p. 348.

27. "How the Candidates Look," *Terre Haute Daily Express*, Aug. 9, 1856, p. 2.

28. Abraham Lincoln, letter, July 10, 1856, in Basler et al., eds., *The Collected Works of Abraham Lincoln*, vol. 2, p. 347.

29. "Hon. Abram [sic] Lincoln," Chicago *Democratic Press*, July 15, 1856, p. 2.

30. Judge's notes, July, 1855, *Ballance V. Forsyth, et al.*, in Benner et al., *The Law Practice of Abraham Lincoln*.

31. Anthony Elliott, in Palmer, *Bench and Bar of Illinois*, p. 642.

32. T.B.D., letter, July 21, 1856, Springfield *Register*, July 24, 1856, p. 2.

33. U. S. Grant, *Personal Memoirs* (New York: Charles L. Webster, 1886), vol. 1, pp. 214–5.

34. Abraham Lincoln, fragment, c. July 1856, in Basler et al., eds., *The Collected Works of Abraham Lincoln*, vol. 2, pp. 349–50.

35. "Lincoln on Disunion" (from the *Galena Advertiser*), reprinted in the *Amboy Times*, August 7, 1856, p. 1.

36. "Proscription Course of the Ultra Republicans," *Chicago Daily Democrat*, June 12, 1856, p. 2.

37. "Convention of What-dy'a-call-ems—Palmer for Congress," Springfield *Register*, July 16, 1856, p. 2.

38. Philip Wheelock Ayres, "The Lincolns and their Neighbors," *Review of Reviews*, Feb. 1918.

39. "Personal Habits and Memories of President Lincoln," *Belvidere Standard*, Apr. 14, 1868, p. 1.

40. Iota [pen-name], "Illinois Correspondence," *Missouri Republican*, Aug. 7, 1856, p. 2.

41. Richard Yates, letter Aug. 3, 1856, Library of Congress, Lyman Trumbull papers.

42. Abraham Lincoln, letter, Aug. 4, 1856, in Basler et al., eds., *The Collected Works of Abraham Lincoln*, vol. 2, 358.

43. Abraham Lincoln, letter, July 28, 1856, in Basler et al., eds., *The Collected Works of Abraham Lincoln*, vol. 2, 356.

44. Herndon and Weik, *Herndon's Life of Lincoln*, p. 304

45. Abraham Lincoln, letter, Aug. 4, 1856, in Basler et al., eds., *The Collected Works of Abraham Lincoln*, vol. 2, 358.

46. Abraham Lincoln, speech, Aug. 27, 1856, in Basler et al., eds., *The Collected Works of Abraham Lincoln*, vol. 2, p. 363.

47. "Personal Memory of Lincoln," *Paris Daily Beacon*, Feb. 12, 1909, Lincoln Collection, ALPLM, Reminiscences file.

48. H.P.H. Bromwell, "A Story of the Lincoln Campaign," *Denver Tribune*, reprinted in Henrietta Bromwell, *Genealogy of the Bromwell Family* (Denver: privately printed, 1910), p. 76.

49. "Personal Memory of Lincoln," *Paris Daily Beacon*, Feb. 12, 1909, Lincoln Collection, ALPLM, Reminiscences file.

50. Ibid.

51. Ibid.

52. H. P. H. Bromwell, "A Story of the Lincoln Campaign," p. 75.
53. Ibid., p. 76.
54. Ibid.

CHAPTER 11

1. DeWitt Smith, typescript, Lincoln Collection, ALPLM, Reminiscences file.
2. Ibid.
3. Shelby [pen-name], letter, Springfield *Register,* Aug. 19, 1856, p. 2.
4. Orland Kay Armstrong, "Comrade of Lincoln in his Youth," *Cincinnati Enquirer,* Feb. 8, 1931, Lincoln Collection, ALPLM, Reminiscences file.
5. DeWitt Smith, typescript, Lincoln Collection, ALPLM, Reminiscences file.
6. William Bennett, typescript, Lincoln Collection, ALPLM, Reminiscences file.
7. Robert J. Havlik, "Abraham Lincoln and the Reverend Dr. James Smith: Lincoln's Presbyterian Experience in Springfield," *Journal of the Illinois State Historical Society,* 92–3, Autumn 1999, pp. 222–5.
8. Herndon and Weik, *Herndon's Life of Lincoln,* p. 339.
9. Thomas Lewis, letter, *Springfield State Register,* July 10, 1899, p. 8.
10. Temple, *By Square and Compass,* pp. 130–1.
11. N.B. Archer, letter, Aug. 11, 1856, Library of Congress, Lyman Trumbull papers.
12. Noah Brooks, "Personal Reminiscences of Lincoln," *Scribner's,* Feb. 1878, p. 562.
13. "Former Ogle County Citizen Writes on His Recollections of Lincoln," clipping, no citation, Lincoln Collection, ALPLM, Reminiscences file.
14. Herndon and Weik, *Herndon's Life of Lincoln,* p. 305.
15. Noah Brooks, "Personal Reminiscences of Lincoln," *Scribner's,* Feb. 1878, p. 562.
16. "Some Reminiscences of Abraham Lincoln," *Daily Marysville [Calif.] Appeal,* Nov. 4, 1860, p. 1.
17. Brooks, "Personal Reminiscences of Lincoln," p. 562.
18. "Alton Correspondence," *Missouri Republican,* Sept. 18, 1856, p. 2.
19. Abraham Lincoln, speech, Aug. 27, 1856, Basler, et al., eds. *The Collected Works of Abraham Lincoln,* vol. 2, p. 361.
20. Abraham Lincoln, letter, Sept. 8, 1856, in Basler et al., eds., *The Collected Works of Abraham Lincoln,* vol. 2, p. 374.
21. Ibid.
22. Charles S. Zane, *Sunset,* Oct. 1912.
23. Dr. George M. Angell, undated clipping, Lincoln Collection, ALPLM, Reminiscences file.
24. "Recollections of Lincoln," clipping, no citation, Lincoln Collection, ALPLM, Reminiscences file.
25. Iota [pen-name], "Springfield Correspondence," *Missouri Republican,* Sept. 29, 1856, p. 2.
26. Benjamin S. Edwards, letter, July 24, 1856, Library of Congress, Lyman Trumbull papers.
27. Justice of the Peace transcript, *People v. Johnson,* in Benner et al., *The Law Practice of Lincoln.*
28. Whitney, *Life on the Circuit,* pp. 419–20.

29. T. Lyle Dickey, letter, Dec. 8, 1866, in Wilson et al., *Herndon's Informants*, pp. 504–5.

30. Chrisman, *Memoirs of Lincoln*, p. 56.

31. Ibid.

32. Ibid.

33. Ibid.

34. Whitney, *Life on the Circuit*, p. 420.

35. Iota [pen-name], "Springfield Correspondence," *Missouri Republican*, Sept. 29, 1856, p. 2.

36. Wide Awake [pen-name], "Alton Correspondence," *Missouri Republican*, Sept. 27, 1856, p. 2.

37. "Springfield Correspondence," *Missouri Republican*, Sept. 29, 1856, p. 2.

38. "Would Shake Hands with the Devil," *Missouri Republican*, Sept. 30, 1856, p. 2; another contemporary source (Iota [pen name], *Missouri Republican*, Sept. 29, 1856) recorded Edwards' quote as "Fuse with Lovejoy—I'd fuse with the devil if he . . ." but the wording that was remembered during the campaign and for years afterward was the former.

39. Milton Hay and David Littler, interview, in Wilson et al., *Herndon's Informants*, p. 717.

40. "Would Shake Hands with the Devil," *Missouri Republican*, Sept. 30, 1856, p. 2.

41. Abraham Lincoln, letter, Sept., 27, 1856, in Basler et al., eds., *The Collected Works of Abraham Lincoln*, vol. 2, pp. 378–9.

42. "Springfield Correspondence," *Missouri Republican*, Sept. 29, 1856, p. 2.

43. Chrisman, *Memoirs of Lincoln*, p. 58.

44. Ibid.

45. Ibid.

46. Judgment docket, Sept. 30, 1856, *Davin v. Scates*, in Benner et al., *The Law Practice of Lincoln*.

47. "State Fair—Alton," *Quincy Daily Whig*, Oct. 4, 1856, p. 2.

48. "The Alton State Fair," *Chicago Daily Journal*, Oct. 4, 1856, p. 2.

49. "State Fair—Alton," *Quincy Daily Whig*, Oct. 4, 1856, p. 2.

50. "The Great Fremont Demonstration," *Alton Weekly Courier*, Oct. 9, 1856, p. 2.

51. Ibid.

52. "The Fremont Meeting Last Night," *Peoria Weekly Republican*, Sept. 19, 1856, p. 1.

53. "Abram Lincoln," *Peoria Weekly Republican*, Oct. 3, 1856, p. 2.

54. "Personal Reminiscences of Abraham Lincoln," Noah Brooks, *Scribner's*, Feb. 1878, p. 561.

55. "Caught at a Mean Trick," *Springfield Conservative*, Oct. 9, 1856, p. 3.

56. "Fremont Leads the Van," *Peoria Weekly Republican*, Oct. 17, 1856, p. 2.

57. John Kirkpatrick, letter, Sept. 26, 1856, *Urbana Constitution*, Oct. 18, 1856, p. 3.

58. B.J. Radford, "Lincoln Reminiscences," *Lima [Ohio] Weekly Eagle*, May 15, 1931, Lincoln Collection, ALPLM, Reminiscences file.

59. "Q" [pen-name], *Missouri Republican*, Sept. 24, 1856.

CHAPTER 12

1.   Abraham Lincoln, letter, Oct. 28, 1856, in Basler et al., eds., *The Collected Works of Abraham Lincoln*, vol. 2, p. 380.

2.   "N.P. Banks at Belleville," *Alton Weekly Courier,* Oct. 16, 1856, p. 1.

3.   Koerner, *Memoirs,* vol. 2, p. 33.

4.   "Republican Mass Meeting of Saturday," *Weekly Belleville Advocate,* Oct. 22, 1856, p. 2.

5.   Ibid.

6.   Koerner, *Memoirs,* vol. 2, pp. 32–3.

7.   "Republican Mass Meeting of Saturday," *Weekly Belleville Advocate,* Oct. 22, 1856, p. 2.

8.   Koerner, *Memoirs,* vol. 2, p. 33.

9.   Ibid.

10. Whitney, *Life on the Circuit,* p. 75.

11. Allen H. Wright and W.H. Somers, *A New Light on Abraham Lincoln as an Advocate* (San Diego: privately printed, 1925), p. 2.

12. Whitney, *Life on the Circuit,* p. 420.

13. Chiniquy, Charles, *Fifty Years in the Church of Rome* (London: Protestant Truth Society, 1948), pp. 364–5.

14. "A Question for the Laboring Man," *Urbana Our Constitution* Oct. 25, 1856, p. 2.

15. Abraham Lincoln, letter, Oct. 21, 1856, *Spink v. Chiniquy,* in Benner et al., *The Law Practice of Lincoln.*

16. Whitney, *Life on the Circuit,* p. 421.

17. Chiniquy, Charles, *Fifty Years in the Chrch of Rome* (London: Protestant Truth Society, 1948), p. 365.

18. Whitney, *Life on the Circuit,* p. 420.

19. Joseph Gillespie, introduction, in Linder, *Reminiscences,* p. 19.

20. U.S. Grant, *Personal Memoirs,* vol. 1, p. 215.

21. Ibid.

22. Ibid.

23. William H. Furness, letter, Nov. 9, 1856, quoted in Luthin, *The First Lincoln Campaign,* p. 4.

24. Actual result figures are from Blaine Brooks Gernon, *Lincoln in the Political Circus* (Chicago: Black Cat Press, 1936), p. 136.

25. Abraham Lincoln, letter, Aug. 4, 1856, Basler, ed. *Collected Works,* III, p. 358.

26. Theodore Parker, letter, Nov. 17, 1856, in Newton, *Lincoln and Herndon,* p. 100.

27. B. Edwards, letter, Nov. 14, 1856, *People v. Anderson & Anderson,* in Benner et al., *The Law Practice of Lincoln.*

28. James S. Ewing, speech, Feb. 12, 1909, in Angle, *Abraham Lincoln By Some Men Who Knew Him,* p. 40.

29. Palmer, *Bench and Bar of Illinois,* p. 186.

30. Whitney, *Life on the Circuit,* p. 470.

31. Documents and reports, *People v. Delny,* in Benner et al., *The Law Practice of Lincoln.*

32. Wright et al., *A New Light on Abraham Lincoln as an Advocate,* p. 2.

33. *History of Sangamon County,* (Chicago: Interstate Publishing, 1881), p. 225.

34. Thomas Lewis, letter, *Springfield State Register,* July 10, 1899, p. 8.

35. Joseph Wallace, "Philemon Stout," *Past and Present of the City of Springfield and Sangamon County, Illinois* (Chicago: S.J. Clarke, 1904).

36. Testimony of Thomas Connor, transcript, *Illinois State Journal,* Nov. 22, 1856, p. 2.

37. Testimony of F.I. Dean, transcript, *Illinois State Journal,* Nov. 24, 1856, p. 2.
38. Ibid.

CHAPTER 13

1. Whitney, *Life on the Circuit,* p. 180.
2. Joseph Gillespie, introduction, in Linder, *Reminiscences,* p. 13.
3. Linder, *Reminiscences,* p. 184.
4. Joseph Gillespie, introduction, in Linder, *Reminiscences,* p. 13.
5. Linder, *Reminiscences,* p. 184.
6. Ibid.
7. Testimony of John Armstrong, "The Anderson Murder Trial," *Illinois State Journal,* Nov. 24, 1856, p. 2.
8. Ibid.
9. Testimony of J.C. Woods, transcript, *Illinois State Journal,* Nov. 25, 1856, p. 2.
10. Testimony of Samuel Harvey, transcript, *Illinois State Journal,* Nov. 25, 1856, p. 2.
11. Testimony of Council Sampson, transcript, *Illinois State Journal,* Nov. 25, 1856, p. 2.
12. John J. Duff, *A. Lincoln, Prairie Lawyer* (New York: Rhinehart, 1960), p. 331.
13. Daniel W. Stowell, "Her Day in Court: The Legal Odyssey of Clarissa Wren," in Daniel Stowell, ed., *In Tender Consideration: Women, Families and the Law in Abraham Lincoln's Illinois* (Urbana: University of Illinois Press, 2002), p. 204.
14. Testimony of Cyrus Youst, from transcript, *Illinois State Journal,* May 22, 1856, p. 3.
15. Ibid.
16. Mary Lincoln, letter, Nov. 23, 1856, in Henry B. Rankin, *Personal Recollections of Abraham Lincoln* (New York: Putnam, 1916), p. 196.
17. "Springfield Correspondence," *Missouri Republican,* Nov. 26, 1856, p. 1.
18. Testimony of John Armstrong, "The Anderson Murder Trial," *Illinois State Journal,* Nov. 25, 1856, p. 2.
19. Testimony of O.N. Stafford, transcript, *Illinois State Journal,* Nov. 27, 1856, p. 2.
20. Testimony of Moses Pilcher, transcript, *Illinois State Journal,* Nov. 27, 1856, p. 2.
21. Linder, *Reminiscences,* p. 185.
22. Ibid., p. 184. Also "Springfield Correspondence," *Missouri Republican,* Dec. 3, 1856, p. 1.
23. Linder, *Reminiscences,* pp. 184–5.
24. Springfield Correspondence," *Missouri Republican* Dec. 3, 1856, p. 2.
25. "The Republican Banquet!" *Chicago Daily Journal,* Dec. 11, 1856, p. 2. John B. Drake, co-owner of the Tremont House, had two sons who built the Drake Hotel, still a landmark in the city of Chicago.
26. A. Lincoln, fragment, c. February 1857, in Basler et al., eds., *The Collected Works of Abraham Lincoln,* vol. 2, p. 391.
27. "Republican Banquet," *Chicago Democratic Press,* Dec. 11, 1856, p. 2.

AFTERWORD

1. U.S. Census, 1860, Springfield, Sangamon, Illinois; roll M653_226, citation is misspelled. "Jame" Anderson; Ibid., East Windsor, Mercer, New Jersey, roll M653_697.

2.   "Death of Gov. Bissell," *Chicago Journal,* Mar. 19, 1860, p. 1.
3.   Palmer, *Bench and Bar of Illinois,* p.186.
4.   Ibid., pp. 188–89.
5.   *History of Sangamon County* (Chicago: Interstate Publishing, 1881), p. 225.

SELECTED BIBLIOGRAPHY

Abraham Lincoln: Tributes from His Associates. New York: Thomas Y. Crowell, 1895.

Angell, George M. undated clipping Lincoln Collection, Abraham Lincoln Presidential Library and Museum (ALPLM), Springfield, Ill., Reminiscences file.

Angle, Paul M. *Abraham Lincoln by Some Men Who Knew Him.* Chicago: Americana, 1950.

———. *Here I Have Lived: A History of Lincoln's Springfield.* New Brunswick, N.J.: Rutgers University, 1935.

———. *Lincoln: 1854–1861.* Springfield, Ill.: The Abraham Lincoln Association, 1933.

Arnold, Isaac. *Reminiscences of the Illinois Bar Forty Years Ago.* Illinois State Bar Association, 1881.

Bartlett, David W. *Life and Public Services of Hon. Abraham Lincoln.* Freeport, New York: Books for Libraries, 1969. Originally published New York: H. Dayton, 1860.

Basler, Roy P., Marion D. Pratt, and Lloyd A. Dunlap, eds. *The Collected Works of Abraham Lincoln.* New Brunswick, N.J.: Rutgers University, 1953.

Baxter, Maurice. *Orville Browning.* Bloomington, Ind.: Indiana University Press, 1957.

Benner, Martha L., Cullom Davis, Daniel W. Stowell, Susan Krause, John A. Lupton, Stacy Pratt McDermott, Christopher Schnell and Dennis E. Suttles., eds. *The Law Practice of Abraham Lincoln: Complete Documentary Edition,* DVD-ROM. Urbana, Ill.: University of Illinois Press, 2000.

Beveridge, Albert. *Abraham Lincoln, 1809–1858.* Boston: Houghton Mifflin, 1928.

Braden, Waldo W. *Abraham Lincoln, Public Speaker.* Baton Rouge, La.: Louisiana State University, 1988.

Bromwell, Henrietta E. *Bromwell Genealogy.* Denver, Colo.: Privately printed, 1910.

Browning, Orville H. *Diary of Orville H. Browning.* Springfield, Ill.: Illinois State Historical Library, 1925.

Carman, Harry J. and Luthin, Reinhard. "Some Aspects of the Know-Nothing Movement Reconsidered." *South Atlantic Quarterly,* vol. 39, no. 2, April, 1940.

Chrisman, Herring. *Memoirs of Lincoln.* Privately printed, 1930.

Crissey, Elwell. *Lincoln's Lost Speech.* New York: Hawthorn Books, 1967.

Crossley, Frederic B. *Courts and Lawyers of Illinois.* Chicago: American Historical Society, 1916.

Cunningham, J.O. "The Bloomington Convention of 1856 and Those Who Participated In It." *Transactions of the McLean County Historical Society,* 1905.

———. *Some Recollections of Abraham Lincoln.* Norwalk, Ohio: The Am. pub. co., n.d. [1909?].

Donald, David. *Lincoln's Herndon.* New York: Alfred Knopf, 1948.

Dwyer, Orville. "Lincoln's 'Lost Speech' Quoted After 73 Years." *Chicago Daily Tribune.* Feb. 11, 1929 (also in Lincoln Collection, ALPLM, Reminiscences file).

Emerson, Ralph and Adaline T. Emerson. *Mr. and Mrs. Ralph Emerson's Personal Recollections of Abraham Lincoln.* Rockford, Ill.: Wilson Bros., 1909.

Fraker, Guy. *Men of Influence.* Bloomington, Ill.: Bloomington Pantagraph, 2003.

Gernon, Blaine Brooks. *Lincoln in the Political Circus.* Chicago: Black Cat Press, 1936.

Guelzo, Allen C. "Come-outers and Community Men: Abraham Lincoln and the idea of Community in Nineteenth Century America." *Journal of the Abraham Lincoln Association,* vol. 21, no. 1, 2000.

Hamilton, Charles Granville. *Lincoln and the Know Nothing Movement.* Washington: Annals of American Research, 1954.

Hart, Richard E. *Lincoln's Springfield: 1860* [Typescript]. Springfield, Ill.: Richard E. Hart.

Herndon, William H. and Jesse W. Weik. *Herndon's Life of Lincoln.* New York: Fawcett, 1965. [Reprint of: Chicago: Belford, Clarke & Company, c1889].

Hertz, Emanuel. *Abraham Lincoln: His Law Partners, Clerks and Office Boys.* Privately printed, 1930.

History of Sangamon County. Chicago: Inter-state Publishing Company, 1881.

Julian, George W. "The First Republican National Convention." *American Historical Review,* vol. 4, no. 2, Jan. 1899.

King, Willard. *Lincoln's Manager: David Davis.* Cambridge, Mass.: Harvard University Press, 1960.

Koerner, Gustave. *Memoirs of Gustave Koerner, 1809–1896,* Thomas J. McCormack, ed. Cedar Rapids, Iowa: The Torch Press, 1909.

Lamon, Ward H. *Life of Abraham Lincoln: from his birth to his inauguration as president.* Boston: James R. Osgood, 1872.

Lincoln Collection, Abraham Lincoln Presidential Library (ALPLM), Springfield, Ill.

Linder, Usher F. *Reminiscences of the Early Bench and Bar of Illinois.* Chicago: The Chicago Legal News Company, 1879.

Lovejoy, Owen. *His Brother's Blood, Speeches and Writings, 1838–1864.* William F. Moore and Jane Ann Moore, eds. Urbana, Ill.: University of Illinois Press, 2004.

Lowry, Thomas. *Personal Reminiscences of Abraham Lincoln.* Privately printed, 1910.

Luthin, Reinhard H. "Abraham Lincoln Becomes a Republican." *Political Science Quarterly,* vol. 59, no. 3.

Luthin, Reinhard H. *The First Lincoln Campaign.* Cambridge, Mass.: Harvard University Press, 1944.

Magdol, Edward. *Owen Lovejoy: Abolitionist in Congress.* New Brunswick, N.J.: Rutgers University, 1967.

Matthews, Elizabeth W. *Lincoln as a Lawyer: An Annotated Bibliography.* Carbondale, Ill.: Southern Illinois University Press, 1991.

Memorials on the Life and Character of Stephen T. Logan. Springfield, Ill.: H.W. Rokker, 1882.

Newton, Joseph. *Lincoln and Herndon.* Cedar Rapids, Iowa: Torch Press, 1910.

Nightingale, Joseph R. "Joseph H. Barrett and John Locke Scripps, Shapers of Lincoln's Religious Image." *Journal of the Illinois Historical Society*, 92–3, Autumn, 1999.

Oakleaf, Joseph Benjamin. *Abraham Lincoln as a Criminal Lawyer.* Rock Island, Ill.: Augustana Book Concern, 1923.

Palmer, John M., ed. *The Bench and Bar of Illinois, Historical and Reminiscent* Chicago: Lewis Publishing Co., 1899.

Pratt, Harry E. "Abraham Lincoln in Bloomington, Illinois." *Journal of the Illinois State Historical Society*, vol. 29, no. 1, April. 1936.

———. *Personal Finances of Abraham Lincoln.* Springfield, Ill.: The Abraham Lincoln Association, 1943.

Prince, Ezra M., ed. *Transactions of the McLean County Historical Society.* Bloomington, Ill.: Pantagraph, 1900.

Randall, Ruth Painter. *Lincoln's Sons.* Boston: Little, Brown, 1955.

Rice, Allen Thorndike. *Reminiscences of Abraham Lincoln.* New York: North American Review, 1883.

Steiner, Mark. "The Lawyer as Peacemaker: Law and Community in Abraham Lincoln's Slander Cases." *Journal of the Abraham Lincoln Association*, vol. 16, no. 2, 1995.

Stevens, Walter B., edited by Burlingame, Michael. *Reporter's Lincoln.* Lincoln, Neb.: University of Nebraska, 1998.

Stowell, Daniel W., ed., *In Tender Consideration: Women, Families and the Law in Abraham Lincoln's Illinois.* Urbana, Ill.: University of Illinois Press, 2002.

Strozier, Charles B. "Lives of William Herndon," *Journal of the Abraham Lincoln Association*, vol. 14, no. 1, 1993.

Stuart-Hay Collection, Abraham Lincoln Presidential Library (ALPLM), Springfield, Ill.

Temple, Wayne C. *By Square and Compass; Saga of the Lincoln Home.* Mahomet, Ill.: Mayhaven Publishing, 2002.

Wallace, Joseph. *Past and Present of the City of Springfield and Sangamon County, Illinois.* Chicago: S.J. Clarke, 1904.

Wallace, Mrs. Frances. *Lincoln's Marriage.* Privately printed, 1917.

White, Horace. *Life of Lyman Trumbull.* Boston: Houghton Mifflin, 1913.

Whitney, Henry C. *Life on the Circuit with Lincoln.* Caldwell, Idaho: Claxton Printers Ltd., 1940.

Wilson, Douglas L. "William H. Herndon and His Lincoln Informants." *Journal of the Abraham Lincoln Association*, vol. 14, no. 1, 1993.

Wilson, Douglas L. and Rodney O. Davis. *Herndon's Informants.* Urbana, Ill.: University of Illinois, 1998.

Wilson, Rufus R. *Lincoln Among His Friends.* Caldwell, Idaho: Claxton Printers Ltd., 1942.

Wright, Allen, and W.H. Somers. *A New Light on Abraham Lincoln as an Advocate.* San Diego, Calif.: Privately printed, 1925.

Zane, Charles. "Lincoln as I Knew Him." *Sunset*, vol. 14, no. 1, Apr. 21, 1921.

INDEX